to
Maureen Angela Jane

Those who are enamoured of practice without
science are like a pilot who goes into a ship without
rudder or compass and never has any certainty
where he is going.

LEONARDO DA VINCI
1452–1519

This writing seemeth to me, as far as a man can judge of
his own work, not much better than that noise or sound
which musicians make while they are tuning their instruments;
which is nothing pleasant to hear, but yet is a cause why
the music is sweeter afterwards. So have I been content
to tune the instruments of the muses that they may play
that have better hands.

SIR FRANCIS BACON
1561–1626

DYSON'S MECHANICS OF ATHLETICS

To Robbie,

A small token of my love.

Love Chris

X X X
X X
X

Dyson's
Mechanics
of
Athletics

GEOFFREY H. G. DYSON, O.B.E.

Eighth edition revised by

B. D. WOODS, M.Sc., MCSP, DLC, *Lecturer in PE,*
St. Luke's College, Exeter University

P. R. TRAVERS, MB, BS, MRCS, LRCP, D.Phys. Med.,
Researcher, School of Education, Exeter University

HODDER AND STOUGHTON

LONDON SYDNEY AUCKLAND TORONTO

British Library Cataloguing in Publication Data

Dyson, Geoffrey H. G.
  Dyson's Mechanics of Athletics.—8th ed.
  1. Track-athletics   2. Human mechanics
  I. Title   II. Woods, B. D.   III. Travers,
  P. R.   IV. Dyson, Geoffrey H. G. Mechanics
  of athletics
  796.4′01′531   GV1060.5

  ISBN 0 340 39172 3

Printed and bound in Great Britain for
Hodder and Stoughton Educational
a division of Hodder and Stoughton Ltd,
Mill Road, Dunton Green, Sevenoaks, Kent
by Biddles Ltd, Guildford and King's Lynn

Preface to the Eighth Edition

For many years now *The Mechanics of Athletics* has served as a basic text introducing the broad principles of human motion and in particular explaining those principles pertinent to athletic techniques. Since its first edition it has done a great deal to remove the mystique from coaching and set a sound scientific foundation on which a coach, teacher or athlete could confidently rely when endeavouring to improve skill performance.

Since 1962 the book has been regularly revised and expanded as knowledge has advanced and changes in technique have dictated. In this eighth edition the editors have continued the updating process, yet have set out to maintain the essential framework and ethos of Dyson's classical work.

Exeter
October 1985

B. D. W.
P. R. T.

Acknowledgments

The mechanics of track and field athletics have been a special interest of mine for more than twenty-five years, and I welcome this opportunity to express gratitude to the many who, through writing, lecturing or discussion, have taught me most of what I have learned.

In particular, I am indebted to three friends. First, Mr. C. Arrowsmith, B.Sc., A.M.I. Mech.E., now Deputy Head of the Department of Mechanical Engineering, Loughborough College of Technology, whose patient, clear explanation helped me in the beginning. Second, Mr. A. D. Munrow, B.Sc., Director of Physical Education in the University of Birmingham, a constant source of advice and encouragement. And third, Mr. E. F. Housden, O.B.E., M.C., M.A., to whom I am especially beholden for generous and invaluable comment in the preparation of this book.

G.H.G.D.

LONDON

April 1962

Contents

ix

PART II

CHAPTER ONE

Introduction

An important feature in the development of Track and Field athletics coaching has been the spreading of a knowledge of the mechanical principles essential to its skills. For human motion, with its boundless variability, obeys the laws of all motion; and athletic skill at the highest level always applies these same principles to advantage.

The scientifically-minded youth of today are ready to accept the truths of mechanics and, certainly, the subject as applied to sport is of considerable interest to young people. In the classroom it can be used to relate physics to physical education, for athletic examples are more 'alive' and meaningful than many normally used in the physics lesson.

However, in the teaching of skill on the sports ground, in the gymnasium or in the swimming pool mechanical explanation should be used with discretion, for athletes differ widely in intelligence, education and interests; while some will be intellectually stimulated and athletically improved by it, others will be confused.

Because athletes learn their skills through their kinaesthetic sensations, translating what they see or what they are told in terms of 'what it feels like' to do, more descriptive (if mechanically inaccurate) language is often preferable to the jargon of mechanics. Herein lies the art, as opposed to the science, of coaching athletics.

Again, the value of this kind of explanation to the performer varies from event to event. For example, the mechanics of running are extraordinarily complex, yet most good middle and long-distance runners develop an efficient style without giving the matter much thought. On the other hand, sprinters, hurdlers and field event athletes need a more technical, analytical approach to the mastering of skill.

Speaking generally, all athletes are best left unaware of the exact nature of their movements and need only sufficient detail to correct faults, satisfy curiosity and inspire confidence.

Teachers and coaches, however, should not be shy of complexity if it serves a real need. With them, a knowledge of mechanics is an essential tool with which to distinguish between important and unimportant, correct and incorrect, cause and effect, possible and impossible. With such knowledge they can observe and deduce much more than otherwise from athletic performance; and whereas the many skills of track and field are too frequently viewed as isolated experiences, each with its quite separate picture and puzzle, through a knowledge of mechanics teachers and coaches can recognise and explore likenesses, seeing what is general in what is particular, and so create a unity. It can also help towards a better understanding of other subjects, e.g. weight training, which count in the training of the athlete.

The mechanics of athletics is a comparatively undeveloped field in which, because of a multiplicity of unknown or only partially known factors, precise calculation is often impossible; here, too, principles applicable to rigid bodies are being applied to bodies that are far from rigid.

Athletes differ in their masses, skeletal formations, leverages and flexibilities; the magnitude, direction and effectiveness of their various body forces are often difficult or impossible to determine exactly; and accuracy has sometimes to be sacrificed in order to reduce the irregular human shape to more convenient geometric forms.

Even so, such deductions and rough estimates can be of sufficient accuracy to be of real practical value to the athletics coach or teacher— but they must be the result of careful observation and unbiased interpretation, and allowance must be made for laws other than mechanical ones (e.g. biological laws) which also play a part in the analysis of human motion.

It is hoped, therefore, that this book, although lacking in theoretical perfection, will yet achieve something of practical significance. Its contents are based upon the estimated needs of coaches of track and field athletics and physical educators. It assumes no previous knowledge of mechanics, yet it is hoped also to interest the expert.

Part I deals with matters of fact. It attempts to define relevant fundamental mechanical principles, taking many examples from familiar sporting experiences. Deliberately, its content arrangement does not conform to that of the normal mechanics textbook. Also deliberate is the avoidance of formulae wherever possible, as these are not always essential to clear explanation, and people untrained in mathematics are often confused by them; contrary to popular belief, an insight into the physical world can be obtained without the use of highly mathematical language. But, in the absence of formulae, words carry an extra burden and must be read carefully for their full meaning.

Part II, in which the techniques of the various track and field events are analysed, is less factual—for we have so much more to learn. Here, often, the thesis is mere speculation—a hypothesis to be tested and discussed against further lines of research. For the search for knowledge is an unending adventure at the edge of uncertainty.

It must be emphasised that an analysis of mechanical principles is but one aspect of the examination of athletic performance. In our quest for the complete picture we must seek the help of other sciences which arrive at somewhat different conceptions, for they can deduce only those facts obtainable through their special methods.

Thus, to the physiologist, athletic performance is a phenomenon of cells, humours, tissues and nutrient fluids obeying organic laws. The psychologist sees the athlete as a consciousness and a personality, while, to the physicist, he suggests a machine unique in its organisation, adaptiveness and complexity.

To the imaginative student of athletics, the borders of the various specialities are seen to overlap; the techniques of one science become meaningful and illuminating in others.

Motion[1]

All motion in track and field athletics, whether of an athlete's whole body, a part of it, or the movement of some object of athletic apparatus (like a pole or shot) behaves in accordance with certain well-established principles, and is subject to the same mechanical laws[2] as everything else on earth, animate and inanimate. Motion is of two kinds, *linear* and *angular*.

Linear motion

Linear (sometimes referred to as translatory or rectilinear) motion is characterised by the progression of a body in a straight line, with all its parts moving the same distance, in the same direction and at the same speed. One seldom sees pure linear motion in track and field events, but it is a factor to be taken into account, none the less. Fig. 1 gives an example of it in another sport, tobogganing. However, in so far as a sprinter's

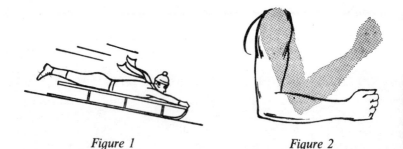

Figure 1   *Figure 2*

---

[1] The modern theory of motion was largely the creation of Galileo Galilei; and the century following his death in 1642 saw the establishment of the principles of Motion (the work of several great minds) along lines initiated by him.

[2] The branch of mechanics which deals specifically with motion resulting from the action of force is called *dynamics*; that branch which deals with a study of balanced forces is called *statics*.

movements in a 100 metres race can be thought of as being in a straight line, from start to finish (i.e. ignoring the rotational movements of arms, legs and trunk), linear movement *is* apparent, and there are many other such examples in athletics.

Angular motion

Angular or curvilinear motion is far more common in all human and animal locomotion because, mechanically speaking, such motion is dependent upon a system of levers of which they are constructed. It is of such importance in track and field athletics that a special chapter is devoted to it later in this book (pages 65–123).

Meanwhile, the chief difference between angular and linear motion is that whereas in angular movement one part of the object—the axis—remains fixed in relation to the others (as, for example, when the arm rotates about the shoulder joint (Fig. 2) or a discus rotates in the air (Fig. 3)), in linear motion every particle of the object travels the same distance simultaneously, moving from one location to another.

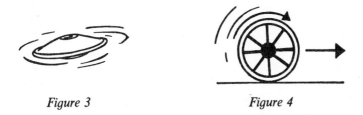

Figure 3   Figure 4

A body can perform linear and angular movements simultaneously: when, during its rotations or angular displacements, its axis moves along a certain path. The motion of a rolling wheel (Fig. 4) is an example of this. The wheel's hub moves in a linear fashion because of the rotations of the rim: an example of the many objects, including animals and human beings, which move *as a whole* in a straight path as a result of rotational movement (a single rotation or a combination of several rotations) of some part. A sprinter obtains linear movement through the rotary action of his feet; in throwing or putting, the rotational movements of an athlete's body can be co-ordinated to impart linear motion to the missile.

In all athletic activities the best results call for a blending of linear and rotational motion; in soccer, the speed with which the foot kicks the ball is a function not only of the rotations of the leg about its hip and knee, but also of the linear motion of the body as a whole; the sprinter's rotational foot movements must be co-ordinated with the linear vertical motion of his whole body; similarly, the hammer-thrower's forward movement across the circle must be co-ordinated with his turns.

Uniform and non-uniform motion

The motion of a body is said to be *uniform* when equal distances are covered in equal times. It is *non-uniform* when unequal distances are covered in equal times. Thus, an athlete running 1500 metres in 4 minutes at even pace would run with uniform motion (i.e. 16 sec per 100 metres); but a sprinter with intermediate times of 5.8 sec (50 m), 6.8 sec (60 m), 7.7 sec (70 m), 8.8 sec (80 m) and 11.1 sec (100 m) would be travelling with non-uniform motion.

The sprinter's motion from 60 to 70 metres would be described as *accelerated* as he covers the 10 metres distance 0.1 sec faster than the 10 metres immediately preceding (i.e. 50 to 60) and as he loses speed from the 70 metres mark his motion from then on is *retarded*. These are both loose analogies, since the process of taking even a single running stride involves acceleration and retardation.

Velocity

In mechanics a distinction is made between velocity and speed, although, in track and field athletics, for most purposes the terms are synonymous and, for the athlete, the term 'speed' is more meaningful than 'velocity'. *Velocity* includes the *direction* of travel as well as the *rate* at any instant. A runner may move at a speed of 24 m.p.h. (38.6 km.p.h.), but to state his velocity we must find in which direction he is travelling; he may have a velocity of 24 m.p.h. (38.6 km.p.h.) due north.

The rate of motion or the speed of an object is given in units of length and time. Thus a speed of 24 m.p.h. may also be stated as 35.2 ft per second (or 10.72 m/s).

Possessing *magnitude* and *direction*, velocity is a *vector quantity* and can therefore be represented diagrammatically by straight lines (pages 11 and 12).

Acceleration

Very rarely in athletics are velocities constant; more often they change in their speed or direction, or both at once. As we have seen, when the velocity of an object (e.g. an athlete or a missile) changes in speed it is said to be *retarded* or *decelerated* (if it continually decreases) or *accelerated* (if the velocity continually increases).

But the term *acceleration* is used in mechanics in either the gaining or losing of speed. Whenever the acceleration of an object is opposite in direction to its velocity (as when our sprinter lost velocity after reaching 70 metres) the term *negative acceleration* is used, and when acceleration and velocity are in the same direction (as when the sprinter picks up speed initially) the acceleration is called *positive*.

By 'acceleration', therefore, is meant *the rate of change of velocity*.

The following is an example of positive acceleration: let us suppose that an athlete running at a rate of 5 m/s (i.e. 18 km.p.h.) increases his speed so that it reaches 7.5 m/s (i.e. 27 km.p.h.) in 5 seconds. His change in speed is 7.5 minus 5, or 2.5 m/s. But this is not his acceleration; it is only the change in velocity.

The change in velocity, 2.5 m/s, occurred in 5 seconds, so the change in velocity *per second* is 2.5 m/s divided by 5, or 0.5 m/s every second. Each second the velocity increased by 0.5 m/s. The acceleration—the 'pick-up' to use sprinting parlance—was therefore 0.5 m per second per second (usually abbreviated to 0.5 m/s^2).

Thus every statement of acceleration must contain two units of time: one for velocity and one for the time during which that change in velocity occurred.

What has been said concerns *uniform acceleration*, but in athletics acceleration is often of a non-uniform character. However, we can only calculate the true value of an acceleration at any instant by taking as a basis the change of velocity during a period of time, making the latter as small as possible—ascribing an *instantaneous acceleration* to an object or athlete, which may be different at different times.

Being a vector quantity, acceleration has *direction* as well as magnitude; a runner taking a bend (Fig. 38), for example, is accelerating even if his speed is constant—because of his continuous change in velocity towards the inside of the bend at right angles to his running direction. Likewise, a hammer rotating at uniform speed has an acceleration towards its axis. (See page 47 and pages 226–32.)

So a change in either speed or direction constitutes an acceleration.

Motion of freely falling bodies

As performance in every athletic activity is influenced by the force of gravity, the laws of freely falling bodies apply to all track and field events. Strictly speaking, these laws are applicable only to motion in air-free space, but in athletics, if we exclude the javelin and discus, air resistance in falling can for all practical purposes be ignored, as can the decrease in acceleration with altitude (see page 49).

The actions of the efficient runner reduce to a minimum the dropping of body weight on each stride and, therefore, the degree of upward movement which would otherwise be wasted on raising it again. The good hurdler takes his obstacles with little to spare in order to return to ground quickly. The high-jumper trains to improve both the power and direction of his take-off drive to gain more height, 'defying' gravity. Again, the time during which shots, javelins, hammers and discoi are in flight is largely governed by these same laws.

For a hundred and more centuries, between the earliest civilised man and the time of Galileo, it was believed that heavier things fall faster in proportion to their weight. However, two bodies let fall simultaneously side by side (starting from rest) fall equally quickly, regardless of weight. In actual practice it is found that dissimilar bodies do not always accelerate under the influence of gravity at exactly the same rate. Any observed difference is due to the influence of air resistance. Newton demonstrated this most aptly in a classical experiment in which a feather and a golden guinea were released simultaneously from the top of a tall enclosed glass jar. As one would expect, the guinea reached the bottom of the jar before the feather. The experiment was then repeated after most of the air had been evacuated from the jar. On release, the feather and the guinea hit the bottom of the jar at the same time.

Obviously, bodies that are expanded to give a large surface area are going to be more affected by air resistance than bodies that are compact and streamlined. This is entirely due to the fact that a larger mass of air has to be displaced from in front of the larger surface and fill in behind it.

Near the earth's surface the vertical velocity of a freely falling object increases by 32 ft (9.8 m) per second every second (Fig. 5a); i.e. it is travelling 32 ft (9.8 m) per second faster at the end of each one second interval than it was at the beginning; and in rising it loses vertical velocity at the same rate.

The distance it falls is proportional to the square of the time—i.e. in one unit of time, 1: in two units, 4: in three units, 9 and so on—and can be calculated from the formula $d = \frac{1}{2}gt^2$, where d is the vertical distance of rise or fall, measured in feet or metres, $g = 32$ ft or 9.8 m and $t =$ the time in seconds.

An object falling for three seconds will therefore drop 144 ft (44.1 m)—i.e. 16 ft (4.9 m) × 9; will have a final speed of 32 ft (9.8 m) × 3,

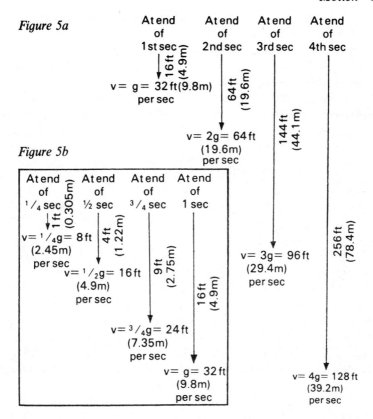

Figure 5a

Figure 5b

Board (metres)	Height C. of G. raised from take-off ft (m)	C. of G. time above board sec	C. of G. time below board sec	Time for whole flight sec	Speed of entry m.p.h. (km.p.h.)
1	4 (1.22)	1.16	Hands enter as C. of G. passes board	1.16	15 (24.1)
3	4 (1.22)	1.16	0.28	1.44	20 (32.2)
3	1 (0.305)	0.75	0.33	1.08	18 (29.0)
3	2 (0.6)	0.91	0.30	1.21	19 (30.6)
5	2 (0.6)	0.91	0.50	1.41	23 (37.0)
10	2 (0.6)	0.91	0.92	1.83	32 (51.5)

or 96 ft (29.4 m) per second; and its average speed will be half of this, i.e. 48 ft (14.7 m) per second.

The distance it falls in this time will be the average speed multiplied by the time of falling, i.e. 48 ft (14.7 m) × 3, or 144 ft (44.1 m). Released vertically with an initial upward speed of 96 ft (29.4 m) per second from a point 144 ft (44.1 m) below its original level, the object will take exactly the same time to reach this level, when its speed will again be zero.

The formulae $t = \sqrt{\dfrac{2h}{32}}$ (ft) and

$$t = \sqrt{\frac{2h}{9.8}} \text{(m)}$$

connect the vertical distance of rise or fall with the time taken, where t = the time in seconds and h the height in feet or metres, depending upon the chosen units of measurement.

Therefore, when an object drops 144 ft (44.1 m) the time taken is:

English $\sqrt{\dfrac{2 \times 144}{32}}$ sec $= \sqrt{\dfrac{288}{32}}$ sec $= \sqrt{\dfrac{9}{1}} = 3$ sec

Metric $\sqrt{\dfrac{2 \times 44.1}{9.8}}$ sec $= \sqrt{\dfrac{88.2}{9.8}}$ sec $= \sqrt{\dfrac{9}{1}} = 3$ sec

Similarly, if a high jumper rises 4 ft (1.23 m) from take-off to the high point of his jump (a greater height than so far achieved) the time taken will be:

English $\sqrt{\dfrac{2 \times 4}{32}}$ sec $= \sqrt{\dfrac{8}{32}}$ sec $= \sqrt{\dfrac{1}{4}}$ sec $= 0.5$ sec

Metric $\sqrt{\dfrac{2 \times 1.23}{9.8}}$ sec $= 0.5$ sec

Fig. 5*b* illustrates the distances an object drops in $\frac{1}{4}$ sec, $\frac{1}{2}$ sec, $\frac{3}{4}$ sec and 1 sec.

The table at the foot of page 9 shows the periods of time for the performing of fancy dives from boards of competition height, based on the assumption that the diver's Centre of Gravity is the same height above the board at take-off as it is above the water at the moment of entry.[1] Speeds of entry are also given.

---

[1] A. F. Ball, 'The Mechanics of Diving', unpublished thesis, Loughborough College, England.

The table indicates the value of height gained above the board; the height of the board itself is of less importance. For example, on a 3 m board a change in Centre of Gravity peak height from 2 ft (0.61 m) to 4 ft (1.22 m) will add 0.23 sec to the flight time; alternatively, only 0.20 sec if the board is raised to 5 m. To match a 0.23 sec increase in flight time, a diver's 10 m take-off would need to be raised to as much as 20.7 m (67 ft 10.7 in). Clearly, because of the acceleration of freely-falling bodies, height gained 'on the way up' in diving can be of greater value than a raising of the board to increase distance 'on the way down'.

Parallelogram and resolution of velocities

In the course of taking a running stride, high-jumping or releasing a shot (to take only three of countless examples) (Fig. 6) an athlete imparts to his body and/or the missile two motions simultaneously—one upward and the other forward. These are called *component velocities* because combined together, they produce a *resultant velocity*, i.e. the actual velocity of the body or missile. These two simultaneous component motions do not affect each other, can be considered separately, and for the purpose of athletic analysis it is often useful to treat them as such.

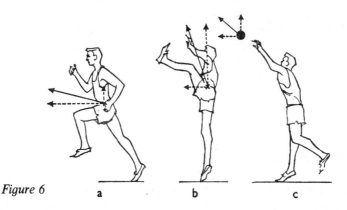

Figure 6   a   b   c

If the magnitude of each of these components is known, then both the direction and magnitude of the resultant velocity can be illustrated diagrammatically by the parallelogram method (Fig. 7). A spot is first marked on paper representing the point of release (in throwing) or the Centre of Gravity (see page 53) (in running, jumping and vaulting). From this two lines called *vectors* (from the Latin verb meaning to carry or convey) are drawn at right angles to each other; these indicate the two components, the length of each line from its point of origin to the arrowhead representing the magnitude of each velocity (Fig. 7*a*).

Using these as two sides of a parallelogram, the missing sides are constructed by simple geometric methods (Fig. 7*b*). A diagonal is finally drawn from the point of origin to the opposite corner, representing in its length and direction both the magnitude and direction of the resultant velocity (Fig. 7*c*).

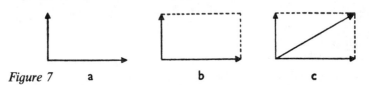

Figure 7   a   b   c

Conversely, when the magnitude and direction of the resultant motion are known it is simple enough to resolve this into its vertical and horizontal components (Fig. 8).

Component motions do not always operate at right angles to each other (see Fig. 171). In determining a resultant the parallelogram method can also be applied when angles are obtuse or acute (Fig. 9*a* and *b*). Here it is important to note that in the resolving of a resultant either the directions or the magnitudes of both components, or the direction and magnitude of one component, must be known in advance. Otherwise the problem is capable of many different solutions, since there are many parallelograms with the same diagonal.

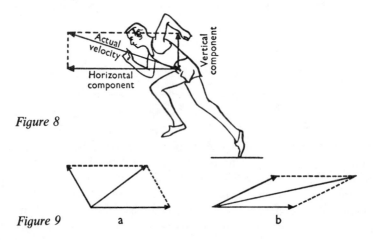

Figure 8

Figure 9   a   b

Quantities like velocity which have both magnitude and direction (e.g. force, acceleration and momentum), are also called 'vector quantities' and can be combined by the parallelogram method. Other qualities (e.g. mass, speed, power and energy) which have only *size*, without specific direction, are called *scalars*.[1] Track distances are usually treated as scalar quantities. We speak of a runner as having covered a distance regardless of the direction in which he travels. (See also pages 37–40).

In such a method as has been described accuracy depends on the quality of draughtsmanship and the scale of the drawings. Those with the necessary trigonometrical background will be freed from these limitations.

Path of Projectiles

As soon as throwing implements are released or athletes break contact with the ground they begin to fall, in the sense that gravity then changes their direction of motion. Hence, greater distance in throwing or jumping can be obtained when the initial velocity contains an upward as well as a forward component. For in this case the missile or athlete is in the air longer, permitting greater horizontal travel before return to ground.

In air-free space a combination of inclined-upward initial velocity and gravity causes the object's Centre of Gravity (see page 53) to describe a perfectly regular curve called a *parabola*. When the emphasis is on horizontal motion, as in long-jumping (Fig. 10), the curve is long and low, but in the high jump, where vertical movement is stressed, it is short and steep (Figs. 11 and 12).

It is important to note that in track and field athletics, where neither jet propulsion (where force is derived from the reaction to escaping gases) nor a mid-air change in weight take place, the movements of an athlete off the ground cannot disturb the smooth curve of his Centre of Gravity.

Again, in air-free space the horizontal component remains constant throughout flight; the long-jumper's forward speed on landing will be the same as at take-off. However, the vertical component, being subject to the laws of freely falling bodies, will be zero at the high point of the jump or throw and then the athlete or missile will fall with gravitational acceleration.

In fact, a jumper or missile may be regarded as having two independent motions (Fig. 12); an initial, uniform inclined-upward

[1] From the Latin *scala*, meaning a ladder; a symbol for increasing or decreasing magnitudes reminiscent of a musical scale.

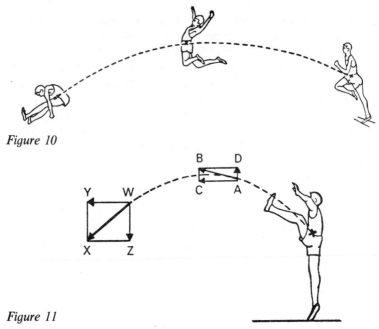

Figure 10

Figure 11

motion continuing along the line AB, and a free-fall measured at successive points (here, at 1/8 second intervals) along this line.

Note that our high jumper moves *horizontally* at a steady speed, while a decreasing upward motion to the high point of his jump is matched by an increasing downward motion from then on.

Fig. 11 shows how, through the use of vectors (page 11), the proportion of a jumper's horizontal and vertical motion can be illustrated at any point along the flight path of his Centre of Gravity. Thus, at point A, the *tangent* AB (i.e. the straight line at right angles to the radius of the flight path at this point) represents the athlete's velocity *at that instant*; while the vectors AC and AD denote his horizontal and vertical velocities, respectively.

Note that while the horizontal components AC and WY are equal, the vertical velocities (at points A and W) differ not only in direction, but also in magnitude.

In practice, of course, an object in flight pushes air aside, encountering air resistance, a force which slows down motion and distorts the flight path, causing the Centre of Gravity to travel in a curve,[1] somewhat as

---

[1] A so-called *ballistic curve*, with its descending part steeper than its ascending part.

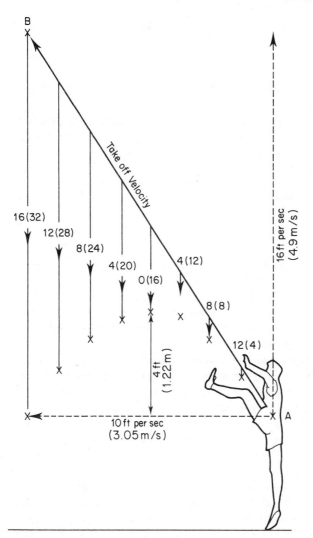

Figure 12

The resultant vertical velocities in feet per second are shown at $\frac{1}{8}$ second intervals. The free-fall component is in brackets. Up to 0.5 sec. the upward velocity component is greater than the free-fall velocity. At 0.5 sec. the two opposing components are exactly equal, after which the free-fall component exceeds the upward velocity and the body begins to accelerate downwards.

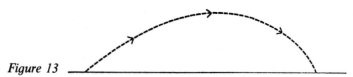

Figure 13

shown in Fig. 13. The affect of air resistance depends upon the size, shape, mass and velocity of the moving object, together with the time that it is in flight. In the jumping events, even though the body presents a considerable area, the flight paths are essentially regular because of the brevity of the flight time and the large mass of the body.

In the throwing events there is likely to be some variation in the parabola patterns. In the case of the shot and the hammer, resistance is proportional to $\dfrac{\text{diameter}}{\text{mass}}$. In both cases the diameters are relatively small and the masses high, so air resistance will be small. It can be shown by high speed photography that above the release point the shot describes an almost perfect parabola as would be expected. Similarly, the hammer's flight path is only likely to be distorted slightly even though the flight time is longer and the trailing cable and handle will tend to increase resistance.

The discus and javelin both have aerodynamic properties which will result in the development of left forces if correctly thrown. The presence of a left force is bound to change the trajectory of these projectiles.

Theoretically the optimum angle of release for a projectile regardless of release velocity is 45°, but this does not take into account the influence of air resistance, possible lift forces, as already mentioned and the fact that all implements are released at some distance above ground level. The hammer probably corresponds closest to the theoretical ideal as it experiences no lift forces, is relatively unaffected by air resistance and the release height is low compared to the distance thrown. The aerodynamic nature of the javelin and discus considerably modifies the ideal angle of release, as will also the presence of a head or following wind. Once again, the height of release is of little importance as the distances thrown are considerable. In shot putting the range obtained is much less than in the other throwing events and consequently the height of release becomes more important.

Fig. 15 illustrates diagrammatically how, in releasing the shot from a point 7 ft (2.13 m) above the ground, the optimum angle varies with the velocity; a low velocity necessitates the use of a comparatively low release

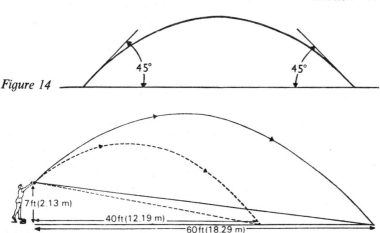

Figure 14

Figure 15

Projecting from a height of 7 ft (2.13 m)

For 60 ft (18.29 m) 41° 41′ from the horizontal

For 40 ft (12.19 m) 40° 2′ from the horizontal

angle, and vice versa. On the other hand, Fig. 16 shows how a short man, theoretically, must put more steeply than a tall one and use more velocity to attain a given distance. In this event it is, therefore, upon *height* and *velocity* of release that optimum angles depend.

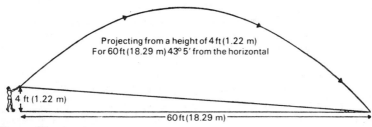

Projecting from a height of 4 ft (1.22 m)
For 60 ft (18.29 m) 43° 5′ from the horizontal

4 ft (1.22 m)

60 ft (18.29 m)

Figure 16

In the long-jump, where the athlete relies mainly on controlled sprinting speed to build up a high take-off velocity, this is done at the expense of vertical speed, horizontal motion being so marked that in the best jumps the athlete's Centre of Gravity (see page 53) is projected at take-off at an angle below 30 deg. (see page 177). Here, as in shot putting, the point of projection of the Centre of Gravity is above the landing level.

CHAPTER THREE

Forces (1): Newton's Laws

Force is that factor which produces or tends to produce motion. Motion in athletics can be produced only when force has been applied, but it is nevertheless possible to have force without motion. In track and field athletics the main sources of force are (*a*) internal, the muscular actions of the athlete, and (*b*) external, the downward pull of gravity, the friction and upthrust of the ground and the resistance of the air. As Sir Isaac Newton's Laws of Motion are fundamental to the whole science of force—even today's rocket and missile discoveries are based upon his theories—they will be discussed first.[1]

Newton's First Law (Law of Inertia)

It was as long ago as 1687 that Newton, in his *Principia Mathematica Philosophiae Naturalis*, enunciated the first of his three laws in the now famous words:

'*Every body continues in its state of rest, or of uniform motion in a straight line, except in so far as it may be compelled by impressed forces to change that state.*'

This is known as the Law of Inertia, inertia (the Latin for idleness or laziness) being the property innate in all bodies, animate and inanimate, by virtue of which they obey this law.

Expressed in simpler language, it says that everything in the universe is lazy, so lazy that force is necessary to get it on the move, when it then travels in a straight line with constant speed; so lazy that, once in motion, further force must be applied to slow it down, stop it, speed it up or change its direction.

---

[1] The discrepancies that exist between Newtonian (i.e. classical) mechanics and the physical universe are quite undetectable by ordinary means and, generally speaking, are important only in investigating the motions of bodies of sub-atomic size or those with a speed approaching that of light. As Albert Einstein himself wrote, 'No one must think that Newton's great creation can be overthrown by Relativity or any other theory.'

Thus, a shot rolling along level ground would continue to roll for ever in a straight line were it not for ground and air friction. An athlete moving through space would continue to travel for ever in a straight path were it not for air resistance and the downward pull of gravity. The law applies also to spinning motion. A hammer thrower would go on and on turning were it not for friction and the forces subsequently applied in releasing the missile.

Direct proof of the correctness of Newton's assumption is impossible here on earth, since we cannot remove a body completely from external influences, but in its logical results the law is never at variance with experience; and, of course, of recent years it has been demonstrated and confirmed practically in space research.

Inertia, therefore, is concerned with a body's resistance to change in movement and is an important—often determining—factor in problems involving energy-expenditure and fatigue in exercise. It is a property always present in an object and is never 'overcome' (*in the sense that it is destroyed*) once that object has been set in motion, as is frequently supposed.

The claim 'to get an object on the move one must overcome its inertia' is based on the common experience whereby it is more difficult to start an object moving than to keep it in motion; but this is due to the fact that, to start it, force must be used against both its inertia *and* the frictional ground and air forces, whereas to maintain a constant speed only the frictional forces oppose movement, and less force is therefore required. But to increase the speed again, inertia has still to be 'overcome'. For example, ignoring ground and air friction, when a definite force is applied horizontally, the pressure between the hand and a 16-lb (7.26 kg) shot is exactly the same, whether the shot is moved from rest or is in motion at the time. *In terms of inertia, therefore, rest and uniform straight-line motion are manifestations of the same thing.*

Inertia is proportional to *mass*—the amount of the material of which an object is made. In fact, the terms are often interchangeable. The mass of an object is the measure of its inertia, its resistance to change in motion. The British unit of mass is the pound (lb).[1] The S.I unit of mass is the kilogramme (kg). By way of illustration, if equal forces are applied to a 16-lb (7.26 kg) shot and a 1-lb 12$\frac{1}{4}$-oz (800 gm) javelin, the change in

---

[1] For engineers, the unit quantity of mass is called the 'slug', which is that mass which will be accelerated at the rate of one foot per second per second by a force of one pound weight. A slug is therefore approximately 32 lb (14.5 kg).

motion of the javelin (i.e. its acceleration) will be much greater. Mass must not be confused with *weight*; they are not the same (page 50).

Newton's Second Law (Law of Acceleration)

By means of the second law, which actually includes the first, we can determine how force can change the motion of an object. It states:

'The rate of change of momentum is proportional to the impressed force, and the actual change takes place in the direction in which the force acts.'

Momentum is the product of mass and velocity: it can be considered as a measure of the quantity of motion possessed by a body. It is a vector quantity, i.e. it possesses both magnitude and direction. A runner having a mass of 140 lb and a velocity of 30 ft/s has a momentum of 4,200 units, and so has a 30-lb object moving at 140 ft/s. Alternatively, a runner having a mass of 65 kg and a velocity of 10 m/s has a momentum of 650 units, and so has a 10 kg object moving at 65 m/s. Thus, a marble can possess the momentum of a cannon ball, given sufficient velocity.

At a definite time the moving runner has momentum, and a period of time is necessary for him to change it. From the law of inertia we know that the velocity of a moving object (i.e. the distance it travels per unit of time in a given direction) remains constant unless a force acts on it. This second law tells us that, *provided we consider a definite period of time*, any change in velocity (positive or negative) will be directly proportional to the amount of force used—assuming it not to be countered by an opposing force[1], and also inversely proportional to the object's mass.

For example, consider a definite period of time, say, two seconds; the effective force a runner must use to increase his speed during these two seconds in a race is in direct proportion to his speed increase, i.e. if he wishes to double this speed increase in the two seconds he must double the amount of force he exerts.

If there are two runners, one weighing only half as much as the other, and the same effective horizontal force is exerted by each during the two seconds, the lighter athlete will acquire double the speed increase of the heavier one—demonstrating that the change in velocity is inversely proportional to the mass of the object. This second law therefore generalises the obvious fact that one can throw a cricket ball farther and faster than a 16-lb (7.26 kg) shot. (See also page 30.)

---

[1] In the analysis of human motion the term 'force' usually refers to a *net* or *resultant* force.

It should be noted, however, that a force need not act through an object's Centre of Gravity to produce a given linear acceleration, for the force will create the same linear acceleration whether or not so directed. Should the force *not* pass through the Centre of Gravity, that point will change speed in a direction parallel to the direction of the force while, simultaneously, the object will rotate about an axis passing through its Centre of Gravity (see also 'Moments', pages 70–72).

Newton's Third Law (Law of Reaction)[1]

One cannot exert a force without opposition; a single, isolated force is therefore an impossibility. For every force acting anywhere there is always an equal force acting in an opposite direction. Forces always work in pairs, as 'twins' opposing each other. This is the meaning of Newton's Third law, which states: '*To every action there is an equal and opposite reaction; or the mutual actions of two bodies in contact are always equal and opposite in direction.*'

The effect upon one body is known as the *action* and that upon the other the *reaction*, but it is often a matter of choice or opinion as to which is which. In mechanics the two forces are of equal importance and exist simultaneously; but obviously, in the analysis of human motion we have often to think of *Man* as originating the force.

To the question, 'Why don't the opposing forces cancel out, leaving no force at all?' the answer is that they *do* when they arise *in the same body*. That is why a body is unaffected by mutual actions between its parts. In athletics, however, this Third Law often involves equal and opposite forces *in two separate bodies*.

For example, if two spring balances are hooked together and then pulled in opposite directions (Fig. 17) the readings on them will be identical. A man standing on the ground is pulled down on it with his weight and the ground pushes up with a force (often referred to as *ground reaction*) equal to his weight (Fig. 18). When a bird beats downward with

Figure 17 7   ←——— F1   ===   ——— F2 →

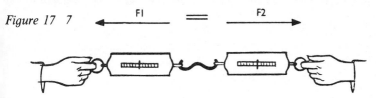

---

[1] Newton's own, particular contribution to the theory of motion; for the First and Second Laws had been effectively applied earlier by Galileo.

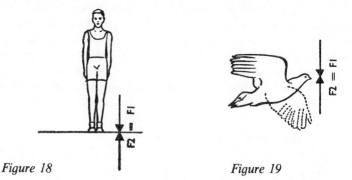

Figure 18   Figure 19

its wings in flight, its body and the air struck experience equal but opposite forces (Fig. 19). And when a sprinter leaves his blocks (Fig. 20) he drives backward with a force equal to that which propels him forward; for not only does this third law hold for bodies in equilibrium—it is equally true in acceleration.[1]

Figure 20   Figure 21

For as long as a runner or jumper *accelerates* his swinging leg upward at take-off, the tendency will be for the rest of his body to be pulled down; hence he could be considered effectively heavier at that instant (Fig. 21). If the leg ceases to accelerate, but continues upward with a uniform motion, then his take-off foot presses against the ground with a force equal to his weight; *and when it slows down momentarily he loses weight again.* In a reverse movement, with the leg dropping (but with his other foot still in contact with the ground) the pressure between his supporting foot and the ground decreases and then increases. These examples of

---

[1] But some would say it applies only to *dynamical* systems. They would accept the instances of bird and sprinter but would regard the spring balances and standing man as examples of a static equilibrium of forces.

action and reaction and the two-way action of forces can be demonstrated on a weighing machine or, more scientifically, on a force platform. (For more detailed treatment, see Chapter 8, pages 155–164).

When a force sets an object in motion the momentum of that object is altered. As, according to this Third Law, forces always work in opposing pairs, a change in momentum in one object must be accompanied by the same change in momentum of another object in an opposite direction and *the momentum of the system as a whole therefore remains the same.*[1] Hence, when a gun is fired, the explosion gives the bullet momentum in a forward direction equal but opposite to the gun's 'kick' against the shoulder (Fig. 22).

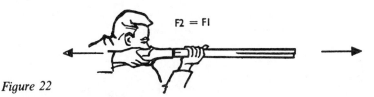

Figure 22

Again, a high-jumper's momentum at take-off is equal to the change in the earth's momentum in an opposite direction (Fig. 11). But the reaction of the earth is not noticeable because of its enormous mass. Likewise, such is the law of reaction, the earth moves up to meet the athlete as he falls towards the earth. The earth's mass is so great in comparison that both movements can be neglected.

The principle holds good, too, for mid-air movements of parts of an athlete's body. Although, in the air, he can do nothing to change the momentum of his body as a whole[2] (see *Path of projectiles*, page 13) nevertheless he can move a part of it against some other part, producing similar reactions within the body. See also Chapter Five (pages 100–123).

It should be noted, however, that to exert a *maximum* of body force in running, jumping or throwing the athlete must be in contact with firm, resisting ground. If, for example, in shot putting he breaks contact before completing the delivery, then he can only impart additional speed to the shot by giving his body backward speed in reaction. His final arm thrust is made at the cost of reducing the shoulder's forward speed; thus, the force and range of arm movement are reduced (pages 201–206 and 239).

---

[1] *The Law of the Conservation of Momentum.* Something that is conserved is protected, kept safe from depletion.
[2] Sky divers and parachutists are different because they use an external force—air resistance—to change their body positions and momentum.

CHAPTER FOUR

Forces (2)

Force

As stated in the introduction to the previous chapter, force is that factor which produces or tends to produce motion.

In athletics all motion is derived from force—force from muscle tensions, from gravity, from the friction and upthrust of the ground and the resistance of the air. In sport we are concerned mostly with the use of force for *changing the state of motion* of athletes and their implements—slowing them down, stopping or speeding them up.

However, there can be force without motion. For example, one can be unsuccessful in trying to move a heavy weight; a javelin or pole can be gripped tightly without its moving; a tennis ball can be flattened a little by squeezing. *Force can, therefore, bring about, or tend to bring about, a change of shape in a body*, causing stresses within, which are the result of its attempt to regain its original shape; *and forces do not affect motion when their resultant is zero.*

Force can be felt but not seen. But its effects can be seen and measured, and it can be described and determined in terms of its *magnitude*, *direction* and *point of application*. Like velocity and momentum, therefore, *it is a vector quantity*, and can be analysed by the use of a parallelogram.

Magnitude. For the measurement and comparison of forces we need unit systems based on *length, mass* and *time*. In the English system, these are the foot, the pound and the second respectively (f.p.s.); the metre, kilogram and the second (m.k.s.) in the now more widely-used Système International d'Unites (S.I.).

With the f.p.s. system, a unit of force (known as the *poundal*) gives an acceleration of one foot per second per second (1 ft/s^2) to a mass of one pound, while the S.I. unit of force (called a *newton*) accelerates kilogramme one metre per second per second (1 m/s^2).

The newton, now used throughout all scientific work, is called an absolute unit because its value is independent of where it is applied. Because the weight of a body varies from place to place (see page 49) a unit dependent on weight is unsatisfactory.[1]

The athlete produces force by the action of muscles working upon the skeletal system. The contraction of muscles produces movement at our joint complexes which brings about movement of the body as a whole. Movement therefore depends upon the physiological characteristics of the muscles themselves and the mechanical effects that muscle action has upon the lever systems of the body.

Muscles are composed of large numbers of muscle fibres which, although being essentially similar, have significant differences in size, structure and function. A confusing variety of ways have been devised over the years for classifying these different types of muscle fibres. A popular contemporary method is to classify according to function and in this system two basic types of fibres have been identified which are functionally opposite. These are known as fast twitch (FT) and slow twitch (ST) fibres. The FT fibres have adaptation for rapid, explosive activity. Their anaerobic capacity is high and they are capable of giving a large power output for short intervals of time. Their activity is limited by the depletion of energy sources within the fibres and the accumulation of waste products. The ST fibres, however, are essentially aerobic in function and are capable of sustained action of lower intensity and consequently are more important in endurance type work.

All muscles have a mixture of both types of fibre. The ratio of FT to ST fibres in muscle is not fixed. Variation occurs according to function. For example, those muscles that are concerned with the maintenance of posture tend to have a larger number of ST fibres because it is necessary for them to work for long periods of time without fatiguing. Variation in the FT, ST balance is also genetic. Some people are born with a general predominance of FT fibres and these people show special aptitude for 'explosive activity'. Our sprinters, jumpers and shot putters are drawn from this group. Conversely, some people have a greater ST element in their muscular make-up and these, as would be expected, excel in the endurance events. The evidence suggests that we are born with a fixed number of muscle fibres in each muscle and a fixed ratio of FT to ST fibres. Although we can hypertrophy the fibres that we have, we cannot develop new ones. Similarly, by employing the correct training pro-

---

[1] Nevertheless, for practical purposes a newton can be considered .225 of the weight of one pound.

cedures we can enhance either FT or ST performance but the fibres themselves are not transmutable. In other words, we cannot change FT to ST fibres or vice versa. Complicating the whole situation is the fact that researchers are identifying fibres that are intermediate in structure and function between the two extremes of the ST and FT types. Within these intermediate types it is suggested that either the explosive or the endurance capacity could be developed.

Traditionally, muscle has been looked upon as a contractile structure which produces force as a result of the capacity to shorten. This is perhaps a rather naive view because muscles not only develop tension in shortening but can also do so in lengthening. Indeed the contractile capacity of a muscle is greatly enhanced by its ability to couple its contractility to its elasticity. Little is known about the elastic function of muscle because it is very difficult to investigate due to its transience, but it is well recognised that large power outputs are often only possible by bringing into play the elastic component.

The magnitude of muscular force that can be brought into play is dependent upon:

(i) the actual ST/FT muscle fibre ratio;

(ii) the size of the muscle or its physiological cross section (i.e. the section through its maximum diameter at right angles to the direction of its fibres;

(iii) the speed at which the muscle fibres actually shorten when acting concentrically. (Concentric contraction occurs when the muscle is actually shortening while in a state of tension.) Fig. 23*a* shows quite clearly that the faster the muscle contracts the less force can be developed. This diagram also shows that muscle can develop even greater force while lengthening (i.e. being stretched) while in a state of tension. A muscle that is compelled to stretch while in active tension is said to be working eccentrically.

(iv) whether the muscles can be put in a state of tension immediately prior to contraction. This 'pretensioning' of muscles is frequently employed when high power outputs are required and suggests that there is a coupling of the elastic capacity of the muscle with its contractile capability.

Within limits, the faster the pretensioning movement the greater will be the overall power output.

In athletics the pretensioning of muscle is brought about by (1) quickly lowering the body on ground contact, (2) abruptly checking its horizontal motion or (3) otherwise increasing its load by accelerating

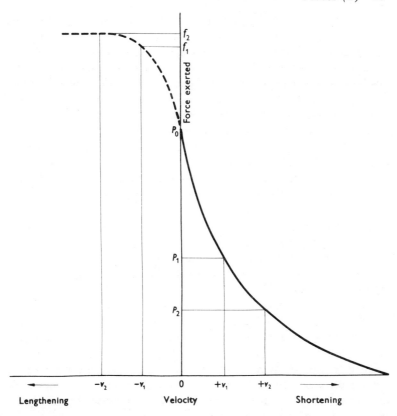

Figure 23a

A diagram of the relationship between force and velocity of shortening for human muscle: P_1 and P_2 are the forces exerted by a single fibre shortening at velocities v_1 and v_2; f_1 and f_2 are the forces when the fibre is being stretched at the same velocities v_1 and v_2; P_0 represents the isometric tension of that fibre.

From B. C. Abbott, Brenda Bigland and J. M. Ritchie, 'The physiological cost of negative work', *Journal of Physiology*, 117 (1952), page 386.

another part of the body, e.g. the arms, a free leg, the hips or the trunk and head.

Thus, a high jumper is able to exert much greater force at take-off as a result of his jumping leg flexing eccentrically immediately before its drive. It is interesting to observe that the amount of flexion seen at the hip and the knee during the take-off thrust is quite small which again suggests that we are using the elastic action of the muscle rather than the generation of contractile force. (Fig. 142 *k-o*) A golfer's trunk is already twisting in the direction of drive before the club head reaches its highest point in the back-swing (Fig. 23*b*). Likewise, good throwers 'lead with the hips' to first stretch resisting trunk muscles. (Fig. 192*d–e*)

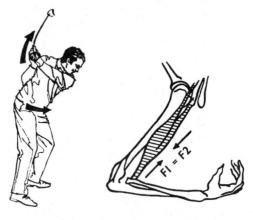

Figure 23b   *Figure 24*

In athletics we are seldom, if ever, concerned with the measurement of force of a single muscle, but rather think in terms of a whole movement, momentarily involving the total force of several muscle groups working against the resistance of the ground (as in running), a missile (e.g. in discus throwing) or, sometimes, against some other part of the body (as in movement which originates in the air).

Certainly, in athletic movement, no muscle—and not even a single muscle group—works alone, for all the muscles of the body are more or less in constant demand, supporting, guiding and generally contributing to force and the control of movement. Where, through weakness in the supporting muscles, joints are poorly stabilized, proper running, jumping and throwing movement is impossible; and in such activities as weight training muscular weakness can cause the body to be moved out of effective position.

Electromyographs monitor the electrical impulses of working muscles—information which can be fed back by means of radio-telemetry. By recording such impulses on the audio-tracks of video-tape machines equipped with instant slow-motion play-back, pictures of athletics in action can be synchronised with the visual images of muscular impulses responsible for that action.

The technique has shown that so-called 'leading-up exercises' and other coaching methods sometimes produce muscular patterns which differ from those required. In particular, the *sequence* of muscle action is not the same, suggesting a need to re-examine some methods of coaching athletic skills.

Direction. When athletic efficiency is at its best force has been properly directed both internally and externally. The direction of the force exerted by a single muscle (Fig. 25) depends upon the relation of the moving bone's long axis to the muscle-insertion. The angle between the muscle's line of pull and the long axis of this bone (the axis being a straight line from the bone's mid-point at either end) is known as the angle of pull, an angle which, with body movement, is constantly changing.

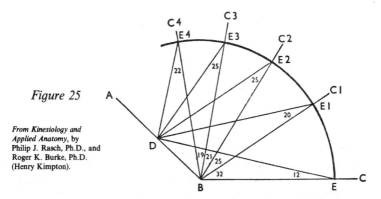

Figure 25

From *Kinesiology and Applied Anatomy*, by Philip J. Rasch, Ph.D., and Roger K. Burke, Ph.D. (Henry Kimpton).

Fig. 25 illustrates the changes in the angle of pull when a muscle shortens. The line AB represents a stationary bone and BC a moving one. With the bone-lever at BC the angle of pull DEB is only 12 deg., but when the bone is moved to BC1 the angle increases to 20 deg.; it is 25 deg. at both BC2 and BC3 and then reduces to 22 deg. at position BC4. Only when the muscle's origin D is farther from the axis B than the insertion E can this angle be at right angles.

From a purely mechanical point of view, a muscle's most effective pull will be at right angles to the moving bone; but as muscle fibres at such an angle are seldom adequately stretched, the greatest effective force is usually obtained when the angle of pull is more acute (Fig. 25). It would seem, therefore, that *physiological laws sometimes work in opposition to mechanical ones*, which points to the futility of trying to analyse athletic techniques on a mechanical basis, muscle by muscle; moreover, in a dynamic situation it is usually impossible to identify the contribution of separate muscles.

As with the assessing of the magnitude of force, it is more convenient to consider the direction of an athlete's *total, resultant* body force exerted against the resistance of the ground or apparatus (and, sometimes, to express this approximately in terms of his own body weight or the weight of the missile he may be throwing). In running, for example, this should be done in such a way as to produce mainly horizontal movement; at take-off in high-jumping force must be directed mainly in a downward direction, so that the athlete shall be thrown almost vertically; and in throwing events the direction of total body force will determine the angle at which the missiles are thrown.

Point of application. The effect of force varies with the point of its application. This characteristic is discussed more fully later (pages 65–7 and 70–79). Meanwhile, it is sufficient to say that, internally, force is applied to the bone levers at the points where muscles originate or are inserted (Fig. 24). As to the total force of propulsion in running and jumping, it is applied where the feet contact the ground (Fig. 20) and, in shot putting, where the missile touches the hand (Fig. 192). The point of application and the direction of force may be combined in the one concept: *the line of action.*

Accelerated motion

As already stated, in track and field athletics we are mostly concerned with the use of force to change the state of motion of athletes and their implements. In this connection, two simple experiments should help to clarify its effects.

First, as in Fig. 26a, two 8-lb (3.63 kg) shots are placed on a smooth, horizontal surface, and between them is set a compressed spring which cannot expand because it is tied. When the thread is broken the spring drives both shots apart with equal force (Fig. 26b) and they collide simultaneously with two wooden blocks set, beforehand, at equal distances from the shots' original positions (Fig. 26c). From this it can be

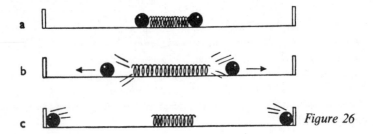

Figure 26

seen that *when equal forces are applied against equal masses they produce the same change in velocity,* and experiments prove that *accelerations given to a body are proportional to the magnitude of the force.*

Then, one of the shots is replaced by a 16-lb (7.26 kg) missile (Fig. 27*a*) and the experiment is repeated (Fig. 27*b*). Now, the larger shot is given only half the acceleration of the smaller one and, in a given time, it travels only half the distance (Fig. 27*c*). From this we can conclude that *when equal forces impart accelerations to unequal masses, the product of mass and acceleration is the same;* which gives us our measurement of *force = mass × acceleration.*

Therefore, under otherwise identical conditions, the acceleration of athletes and their apparatus depends upon their masses which, in turn, are measures of *inertia,* resistance to motion (Newton's First and Second Laws, pages 19–21).

To provide *equal acceleration* in *unequal masses,* the forces applied must be proportional to the masses; for example, if there are two runners, one of mass 120 kg and the other 60 kg, the heavier athlete must exert twice the force of the lighter athlete to produce the same acceleration.

We have seen that, *for a given body,* accelerations are proportional to the magnitudes of the forces producing them; and a force equal to body weight is responsible for an acceleration, *g,* of approximately 32 ft (9.8 m) per second every second. It follows that a force of twice body weight will result in an acceleration of 2*g.*

In establishing this type of relationship between force and acceleration a useful equation is

$$\frac{F}{W} = \frac{a}{g}$$

where F is the force, W the weight of the object or person, a the acceleration related to weight and g either 32 or 9.8, depending on the units chosen for *all* these measurements.

So, for example, we can relate a sprinter's instantaneous horizontal component of drive from his blocks of, say, 200 lb to his weight of 160 lb; and his acceleration can then be calculated *in the same ratio to g*— in this case 5:4, or 40:32—i.e. 40 ft/s^2, the relevant equation being

$$\frac{200}{160} = \frac{40}{32}$$

Again, an athlete whose mass is 70 kg and who exerts a force of 100 kg (more correctly 980 newtons: see pages 50–51) will have an acceleration in the ratio of 10:7, the metric equation being

$$\frac{100}{70} = \frac{14}{9.8}$$

i.e. 14 m/s².

Or where the acceleration is known, and then related to g, we can assess the instantaneous drive relative to body weight.

Just as the Force of Gravity is responsible for a constant free-fall acceleration which, in 1, 2, 3, etc. units of time produces vertical distances in the proportions of 1, 4, 9, etc. (pages 7–8) so does a similar relationship between time and distance apply to an object or athlete moving *in any direction* as a result of the application of *any constant force in* that direction.

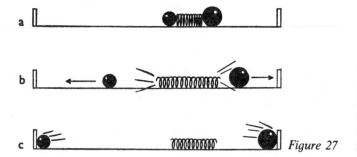

Figure 27

Impulse

The change in speed of an athlete, discus, shot, javelin or hammer does not merely depend upon the force applied, but also upon the *time* for which it operates, its *impulse*. In starting from blocks, for example, an athlete should adjust his position not only to increase his driving force but also to lengthen the time during which it is exerted, thus increasing his starting velocity (Fig. 132). And in the throwing events, also, the best techniques are those in which maximum muscular force is exerted for the longest possible time in the right direction.

The same change in speed (and, therefore, the same impulse) can be produced by a small force acting for a long time, or a very large force acting for a short time. In building their impulses (for a given sequence of muscular activity) athletes certainly differ in combining force with time—yet, for any one individual, the impulse pattern is markedly similar over consecutive trials of that activity.

In athletics, an increase in force often requires a more rapid action, resulting in a decrease in *time* of operation—unless the distance over which the force operates is increased. With human motion, the bigger the force, the faster the limb extension and the sooner a movement ends. So *distance* (determined, usually, by the range of body and limb extension) rather than *time* is the limiting factor. Fortunately, however, increases in force are often effectively greater than decreases in time—so total impulse is improved.

The impulse of a force is equal to the momentum (mass × velocity) of the mass moved from rest by the force. Of academic interest only, the impulse given to a high-jumper at take-off is also given to the earth, but in an opposite direction. Their momenta are therefore equal. Likewise, an athlete's momentum from the blocks in a sprint start is equal but opposite to the earth's, for the impulse is the same. In fact, *the concept of momentum is often used as equivalent to that of impulse.*

In the analysis of athletic movement it is often convenient to distinguish between a *controlled* impulse, due to direct muscular effort and joint leverage, as with the leg-drive in sprint-starting, and a *transmitted* impulse produced, for example, by the bracing of a comparatively unyielding leg against the ground during the initial stages of a high-jump take-off, where the magnitude and direction of impulse are more determined by the action of the free leg and arms—not through muscular action of the supporting leg itself (Fig. 100). Almost invariably, *in track and field athletic techniques transmitted impulses precede the smaller controlled impulses.* (See also pages 159–65.) Because it involves force, impulse is a vector quantity.

Effective force

In track and field athletics there are many examples of the impossibility of exerting full force against a fast-moving object, for the feet (in running) and the hand (in throwing) cannot be moved fast enough. In such cases, the speed of movement of the source of resistance reduces not only the ability to apply muscular effort, but also the time for which that effort can be applied. These two factors may place quite a low limit to the size of the *effective force*, i.e. the force 'received' by the ground or implement. For this reason, in most athletic events, acceleration has its greatest value at the beginning, when the athlete's body and/or the missile he holds is moving slowly.

Sprinting is a good example. At the start, where the opposing force of air resistance is small because the athlete's movement over the ground is comparatively slow, most of the considerable horizontal force of his leg drive is effective in producing a marked change in speed. But as his speed increases the opposing forces also increase, and therefore a progressively smaller fraction of his limited leg drive is available to add to his speed.

It is difficult to exert a forceful backward thrust against the ground which, to the athlete, appears to be moving in an opposite direction. Top speed is reached when the effective force of the leg drive equals all the opposing forces. Up to this point in the race his speed has increased, but by a progressively diminishing degree. For, with each stride taken, foot contact is of shorter and shorter duration; impulse is successively reduced and even without an actual reduction in horizontal thrust (and reduction is certain) each successive increase in speed is smaller.

A second example can be taken from shot putting where, as soon as the movement across the circle begins, pressure between the shot and the athlete's fingers increases; for force is being applied to accelerate it, and this pressure will aways be equal to the force exerted. A further increase in applied force would result in another increase in pressure, but in practice shot putters find the pressure *reduced* in the final arm-thrust; they find it *easier* to move, whereas if it were possible to impart a constant acceleration it would be as difficult to put at the end as at the beginning. This is because of the difficulty of 'keeping up with' the shot.

In fact, to be able to accelerate his body or a throwing implement an athlete must be capable of moving at a greater speed than the ground or the missile moving away from him. And the greater his speed, in comparison, the greater his effective force will be. Clearly, then, *the ability of an athlete to apply force depends not only upon strength but also upon speed.* (See also pages 70–71, 'Moments in Rotation and Spin.')

Summation of forces

From a purely mechanical point of view it is immaterial whether a succession of forces is applied one by one or simultaneously; the resultant is the same. However, this is not so in human motion. Where human beings are concerned the strongest parts of the body are the heaviest, and have a correspondingly greater inertia: consequently they are less speedy in their movements. With the athlete it is a question of using the different muscles when they are capable of sufficient speed to apply full force.

Again, because the force exerted externally by human muscle diminishes with the speed of limb movement, both *force* and *time*, the constituents of impulse, can be increased *through the simultaneous action of various muscles and levers; for, then, each is prevented from moving more rapidly by the accelerations of others.*

This principle is of particular importance in jumping, where the aim is to impart vertical speed to the athlete's body; but it can also apply to a thrower's downward thrust, evoking an upward counter thrust from the ground. These factors call for a definite sequence and timing of forces. Although, for maximum impulse, all parts of an athlete's body should, in theory, begin their accelerations simultaneously, *in practice* the strongest but slower muscles surrounding the body's Centre of Gravity begin, to be joined by the muscles of the thighs and then by those of the weaker, lighter but faster extremities—*ideally, with all the forces ending together.* This principle, as it applies to high jumping, is illustrated in Fig. 28.

But in throwing (where the final aim is to impart maximum speed *to the missile,* not to the athlete himself) *angular summation* is of special

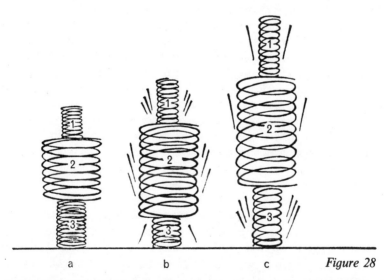

a　　　　　b　　　　　c　　　　*Figure 28*

The numbered springs represent a high jumper's arms (1), trunk and free leg (2), and jumping leg (3). In (A) the spring-system is at rest. In (B) very considerable upward acceleration of the free leg, trunk and arms place a heavy burden on the supporting leg—tending to compress (pretension) it. Only when these accelerations are reduced (*reduced,* not finished, if the greatest possible impulse is to be exerted against the ground) can the jumping leg extend (C).

significance. Here, the principle of the flail applies, where as much energy as possible (and, therefore, as much speed) is 'fed' into the implement.[1]

In a discus throw, for example, (from a wound-up position where hips precede trunk and shoulders which, in turn, lead the arm) the body unwinds in sequence. First the hips (carrying with them an equal rotation of the trunk, shoulders and arm); then, as the hips attain their top speed, the shoulders begin to twist with respect to the hips, *slowing the latter down*. (For when one part of the body moves in a clockwise direction it will have the effect of moving an adjoining part counter clockwise: Newton's Third Law, page 21.) (See Fig. 190*f* and *g* too.) As the legs and hips are checked, something has to happen to the momentum that they possessed. Some will undoubtedly be absorbed as friction between the athlete's shoes and the circle's surface, but a large element will be transferred to the trunk and shoulders. As the trunk, shoulders and arms have a lesser mass than the body as a whole, this injection of momentum will cause them to accelerate, particularly as they are already moving in the same direction as the original movement. The whole process is repeated. As the trunk and shoulders unwind, the throwing arm starts to accelerate and as before this induces a contrary rotational reaction in the trunk which slows down. Momentum now flows from the trunk and shoulders to the throwing arm and in consequence of the momentum differential and acceleration occurs again.

In a mechanically ideal situation the body should be stationary at the instant of release, showing a completely efficient transfer of momentum to the discus. This is never possible in practice. In throwing, particularly, it is sometimes difficult to co-ordinate vertical and angular impulses; e.g. in discus throwing, athletes often break contact with the ground before release because leg and trunk extensions are more rapid than the unwinding movements of the upper body. (See also page 206.)

Of course, the sequence with which an athlete uses the different parts of his body is partly dependent upon the nature of the construction of the human body; and the timing of the various movements can be influenced by the strengths and accelerations of these parts (*see* also pages 202 and 239). This principle of momentum transfer associated with the acceleration and checking of successive body segments with consequent acceleration is extremely important and is fundamental to many throwing, kicking and striking activities. Unfortunately it is not a

[1] A. V. Hill, *Living Machinery* (Bell, 1939), pages 203-5; C. B. Daish, *The Physics of Ball Games* (Hodder and Stoughton, 1972), page 39.

principle that many would naturally adopt and comes to the majority only because of good coaching or as a result of considerable trial and error in practice over a long period.

Opposing forces, parallelogram and resolution of forces

As already stated (page 27) the qualities determining a force are its magnitude, direction and point of application. Force is a vector quantity, therefore, which can be represented diagrammatically by straight lines, as can motion (page 11). Indeed, as, in athletics, all motion is derived through the application of force. Many claims made in Chapter Two in respect of motion apply equally well here.

A line can be drawn, called a *force vector*, with one end representing the point of application, its direction and arrowhead coinciding with the direction of the force, and its length containing as many units of length as the force has units of force (Fig. 7).

Opposing forces. In Fig. 29 (tug o' war) the reactions to the forces exerted on the ground are represented by vector lines, both horizontal, which can be replaced by a single line—a resultant—representing the 250 newtons (see page 27, 50) acting towards the right. When two forces are acting in opposite directions, therefore, the resultant (i.e. *net* force) has the direction of the larger force.

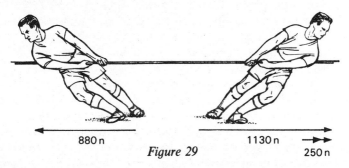

◄———— 880 n	1130 n ———►	
	Figure 29	250 n

Parallelogram of forces. But when several forces acting at a point are not directly opposed and parallel, the problem is more difficult. Forces, like velocities, do not disturb each other; each is separate, and for purposes of analysing movement in athletics it is often convenient to treat them as such.

To take, for example, the directing of a runner's propulsive, muscular force against gravity and air resistance, the relevant point of action of these three forces is the athlete's Centre of Gravity (Fig. 30)—a point

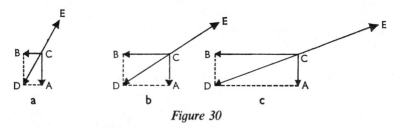

Figure 30

Fig. 30*a, b, c,* above, illustrates the directing of a runner's propulsive force against the force of gravity and air resistance. Point C represents the athlete's Centre of Gravity, the lines CA the force of gravity, the lines CB three strengths of air resistance and the lines CD the magnitude and direction of the resultant of the opposing forces. The propulsive force required to maintain a constant speed is represented by the lines CE.

where, it can be assumed, all the mass of his body is concentrated. (This is discussed more fully on page 53.) At a constant speed these three forces balance each other.

Both gravity (CA) working vertically downwards, and air resistance (CB) acting horizontally against the runner are represented by force vectors. Using these as two sides of a parallelogram, the missing sides are constructed geometrically and a diagonal is drawn from the point of origin—i.e. the Centre of Gravity—to the opposite corner (CD). This line represents in both length and direction the magnitude and direction of the combined opposing forces. The propulsive muscular force required to maintain a constant speed is therefore represented by the line CE. This, an *equilibrant* needed to balance the other forces, is not necessarily to be identified with the angle of the trunk—the runner's 'body-lean'—but none the less Fig. 30*b* and *c* show the need for greater emphasis on horizontal force when air resistance is increased.

Where more than two forces act upon a point (as, for example, within an athlete's body during motion, when diverse muscular forces are involved) the resultant of two forces is first obtained in the manner already described and then this is combined vector by vector, until a resultant—a single force that can replace them all—is found.

In Fig. 31, for example, the vectors A, B, C and D can be compounded by first finding the resultant R1 for A and B (3). This is then added to C to give R2(4) which in turn is added to D(7) to give the final resultant which represents the original four vectors. Or, more simply, these vectors can be added (in any order) head-to-tail—when their resultant will be the single vector joining start to finish (Fig. 31(7)). If the resultant is zero,

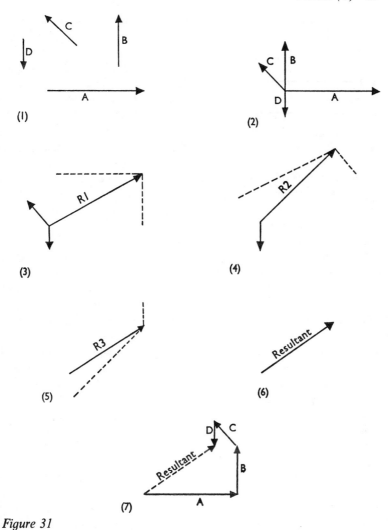

Figure 31

(After Figs. 2–25 and 2–26 of *Physics for the Enquiring Mind*, E. M. Rogers, Princeton University Press, U.S.A.)

the end of the tail-to-head pattern will be back at the starting point. (See also pages 11–13.)

So forces do not satisfy the laws of ordinary arithmetic. One object plus another object will always make two objects—but one force added to another may well be no force at all! Therefore, because forces are vectors, they require different treatment to scalar quantities like mass, length, time, energy, etc.

Resolution of forces. In Fig. 32*a* a long-jumper is shown at take-off with the line of action of a force, at that instant, driving him into the air from his jumping foot (the point of application). Two effects of this force are to project him vertically and accelerate him forward. We know that these component forces may be regarded separately, but in what proportions are they represented? The problem is the reverse of that discussed already.

Again, the geometrical parallelogram method is used; but either the directions or magnitudes of both components, or the direction and magnitude of one component, must be known in advance, otherwise (as there are many parallelograms with the same diagonal) the problem is capable of many different solutions. In this case we know the directions of the components. Two lines are then produced from the point of application (i.e. the foot), one vertical and the other horizontal, and a parallelogram is then made whose diagonal is the vector of the take-off force (Fig. 32*b*). The length of each of these lines in comparison with that of the diagonal represents the magnitude of the components in relation to the take-off drive.

If the take-off force is known, of course, then the line of action can be drawn in units of length corresponding to the units of force, and from the length of the component vectors the magnitude of the horizontal and vertical forces can be calculated.

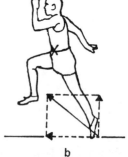

a   *Figure 32*   b

Work and energy

Work. Whereas, in everyday language, 'work' is loosely defined as any kind of effort or exertion maintained for some time, the word as used in mechanics refers to the overcoming of resistance. No matter how hard and exhausting the struggle or the physical benefit derived therefrom, if an athlete attempts to lift a heavy barbell and fails—then he has done no mechanical work! Holding a heavy weight with arm outstretched for several minutes can cause great local muscle fatigue, but in the mechanical sense it is not work. For in order to do work, in the scientific sense, a force must move an object through some distance. *Work = Force × Distance.*

This formula can also be applied (somewhat academically, perhaps, from the point of view of the coach or athlete) to the working of a single muscle. If its force of contraction is unknown then this is computed from its proportional cross-section (see page 28) and the distance is represented by the distance through which the fibres shorten.

Without equipment found only in the laboratory it is impossible to measure accurately the work done by athletes; for in such calculations great care must be taken to ensure that only the force acting in the direction of motion is considered, and to remember that the effective forces exerted in athletic movement are continually changing from one instant to another.

However, it is sometimes useful to make a rough assessment, measuring force in newtons and distance in metres, when the unit of work is the newton-metre (nm) and is called the *Joule (J)*—i.e. *the work done by a force of one newton in moving a mass 1 m is a Joule.*

Thus, from films, it could be calculated approximately that a high-jumper applied his take-off force over a vertical distance of 0.5 m before leaving the ground and if, say, it was estimated that he exerted a force of 1560 newtons, then his work at take-off would be $0.5 \times 1560 = 780$ Joules. Similarly, a javelin thrower who in the actual throwing action pulled the implement over a distance of 2 m, using a force of 580 newtons, would do 1160 Joules of work.

Eccentric contraction, in which active muscle is stretched, entails *the absorption of mechanical work.* When an active muscle exerts a force P and shortens a distance X it performs an amount of *positive work PX*; but if it is stretched a distance X while exerting this force it absorbs work and is said to do an amount PX of *negative work.*[1]

Bending down, lowering a weight, descending stairs, climbing down a rope—all are examples of negative work. In considering the physiological costs of the two types of work it is important to use muscle

---

[1] This is both a physiological *and* a mechanical concept. B. C. Abbott, Brenda Bigland and J. M. Ritchie, 'The physiological cost of negative work', *Journal of Physiology*, 117 (1952), pages 380–90.

movements truly comparable in the two directions—'mirror images', both in placing the limbs and in their time-sequence.

For example, in comparing walking down stairs with walking up, the subject should descend backwards, and both movements should take place at the same speed.

We know that the oxygen consumption of positive work is considerably more costly; that with equal amounts of work, positive work activates more muscle fibres.

Energy. Work must be performed in order to accelerate an athlete or throwing implement. Conversely, a moving athlete, discus, shot, hammer or javelin possesses a certain *capacity to do work* (called *energy*) by giving up velocity, i.e. by coming to rest. The energy an object has by virtue of its motion is called *kinetic energy*; it is the kinetic energy of a javelin which drives it into the ground; a hurdler's kinetic energy sends the hurdle flying when he hits it. This type of energy depends directly on the object's mass; for a given velocity, the greater mass will have more energy. It depends, too, on the square of the velocity; i.e. if an object's velocity is doubled then the kinetic energy becomes four times as great. In linear motion the kinetic energy of a body is given by the formula $e = \frac{1}{2}mv^2$ (i.e. half the product of the mass of an object by the square of its velocity), where v is the linear velocity of the mass. Unlike momentum, energy is a scalar quantity, which explains why kinetic energy can be satisfactorily used, whatever its direction.

There is also the energy of position or condition—*potential energy*. A drawn bow (Fig. 33) or a fibre-glass pole bent from its normal shape are ready to do work and therefore possess potential energy. Likewise, a high-jumper in mid-air, a pole vaulter high over the bar or a shot at the high point of its trajectory—all have potential energy by virtue of their positions.

It appears to be one of the natural laws that energy can be neither created nor destroyed. No machine—and no athlete—can use more energy than has already been absorbed; and, basically, the athlete obtains his from the chemical energy stored in his muscles.[1]

Figure 33

[1] Carbohydrate and fat are his chief fuels; the others are protein and ethyl alcohol. All are plant products. Meat eaters and vegetarians alike depend ultimately on energy derived from the sun.

Since energy is the capacity for doing work, it is measured in units of work—e.g. in Joules. If, for example, an athlete during weight training lifts 90 kg 1.5 m off the floor, the barbell's potential energy is $90 \times 9.8 \times 1.5$ or 1323 Joules. If the barbell is then dropped, its potential energy is changed into the kinetic energy of motion, and at the instant of striking the ground it still has 1323 Joules of kinetic energy; the potential energy has gone. But after the weight has struck the ground the kinetic energy disappears, to be changed into other forms of energy.

When track and field athletic techniques are performed on a sound mechanical basis a maximum result is achieved for a given expenditure of energy. Indeed, the chief factor in many forms of athletics is the supply of energy and its proper and economical utilisation. However, the techniques of sprinting, hurdling, jumping and throwing are best analysed through the concept of *momentum* rather than energy.

Power

In track and field athletics it is not merely the work performed which is important but also the time taken to do it; and in many events an athlete has very little time; a long-jumper moving at great horizontal speed over the eight-inch (20 cm) take-off board, for example, has but a fraction of a second in which to drive downward; he must work very quickly. As the runner increases his speed his feet are a shorter time in contact with the ground to apply force against it.

Even with regard to the development of strength and muscular endurance in training, *the rate of exercising* is important to athletes, for, as Steinhaus maintains in formulating the principle of progressive overloading, 'Muscle hypertrophy is in proportion, not to actual work done, but to the work done per unit of time.'[1]

In mechanics, the rate at which work is done is called *power*. Therefore *power = work ÷ time*. The *more work* that is done in a given time the greater the power; and the *quicker* it is done then the greater is the power used. Here it is important to note the difference between the more precise mechanical meaning and the word's looser meaning in everyday parlance—when, usually, it refers to force.

The measurement of power can be expressed in different ways. Previously kinesiologists, physiologists and others concerned with the analysis of human motion used the foot-pound per second as the smaller unit of measurement and the horse-power as the larger. (It was James Watt, the Scottish inventor, who originally assessed the value of

[1] A. H. Steinhaus, 'The Physiology of Exercise'. Series of lectures, Chicago, U.S.A., 1948.

horsepower at 33,000 foot-pounds per minute, or 550 foot-pounds per second.[1])

To take a simple case: the horse-power of a man running up a flight of stairs can be calculated if his weight, time and the height of the stairs are known. If, then, he weighs 154 lb and takes 4 seconds to climb 14 ft, his rate of working (i.e. his horse-power) is:

$$\frac{154 \times 14}{550 \times 4} = 0.98.$$

Alternatively, if his mass is 70 kg and he takes 4 seconds to climb 4.25 m his rate of working (i.e. his power) is

$$\frac{70 \times 9.8 \times 4.25}{4} = 728.875 \ watts$$

Today it is generally considered that the power unit of measurement should be the *watt*, a metric unit.[2] All our ergometers are calibrated in watts and the majority of published work now uses this unit. *One watt is one Joule per second. One horse-power is equivalent to 745.7 w.*

Wilkie[3] suggests that human muscle, used efficiently, can develop about 250 w for each kilogram; so that from 30 kg of muscle (the approximate amount in an athlete weighing 73 kg (160.6 1b)) 7.5 kw (about 10 horsepower) might be expected. However, not all 30 kg can be made available as an immediate source of power; about half is antagonistic, while much of it contributes indirectly in supporting and guiding movement. The figure for our 73 kg athlete in a 7 ft (2.13 m) high-jump, for example, would be nearer 3 kw (4.02 horsepower). (Incidentally, in such an athlete, approximately 17 kg of muscle will be below the waist, indicating the importance of the lower limbs as a source of power.)

Of power, however measured, it can be said that since it is equal to the product of Force and Velocity, maximum Power cannot be generated when either is too large at the expense of the other. Greatest power is only available between these extremes. In weight training, for example, speed of movement can be improved by lightening the bar; but only where an increase in speed proportionally exceeds a reduction in weight will the lifter's power output have increased.

[1] He tested horses to see how much weight they could lift, through what distance and in what time, pumping water out of coal-mines. When engines replaced horses it was convenient to rate the power of machines in terms of what horses had achieved.

[2] There is nothing inherently *electrical* about a watt!

[3] D. R. Wilkie, 'Man as a source of mechanical power', *Ergonomics*, 3 (1960), page 1.

Hill[1] suggests this happens when the load is about one-third maximum, with the velocity also about a third of what the muscle can achieve maximally. On the other hand, for the development of power through weight training, Travers recommends using two-thirds of the weight that can just be lifted once, and then doing the exercise through a full range as quickly as possible. The lifting of the heaviest possible weight develops 'raw' strength but not speed; the optimum lies between three-quarters and a half maximum—the load being matched to the muscle or muscles required to move it and the length of the limb or lever. For the speed at which muscles operate varies greatly, and the longer the limb the smaller the fraction of maximum weight that can be used to produce the greatest power output.

By lifting progressively heavier weights and timing the lifts, it is possible to obtain a relationship between the weight lifted and the power output. This shows that the greatest power is obtained when lifting sub-maximal weights.

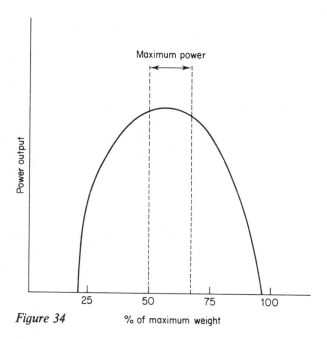

Figure 34   % of maximum weight

[1] A. V. Hill, 'The dimensions of animals and their muscular dynamics', *Science Progress*, 38 (1950), page 209.

Karvinen and Komi[1] recommend contraction speeds for power conditioning corresponding to 30–60 per cent of maximum isometric strength. Their study and all similar studies have so far applied only to *concentric* muscular work; in all probability, figures are much higher for *eccentric* work.

Power output in running is more fully discussed on pages 138–42. Here it is sufficient to say that, under steady-state conditions (e.g. in even paced long distance running) the power used is limited mainly by the extent to which an athlete can absorb oxygen; whereas in sprinting, where much more power is involved, the runner derives his energy from chemical sources stored within the muscle fibres themselves.

From a mechanical standpoint the measurement of power in track and field athletics is exceedingly difficult because, as already maintained, it is usually impossible to assess with accuracy the amount of work—in particular the ever-changing effective force of an athlete's movement. In sprinting, for example, the distance run and time taken are easily come by, but how, without the most complicated of equipment, is the runner's effective force—which changes with each stride and, indeed, throughout the range of movement of a given stride—to be calculated?

Even if it were possible to obtain such figures, the result would make no allowance for additional work against gravity, air resistance, ground friction, positive and negative acceleration of the limbs, and the internal resistances due to muscle viscosity and the friction of various body tissues one against another.

It is for this reason that physiologists find it more convenient to think in terms of the energy used in exercise, using either the body's oxygen uptake or its heat output as a measure of expenditure[2] (see also page 138).

The ability to work quickly—i.e. powerfully—depends partly upon an athlete's neuro-muscular co-ordination and also upon his attitude of mind, e.g., the absence of inhibition through fear of failure or injury, his determination and concentration. However, although muscular effort has so often to be exerted as quickly as possible, it is essential not to lose sight of the importance of *range* in working. Misunderstanding often leads to an omission of whole phases of forceful movement in the build-up of speed. Thus, the athlete fails to attain maximum effect.

[1] E. Karvinen and P. V. Komi, 'Neuromuscular performance' in *Fitness, Heath and Work Capacity*, ed. E. Larson (Macmillan, New York, 1974).
[2] In fact physiologists are interested in five forms of energy: radiant, chemical, mechanical, thermal and electrical.

Centripetal and centrifugal forces

From Newton's Law of Inertia (page 18) we know that objects will continue to move in a straight path unless compelled by force to do otherwise. It follows, therefore, that when an athlete spins with a hammer (to take the best of countless examples in athletics) he must apply force to keep it moving in a near circular path.

By exerting this force—by pulling *on the hammer*—he accelerates it, even if it continues to move with only uniform speed, for by changing the hammer's *direction* of motion he is continually changing its velocity. But as soon as he lets go, the hammer continues steadily along at a tangent; its inertia makes it move in a straight line again, at right angles to the radius of motion at the point of release (Fig. 35).

The pulling-in force exerted by the athlete *on the hammer* is called *centripetal*, the equal but opposite reaction to which is a *centrifugal* force, *acting on the athlete*, pulling outward directly along the radius of motion (Fig. 36)—words derived from Latin phrases meaning 'move towards the centre' and 'flee from the centre', respectively. Speaking generally, in athletics this centrifugal force is a by-product of an effort to increase rotational speed; in itself it is seldom advantageous and is more often an embarrassment to an athlete.

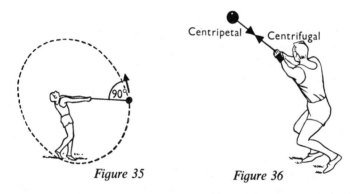

Figure 35   *Figure 36*

The force, f, required to keep an object moving in a circular path (and the equal but opposite centrifugal force) depends upon the *mass, m*, and *velocity, v*, of the object and its *radius* of motion, r, and can be calculated from the formula $f = mv^2/r$. Other things being equal, this force

(i) *is proportional to the moving mass.* Thus, a 16-lb (7.26 kg) hammer is pulled in (and, simultaneously, the thrower pulled outward) with twice the force of an 8-lb (3.63 kg) one;

(ii) *is proportional to the square of the velocity.* If the hammer's speed (i.e. the actual, linear speed) is doubled, the centripetal and centrifugal forces increase four-fold. That is, they are proportional *to the square of the angular velocity* (i.e. the angle described by the hammer per second). For example, if angular velocity is increased three-fold then the hammer needs nine times the original force to be kept moving in a circular path, to which the reaction is nine times the original centrifugal force;

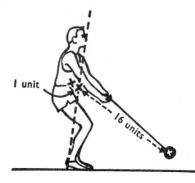

Figure 37

(iii) for a constant angular velocity, *is proportional to the radius of motion.* Again, with hammer throwing as our example: when two men turn with the same angular velocity, the shorter man, with half the radius of motion of the taller, needs only half the centripetal force (and, therefore, half the centrifugal force) to control it. So, by relaxing his arms and shoulders to increase radius, the thrower can increase the speed of the hammer without turning any faster—in which case his centripetal pull must also be increased, but not as drastically as would be necessary through an increase in turning speed.

If, momentarily, both man and hammer head are spinning with equal angular velocity about an axis which passes through the common Centre of Gravity of athlete and hammer (Fig. 37), their respective distances from the axis are inversely proportional to their masses; i.e. if the athlete weighs sixteen times as much as the hammer-head, his radius, relatively, will be sixteen times less (the measurements being made along each radius from the axis to each Centre of Gravity). Under such circumstances the centripetal force pulling on the hammer is equal to the centrifugal force pulling simultaneously on the athlete, but in an opposite direction. An increase in turning speed will increase both forces and there will be no cause to adjust the thrower's position (Fig. 36).

Since almost all athletic movement is angular in character, these principles apply to greater or lesser degree in all events. However, they have a particular significance in hammer and discus throwing and in the pole vault. They apply too, to bend running, where athletes find it more difficult to sprint at top speed in an inside lane than in an outside one (Fig. 38).

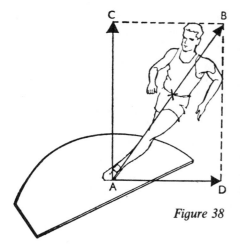

In 'taking' a bend, a runner uses the track surface to supply the necessary centripetal force—which then thrusts sideways against his feet, threatening to topple him outwards. To avoid this he leans inwards.

On a banked curve (Fig. 38) there is less (perhaps no) need of this sideways friction; for a surface tilted sufficiently can then push the athlete straight out with a force AB, the vertical component of which, AC, counteracts his weight, while the horizontal component, AD, provides the necessary centripetal force.

Figure 38

Force of gravity

All athletic performance is influenced in some way by the force of gravity, a centripetal force 'by which bodies tend to the centre of the earth' (Newton.)[1] In Chapter Two (page 8) the acceleration of all freely falling bodies due to gravity (universally symbolised by g) was given as 32 ft (9.8 m) per second each second—a figure sufficiently accurate for most calculations involved in an analysis of track and field techniques.

This might seem to violate Newton's First Law; for why should all objects accelerate vertically downwards at the same rate regardless of their masses if, when projected horizontally by an equal force, their accelerations are strictly determined by their masses? (See page 30.) The answer lies in the perfect balance of gravitation and inertia; *the earth always attracts an object with a force proportional to the mass of that object.* So, doubling the mass of the athlete would double the size of the force between him and the earth.[2]

However, although it is true that at a given point on the earth all bodies fall with the same acceleration, *the pull of gravity diminishes as the distance increases away from the earth's centre and is inversely propor-*

---

[1] He gave no first cause for Gravitation; modern science asks "what" and "how" without knowing the primary "why" for the behaviour of the Universe.

[2] The attractive force between an athlete and the earth depends not only on the mass of the athlete but on the mass of the earth as well, and is proportional to the *product* of their masses, i.e. these multiplied together.

tional to the square of the distance.[1] There is, therefore, a slight variation in gravitational acceleration between the poles and the equator (where the distance from the earth's centre, at sea level, is approximately 13 miles (31 km) greater than at either pole) amounting to 0.54 per cent—just large enough to be detected.[2] (Actually 0.3 per cent of the difference arises because the earth is spinning and, in consequence, a body at the equator tends to move off into space; there is a centrifugal effect.)

Most world track and field athletic records have been made in the temperate zones, where acceleration is 0.36 per cent greater than at the equator. Thus, a 26-ft (7.92 m) long-jump in Germany would be approximately $1\frac{1}{4}$ in. (3 cm) farther in, say, Kenya, and a 255-ft (77.72 m) javelin thrown in New Zealand is worth another $6\frac{1}{2}$ in. (0.17 m) in Ecuador.[3]

The varying gravitational attractions of the sun and moon, which influence the tides, also affect the flight of objects—if only to an infinitesimal extent.

Weight and density

In discussing Newton's Law of Inertia a distinction was made between *mass* and *weight* (page 20). The mass of an object is a measure of its inertia, its resistance to change in motion. This is a property which does not change from place to place; an athlete with mass of 90 kg (weight $90 \times 9.8 = 882$ newtons) would require as much force to obtain a given acceleration in Timbuctoo or Tooting, on the moon as here on earth.

However, because of the slight variation in pull, at the equator an athlete weighs 0.5 per cent less there than in the neighbourhood of the poles, and in the same way, weight, with the pull of gravity, decreases gradually with increasing height above sea-level.

---

[1] This '*inverse square law of gravitation*', almost certainly conceived by Newton in his mother's garden at Woolsthorpe, Lincolnshire, in 1666, '. . . . was occasioned by the fall of an apple, as he sat in contemplative mood' (Stukeley, *Memoirs of Newton's Life*, pages 19–20). What Newton (then 23) saw was not that the apple must be drawn to the earth by Gravity. (That limited concept is at least as old as Aristotle.) What *he* realised was that *all masses attract all other masses*; the same force reached out endlessly into space; the earth's attraction was not unique.

[2] $g = 9.832$ m/s² at the North Pole
    9.780   ″   at the Equator
    9.812   ″   at Greenwich
    9.803   ″   at Wellington, N.Z.

[3] G.T.P. Tarrant, 'Mechanics of human and animal activity', *School Science Review*, England, 78 (December 1938), page 259.

On the moon our athlete would weigh only 147 newtons, for the gravitational pull there is about a sixth of the earth's. (Although the mass of the moon is only approximately an eightieth of the earth's, its diameter is considerably less and its surface, in consequence, is nearer its centre.[1] Because of the inverse square law, the moon's gravity, per unit mass, is therefore relatively greater.) When we speak of 'weight', therefore, we refer to the force of attraction between an object and the earth—an attraction proportional to the object's mass. If we hold a 16-lb (7.26 kg) shot in our hand we must exert a certain muscular force to counteract the earth's attraction; this we call the shot's weight, but it *can* vary, if only fractionally.[2]

Not all 16-lb (7.26 kg) shots are of the same size. Brass shots (which have a lead core) are smaller for their weight than iron ones; a 16-lb shot made from tungsten would be about the size of a tennis ball. Similarly, athletes of different sizes sometimes weigh the same, and vice versa. Obviously, therefore, objects vary in the ratio of their weight (and mass) to volume; i.e. they differ in their *density*. It is as though, in a denser body, matter is the more closely packed. And, with the human body, the density of different parts will vary, e.g. bone is denser than blood.

Weightlessness

When a man stands erect on the ground, the force of gravity acting on his body (i.e. his weight) is cancelled out by an equal upward force exerted by the ground, i.e. '*ground reaction*'; otherwise, obviously, he would accelerate towards the earth's centre (see page 21). This condition also applies to the various *parts* of his body which, in the position shown (Fig. 39) have each to support the body weight above them. Thus, each part experiences a degree of compression which increases from the head downwards. It is of interest to know that this compression will affect our height during the course of a day when we have been standing most of the time. A difference in standing height of 1.5 cms has been measured between morning and evening. Similarly, American astronauts who had been in a gravity free situation for a long period were found to be as much as 5 cms taller on their return to Earth. This compression can be altered by a change in posture; e.g. increasing if the man stands on one leg

---

[1] It is approximately 3–11ths the distance from the surface of the earth to *its* centre.
[2] It is emphasised that weight is a force (best measured in newtons) to be distinguished from mass (measured in kilograms). If m is the mass of a body, then its weight is $m \times g$, where g is the acceleration due to gravity.

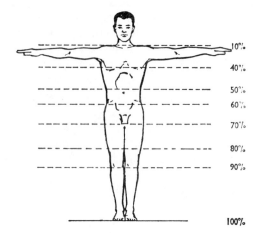

Figure 39

(thereby doubling the vertically upward thrust through that leg) or if he accelerates some part of his body vertically.

However, when he breaks contact with the ground, gaining downward speed or losing upward speed at a rate of 32 ft (9.8 m) per second every second, these states of compression, the sensations associated with them and their effect on the neuromuscular interactions controlling posture and directing movement no longer exist. (For example, in long-jumping, a clumsy initial attempt at a hitch-kick (Fig. 150) can be caused by 'not knowing where the legs are'—because of a lack of pressure on the receptors of the feet and a resulting poor kinesthetic feed-back.) His body, lacking ground reaction, then assumes a condition of transient 'weightlessness' and can move its various parts, or objects carried by it, in ways which, *in a vertical plane*, would otherwise require greater effort— resistance to motion originated in the air being due only to inertia. In a state of 'free fall', for example, the man in the position shown (Fig. 39) will have no sensation of weight in his arms; from the standpoint of mechanics, it requires no effort to hold them in this position, since they and the rest of his body are experiencing the same gravitational acceleration. *Thus, the condition of 'weightlessness' tends to increase mobility at the expense of control, applying not only in jumping, diving and trampolining but even during those brief moments for which runners break contact with the ground on each stride.*

When, in space, a man relaxes completely, he tends naturally to assume a position in which a state of angular equilibrium is reached between the different parts of his body, depending upon the mass and tonus of

Figure 40

his various muscles. Fig. 40 illustrates the resulting posture.[1]

Note also that a floating swimmer (who must displace a weight of water equal to that of his whole body) does not experience 'weightlessness', because his limbs are supported externally—*water reaction* being substituted for *ground reaction*.

Experience of prolonged weightlessness in space has indicated the importance of gravity to human health. With the body no longer subject to its influence, muscles lose their tone while bones lose calcium and become more brittle.

Centre of Gravity

We know that the earth attracts every tiny particle of an object with a gravitational force which is proportional to the mass of each particle. (The direction of the force on each particle is towards the earth's centre, but the distance to that point is so great that, for all practical purposes, the forces can be considered parallel to one another.) If all these separate attractions are thought of as being added together to make one resultant force—i.e. the weight of the object—the point where this force acts will be the *Centre of Gravity*.[2]

In analysing track and field techniques such a point—always indicated by the symbol G – is often used to represent mass as a whole: the body mass of the athlete, a piece of apparatus, or the combined mass of athlete and implement, as in the pole vault or a throwing event. It is here that we can consider all the mass of the object to be concentrated; in fact, a centre of mass or weight from which the body could be suspended in perfect balance in any position.[3]

---

[1] John C. Simons, 'An introduction to surface-free behaviour', *Ergonomics*, England, Vol. 7, No. 1 (January 1964).

[2] 'There is some evidence that Newton, in preparing the *Principia*, was held up almost to the last moment by lack of proof that you could treat a solid sphere as though all its mass was concentrated at the centre, and only hit on the proof a year before publication'. (John Maynard Keynes, 'Newton the man'. From a paper read at Trinity College, Cambridge, in 1946.)

[3] More precisely, a body's Centre of Gravity is always fractionally below its Centre of Mass, for its lower parts experience a slightly stronger gravitational pull than its upper parts (see page 49). The distinction is of no consequence in athletics; here we can assume mass distribution and weight distribution to be one and the same. But note that the concentration of mass *in rotation* is expressed differently (see Fig. 83 and page 112).

However, it is important to realise that this point need not necessarily divide or be surrounded by equal masses. (Only when a body is of uniform density will its Centre of Gravity coincide with its centre of volume.) It is the product of each mass and its distance—i.e. the moments, or turning effects (see page 65)—which must be equal on either side of, or surrounding, the Centre of Gravity.

Fig. 41 and the accompanying tables show the hinge points for the body segments together with their segmental centres of gravity and percentage weights for the male human body. (Note that the anthropometric data given here are weighted toward United States Air Force personnel; the results of other studies have differed slightly.)

Each limb segment has its own Centre of Gravity, lying fairly exactly along the longitudinal axis, always nearer the proximal joint (i.e. the joint nearer the trunk). The tables show the relative *average masses* (average, since these vary in individuals) of different parts of the body, taking the total mass of the body as 100 per cent.

Here, in an erect position with arms to sides, a man's Centre of Gravity (S) averages 55.27 per cent of his height, approximately $1\frac{1}{2}$ inches (4 cm) below the navel, roughly midway between the belly and the back.

Children will average a relatively higher Centre of Gravity in such a position, owing to carrying relatively more weight in their upper body. But, again on average, a woman's Centre of Gravity in this position will be slightly lower, relative to her height, because of her smaller thorax, lighter arms and narrower shoulders, but heavier pelvis and thighs and shorter legs. But the Centre of Gravity lies higher in the trunk of shorter-legged women than in longer-legged males with correspondingly short trunks—an important point when considering the performances of women in high-jumping, hurdling, the running events and in some gymnastic exercises where the body is supported completely by the arms.

The location of the Centre of Gravity for any particular person, in any given position, changes with inspiration and expiration, upon eating and drinking and with any factor that brings about redistribution of body mass. For example the movement of the diaphragm during an increase of fat or age.

For our later observations it will be important to know only the approximate position of this point, and to appreciate that it moves always in sympathy with the movements of the different parts of the body. It is, in fact, a most unstable point in the athlete, and yet, despite its almost continuous motion, it seldom leaves the pelvic cavity.

Motion in contact with the ground. By moving when in contact with the

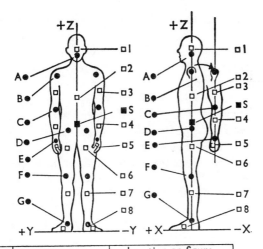

Symbol		Location on figure		
		Coordinates - - %height		
		X	Y	Z
	Hinge Points			
A	Base of skull on spine	0.0	0.0	91.23
B	Shoulder joint	0.0	±10.66	81.16
C	Elbow	0.0	±10.66	62.20
D	Hip	0.0	± 5.04	52.13
E	Wrist	0.0	±10.66	46.21
F	Knee	0.0	± 5.04	28.44
G	Ankle	0.0	± 5.04	3.85

Weight Distribution of the human body
Percent of total body weight

Symbol		X	Y	Z	Percent of total body weight
	Centres of gravity				
1	Head	0.0	0.0	93.48	6.9
2	Trunk-Neck	0.0	0.0	71.09	46.1
3	Upper-Arm	0.0	±10.66	71.74	6.6
4	Lower Arm	0.0	±10.66	55.33	4.2
5	Hand	0.0	±10.66	43.13	1.7
6	Upper Leg	0.0	± 5.04	42.48	21.5
7	Lower Leg	0.0	± 5.04	18.19	9.6
8	Foot	3.85	± 6.16	1.78	3.4
S	Total (whole body)			55.27	100.00

Figure 41

(From the *Bioastronautics Data Book*, National Aeronautics and Space Administration, Washington).

ground an athlete changes the position of his Centre of Gravity both in relation to his mass and to the ground itself. And this applies whether he is in *direct* contact (as, for example, when he is actually touching the ground) or indirect contact (as in pole vaulting, when he is in the air, but holding the pole).

To give examples: if, from the standing position of Fig. 41 he raises his right arm horizontally to the side (Fig. 42*a*) his Centre of Gravity shifts to his right and is raised about $\frac{5}{8}$ in. (1.5 cm); and when the other arm is stretched out similarly (Fig. 42*b*) the Centre of Gravity rises by the same amount again but returns to the body's centre-line.

Then, when both arms are raised directly overhead (Fig. 42*c*) it moves an additional $1\frac{1}{4}$ in. (3.25 cm) higher in the trunk. (In Fig. 42 these movements of the Centre of Gravity have been purposely exaggerated.) In a crouch starting position (Fig. 43) an athlete's Centre of Gravity is lower and brought well forward of the feet, and a pole vaulter who drops his legs while clearing the cross-bar also lowers his Centre of Gravity (if no other movement is involved) while he holds the pole.

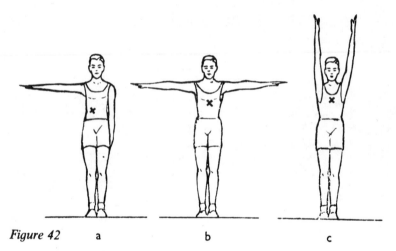

Figure 42   a   b   c

Figure 43

Figure 44

In exceptional forms of movement, however, this point can lie *outside* the body. In the position shown in Fig. 44 the Centre of Gravity might be as much as 3 in. (7.5 cm) outside and below the stomach (varying according to the build and flexibility of the athlete). Variations of this 'piked' or 'jacked' position are sometimes used in pole vaulting, long-jumping, diving, etc.

Motion in the air. We have already seen (page 16) that once an athlete breaks contact with the ground the flight curve of his Centre of Gravity describes a smooth parabola until contact is regained. Certainly no movement of the athlete while off the ground interrupts it.

As an extreme example of this we can take the exploding of a shrapnel shell in the air (Fig. 45). Air resistance apart, the shell's Centre of Gravity describes a smooth curve both *before* and *after* the mid-air explosion, until fragments of it strike other objects. The force of its explosion, working in all directions, leaves the path of its Centre of Gravity unchanged.

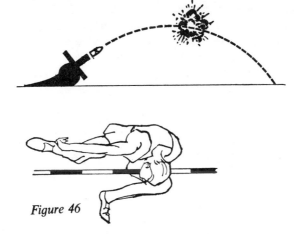

Figure 45

Figure 46

This principle of the maintenance of the path of the Centre of Gravity is exemplified in the hitch-kick (i.e. running-in-the-air) style in long-jumping (Fig. 150) where the athlete cannot alter the flight path of his Centre of Gravity although, for other reasons, his movements have their value (see pages 114–6 and 181–3).

If the long-jumper were permitted to carry weights, he *could* gain additional height and speed by throwing them down and back in the air; for, through the two-way action of force, the impulse so derived would also influence his body, but in an opposite direction—the technique used by the professional athletes of nineteenth-century England, some of whom long-jumped more than 30 ft (13.5 m).[1]

(It is interesting to note that in ancient Greek times when weights (*halteres*) *were* used in jumping for distance, they were *not* released in the air but, with the arms, were swung back prior to the landing. Thus the weights were used mainly to improve the take-off impulse and—to a limited extent—to advance the jumper's heels in relation to the combined Centre of Gravity of athlete and halteres. Their size, shape and weight appear to have been matters of personal preference. Some were made of bronze or lead; others were carved out of stone.)

The modern jumper's movements in the air, therefore, alter his body position only in relation to his Centre of Gravity; they cannot jet-propel him. When in the air, a part of his body moves one way, some other part moves in an opposite direction, simultaneously, so that the product of masses and distances about the Centre of Gravity is unchanged. If, for example, the head and feet move down (as in a dive straddle, Fig. 46) then the hips are made to move up.

But it should be noted that the reaction to a movement in the air need not comprise the units of mass and distance which caused it; e.g. when, using a Western Roll (Fig. 47*a*), a high-jumper reaches towards the pit with his inside arm the simultaneous reaction can be that of a fractional raising of the rest of the body mass (Fig. 47*b*) or, to take the other

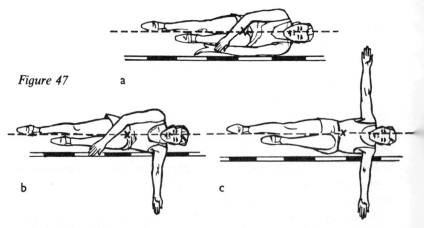

Figure 47   a

b   c

---

[1] However, the discarding of the weights has no effect on the motion of the *common* Centre of Gravity of the closed system, i.e. of weights and athlete combined.

extreme, a pronounced lifting of an even lighter part of the athlete. We see from Fig. 47c that when the arm action is accompanied by a raising of the other arm, the trunk and hips gain no additional height in relation to the Centre of Gravity; one movement cancels out the beneficial effect of the other. Under such circumstances, therefore, it is important which part of the athlete absorbs the reaction.

Friction

Friction occurs when one body moves, or tries to move, in contact with another hindering or opposing motion. The measure of frictional resistance is the force necessary to maintain a body's uniform motion; the acceleration which this force would impart to the body if it acted alone is then equal to the retardation caused by the force of friction. In track and field athletics the term '*friction*' is often used in connection with the movement of the feet on the ground, when frictional force— always acting parallel to the surface—varies with the nature of the ground and shoe surfaces, the force pushing them together, and the relative motion between them.

Surprisingly, perhaps, the area of contact, e.g. the size of the shoe, is unimportant. A small shoe, in comparison with a larger one, reduces the area of contact but, other things being equal, the force pushing it against the ground is greater per unit area. These two effects cancel out each other; frictional force is the same in both cases.

If there were no such thing as friction athletes could not run, jump or throw, but could merely raise or lower their body weight; for the performance of all these activities is partly dependent upon horizontally-directed (i.e. tangential) thrusts against the ground evoking ground reactions of equal magnitude in opposite directions. A sprinter wearing frictionless ball-bearings under his shoes on smooth ice, could not move his Centre of Gravity in any horizontal direction— for even a fraction of a centimetre. *So friction is necessary to stability and progress over the ground.*

These considerations apply to athletes wearing training shoes, basketball boots, etc. (as in shot putting, discus throwing and hammer throwing); but in other events (e.g. sprinting, hurdling, javelin throwing, jumping) an athlete cannot get sufficient horizontal thrust without the use of spikes which enable him to exert a large thrust against the ground without any horizontal movement of his foot.

Friction will oppose the runner when his foot meets the ground at a speed relative to his Centre of Gravity in a backward direction, which is less than the Centre of Gravity's forward speed over the ground. To illustrate, if the sprinter in Fig. 48*a* is travelling at 30 kilometres an hour and, relative to his Centre of Gravity, his foot moves back at 28 kilometres an hour as it contacts the track—then the foot, relative to the ground, moves *forward* at 2 kilometres an hour, braking his forward motion. This happens sometimes when an athlete overstrides.

On the other hand, in Fig. 48*b*, where the foot is moving back at 33 kilometres an hour (for the same 30 kilometre-per-hour body speed), the limb, correctly, drives the body instead of the body driving the limb. Continued acceleration and the maintenance of top sprinting speed largely depend upon the ability to oscillate the limbs rapidly in order to obtain this essential foot speed; at maximum sprinting speed, however, there is little relative movement between foot and ground when touch-down occurs; ground reaction is vertical or nearly so. To re-emphasise: in running, where large amounts of energy can be lost each time a foot lands, it can be as rewarding to reduce such retardation as to attempt to increase leg drive.

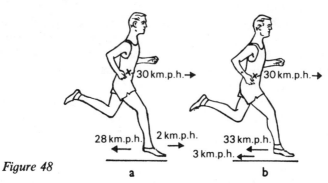

Figure 48

a   b

It must be pointed out that there are in all probability great losses of energy within the human machine due to internal friction but, as yet, nobody has measured them. However, this is mainly a physiological question and does not enter into a consideration of external forces acting on the human body.

Equilibrium[1] or balance

Correct balance—at rest and in motion—is a vital factor in athletic events, and must often be achieved under difficult circumstances.

[1] From Latin words meaning 'equal weights'. The expression is applied to the condition where the effects of forces on a system cancel out, leaving the system unchanged.

Balance and stability at rest. The first consideration for balance (or *equilibrium,* as it is called in mechanics) *is that the resultant of all the forces acting on the object shall be zero.* To take the simple examples in Fig. 49: in both resting positions the force of gravity pulling the brick down is equal but opposite to that of the ground pushing it up. Under such conditions—and this applies to all athletes balanced at rest, too—a vertical line through the Centre of Gravity falls within the base.

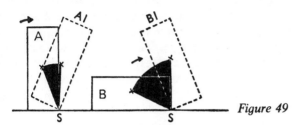

Figure 49

Balanced objects, however, possess varying degrees of firmness or steadiness in their positions; their *stability* varies. We can see at once that it is easier to upset the brick towards the right in position (*a*) than in (*b*); to do this the Centre of Gravity, marked X, must pass over and beyond the far edges, the *angle* through which it must tilt to lose balance in (*a*) being considerably less than in (*b*); less *work* is performed, too, in raising the Centre of Gravity. And the required horizontal *force*, acting through the Centre of Gravity, is also less. But a heavier brick would be more stable in both positions; it would take more work and more force to topple it.

It follows, therefore, that an object's stability depends upon:

    The area of its base
    The height of its Centre of Gravity
    The horizontal distance between the Centre of Gravity and the
    pivoting edge
    Its weight

We speak, then, of *stable* and *unstable equilibrium.* A suspended body in balance (as with the gymnast's vertical position in Fig. 56, assuming it to be motionless) is said to be in stable equilibrium because, if disturbed, it tends naturally to resume its position. But with an axis below the Centre of Gravity unstable equilibrium results; then, if disturbed, a body is disposed to move away from a state of balance.

Figs. 43 and 50 exemplify the application of these principles to track and field athletics. To be steady on his marks (as the rules demand) the sprinter adopts a position where his base is long and fairly broad (Fig. 43), with the Centre of Gravity above it. But for a quick, forceful getaway he crouches with his Centre of Gravity as high and as far forward as circumstances permit; his stability is not great.

On the other hand, an initial position for a standing put (Fig. 50*a*) is much more stable in a forward direction. The base (which includes not only the feet, but also the intervening area) is wider and the Centre of Gravity (common to both man and shot) comparatively far away from the eventual pivot, the front foot. But a vertical line dropped from his Centre of Gravity falls within the base, as with the sprinter.

The athlete of Fig. 50*b* is also balanced, but balanced precariously on one foot. To improve stability and avoid fouling he flexes the supporting leg and lowers his trunk, thus lowering his Centre of Gravity. Body mass outside the base does not upset balance unless it alters the position of the athlete's Centre of Gravity.

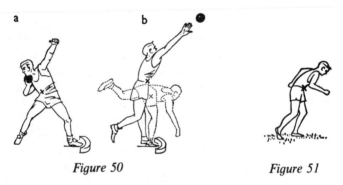

Figure 50   Figure 51

The standing starting position (Fig. 51) is certainly more stable than the thrower's of Fig. 50*b*, but in comparison to a crouched stance (Fig. 43) the base is too narrow and short, and the Centre of Gravity too high—which accounts for the 'rolling' starts seen so often in distance running. In all these positions a heavier athlete, equal in all other respects, will have greater stability.

Although a balanced position is more difficult to attain the higher the Centre of Gravity, the *correction* of balance may be easier—because the moment of inertia of the body (see page 83) is greater and therefore it will take a longer time for the displacing force to bring the Centre of Gravity outside the base and thus it will be easier to sense the developing instability and to effect correcting movements.

Thus, a knife is more easily balanced point downward, by moving the finger, than point upward. But for a *stationary* balanced position the point of the knife should be uppermost.

Balance in motion. Let us consider, for the present, balance in motion to mean that, as a whole, an object or athlete is moving without rotation.

In Fig. 52a a stick is balanced upright in the palm of a hand. When the hand moves forward (Fig. 52b) force is applied to the bottom of the stick, causing it to rotate backward. On a second attempt, however, the stick is tilted forward as the hand accelerates (Fig. 52c). The force of the stick's weight, acting through the Centre of Gravity (now outside the base), tends to rotate it forward, and if the stick leans neither too much nor too little for the force applied by the hand it remains balanced. *Thus, clockwise and counter-clockwise rotations cancel out—the second condition for equilibrium.*

Figure 52

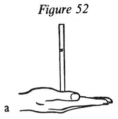

a

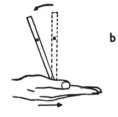

b

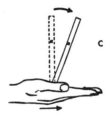

c

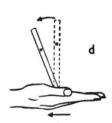

d

When force ceases to be exerted and the motion of stick and hand is therefore uniform, the stick must be upright again to stay in balance (Fig. 52a). Or, if its speed is such by now that air resistance is sufficiently strong, it must lean forward just enough to offset the force of the air.

When the hand applies a braking force, the tendency will be for the stick to fall forward. Now, to stay balanced, it must lean backward (Fig. 52d), and the greater the retarding force the greater this backward lean must be. Finally to remain balanced when the hand is no longer moving, the stick must be upright again (Fig. 52a).

This simple example illustrates an important aspect of the interplay of forces in the maintenance of balance in motion. To take an example from athletics, Fig. 53 depicts a runner's final position in driving his body forward. The reaction to the force of his drive against the ground (here, for simplicity, assumed to pass through his Centre of Gravity) is divided into its forward (F1) and upward (F2) components, which tend respectively to rotate the athlete backward and forward. To run with balance (ignoring air resistance) the force turning him forward at this instant of the stride cycle must exactly counteract the force rotating backward. For balance, any alteration of one of these forces requires an adjustment in the other.

Again, at the start of a sprint the athlete's effective horizontal driving force is much greater than in our previous illustration, for it is easier to push backward with full force against the ground; the tendency to rotate backward is therefore greater. Now, for balanced running the turning effect of the force of the upward component of drive is increased by working at a greater horizontal distance from the Centre of Gravity (Fig. 54). (This principle will be more fully discussed in Chapter Five under *Moments* (page 65) and Chapter Six, *Running*, pages 124–9.)

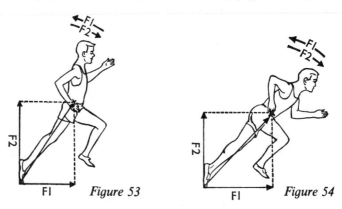

Figure 53   *Figure 54*

Balance in the air—of particular importance to jumpers, vaulters, hurdlers, divers and gymnasts—will be discussed under *Angular Motion*, Chapter Five.

CHAPTER FIVE

Angular Motion

Most of the movement in track and field athletics is of an angular character because the human body, mechanically speaking, comprises a system of levers capable only of rotational motion. And what at first sight often appears to be linear movement is, on analysis, found to be the end product of a series of complex rotations of many parts of the body. It is therefore important, in analysing athletic technique, to be familiar with the principles governing rotational motion.

Moments

It is easier to hold a javelin in a horizontal position at its point of balance (i.e. at its Centre of Gravity) (Fig. 55a) than farther down the

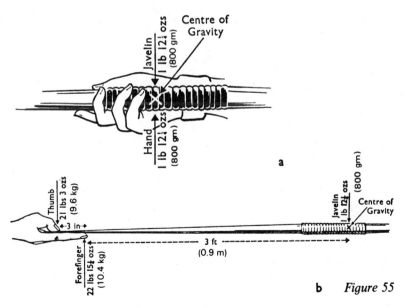

a

b   *Figure 55*

65

shaft, and most difficult of all (if not impossible!) to keep it in this position while grasping the tail end (Fig. 55*b*).

And yet the javelin weighs no more, and the person holding it does not get progressively weaker! The increasing difficulty is due to the tendency for the javelin to rotate—a tendency which grows with an increase in horizontal distance between the force of its weight, acting through the Centre of Gravity, and the hand.

The following are dynamic examples of the same phenomenon; wheels, revolving doors and propellers are easier to turn when force is applied as far away as possible from their axes—the hub, hinge or shaft. A heavy door is progressively easier to close as one pushes farther and farther away from its hinges.

These illustrations indicate that

(i) To turn an object about an axis force must be exerted at a distance from that axis, and the greater the distance, the greater will be the rotational effect. But it is important to note that the distance from the line of action of the force to the axis—the *lever-arm*, as it is called— must be *measured along a perpendicular*, i.e. *at right angles to the direction of the force*. (See Fig. 56.)

(ii) A larger force will produce a greater turning effect.

The product of the force and the lever-arm is called the *moment of the force*, or *torque*[1], and is used as a measure of this turning effect; and the product of torque and the time for which it acts is known as the *angular impulse*.

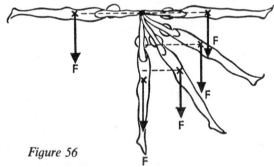

Figure 56

Horizontal bar exercises. The turning effect of the force of gravity on the swinging gymnast is greater when his body is horizontal, and diminishes progressively as he assumes a more vertical position. Obviously, a change in body position during the swing also increases or decreases the lever arm and influences swinging speed.

[1] From the Latin word, meaning 'to twist'.

Moments in equilibrium. In both horizontal positions (Fig. 55) the javelin is in equilibrium, because, *first; the resultant of all the forces acting on it is zero and, second, clockwise and counter-clockwise moments cancel out.* It will help to study this in greater detail.

In Fig. 55a there is no turning effect and the hand merely exerts an upward force equal to the javelin's weight. But in the other position (Fig. 55b) this force by itself will not produce equilibrium, even though the sum of the forces is zero. We must refer to the second condition for equilibrium and take the moments into account.

In this position three forces act on the javelin: (1) the forefinger, acting as the axis or fulcrum, exerts an upward force; (2) the javelin's weight, which has a clockwise moment about this finger; and (3) the downward force exerted by the thumb, which has a counter-clockwise moment. These two moments cancel out.

If we assume the lever-arm of the weight's force to be 3 ft (0.90 m), then its clockwise moment will be 1 lb $12\frac{1}{4}$ oz[1] × 3 (800 gm × 0.90). And if the thumb presses down 3 in. (0.075 m) away from the fulcrum—i.e. $\frac{1}{12}$ th of the distance of the weight's lever-arm—then, for equilibrium, it must exert 12 times more units of force.

$$12 \times 1\,\text{lb } 12\tfrac{1}{4}\text{oz} = 21\,\text{lb } 3\text{ oz or}$$
$$12 \times 800\,\text{gms} = 9.600\,\text{kg or}$$
$$12 \times 7.84 \text{ newtons} = 94.08 \text{ newtons}$$

As the sum of all the forces must be zero, the two downward forces must equal the forefinger's upward pressure of 22 lbs $15\frac{1}{4}$ oz: 10.4 kgs = *101.92 newtons.* So the hand exerts two forces: one upward of *101.92 newtons* and another, downward, of *94.08 newtons.* No wonder the javelin is more difficult to hold in this position!

From the first position in which the javelin was held (Fig. 55a) it can be seen that an object's or athlete's Centre of Gravity is actually a point where the combined moments of the many separate gravitational pulls on all the particles of mass on one side, acting clockwise, equal the combined counter-clockwise moments on the other. (See also page 53.)

Whenever, at rest, a plumb-line can be dropped from the Centre of Gravity to fall within the base (i.e. the hand in Fig. 55a) the various turning effects automatically cancel out—as with the bricks (Fig. 49) and the balanced athletes (Figs. 53 and 54).

Balance in acceleration can be maintained by altering the position of

---

[1] More precisely, the 800 gm of the men's javelin converts to 1 lb 12.218 oz.

the body, thus shifting the Centre of Gravity so as to lengthen or shorten the lever-arms of the component forces applied. For example, the stick in Fig. 57 remains balanced during linear acceleration when the product of upward force-component and its horizontal distance to the Centre of Gravity is equal to that of the forward component and its distance vertically to the Centre of Gravity.

Figure 57

When the stick leans in the direction of the acceleration its Centre of Gravity is lowered, reducing the lever-arm of the horizontal component of drive and the backward-rotating effect it encourages. Simultaneously, the lever-arm of the vertical component is increased, as is the tendency to rotate the stick forward (Fig. 57).

It follows that a sprinter who leans forward too much for the effective force of his leg drive totters, unbalanced, from his marks. Or if he is too upright his legs will seem to move ahead of him and lose their driving effect; this can also happen when a distance runner, surprised by an unexpected challenge, responds without making the necessary adjustment to his body lean.

In efficient running the ratio of forward to upward component of the reaction to leg drive influences the angle of the trunk. At the start, where it is easy to push forcefully backward against the ground, the sprinter needs a pronounced forward lean, but as his speed increases so will the effective force of his drive be reduced, necessitating a progressive modification towards a more erect position. Again, a bounding type of runner, using a comparatively greater vertical drive component, may need a more upright carriage to shorten the lever-arm of the force and so reduce the tendency to rotate forward.

It is quite possible for athletes who enjoy exceptional hip mobility and who possess certain postural characteristics to make the necessary adjustments to the position of the Centre of Gravity without employing the more orthodox forward trunk lean—hence their comparatively upright running positions even during acceleration. The great Jesse Owens springs readily to mind as a good example of this (see also pages 134–8).

We have so far spoken of torque, but in the analysis of balance in athletics it is frequently more convenient to think of *couples*—the essential difference being that whereas the former is the turning effect produced about an axis, a couple (*which exerts a torque*) is *a pair of equal parallel forces acting in opposite directions.*[1] The distance perpendicular to the lines of its parallel forces constitutes the *arm* of a couple, the turning effect of which is found by multiplying *one* of the forces (*they are always equal in size and therefore produce no linear acceleration*) by the arm.

We use a couple when winding a clock, manipulating a corkscrew or spinning a top between the fingers. A pole vaulter's rotation over the crossbar (Fig. 58*a*) is also due to a couple created, in this case, by the reaction to his thrust on the pole (acting vertically upwards) and the force of his weight (pulling vertically downwards). *So a single couple cannot produce equilibrium.*

A body acted on by a couple can be kept in equilibrium only by another couple of the same moment acting in an opposite direction. For example, a hammer thrower's balance in a sagittal plane is partly[2] the result of two pairs of parallel, equal forces acting in opposite directions (Fig. 58*b*). The centrifugal pull acting on the athlete and the equal force of the ground thrusting at an angle against his feet form one couple, tending to rotate him counter-clockwise.

In a clockwise direction, however, the force of the thrower's weight, acting downward through his Centre of Gravity, plus the equal but upward force of the ground under his feet, form a second couple the arm of which is the horizontal distance between the lines of these two vertically directed forces (Fig. 58*b*).

The balance of the stick (Fig. 57) and the accelerating sprinter (page 68) can also be explained in this way. (See also page 113.)

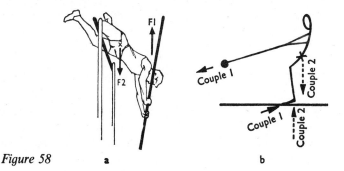

Figure 58   **a**   **b**

---

[1] The terms couple, torque, or moment are often used interchangeably to designate the rotational effects of forces about given axes.

[2] For simplicity, the hammer's weight and the centrifugal forces of the thrower's body have not been considered.

Moments in rotation and spin. In analysing a diver's vertical motion (Fig. 59) we take moments about his Centre of Gravity. When the reaction to his leg thrust (along a straight line drawn between foot and hip) passes directly through his Centre of Gravity, pure translatory motion occurs, i.e. he leaves the board without rotation (Fig. 59a). But as, in successive dives (Fig. 59b and c) he exerts a force at increasing horizontal distances to his Centre of Gravity, the effect is as though more is used progressively in imparting a rotation, while less is available to project his body.

To achieve the same height the diver in Fig. 59b would have to develop *a greater thrust from the board*; greater still for the rotation of Fig. 59c. In both cases the leg-thrust would need to be faster than when delivering a *direct* impulse to the body, reducing the *time* of operation and, consequently, requiring greater force.

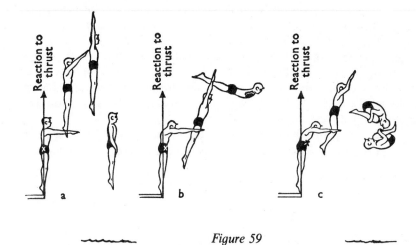

Figure 59

If a body is turning in an *opposite* direction to that in which it will finally be made to rotate by an eccentric thrust, that thrust will be more effective in driving the body linearly, since it will be doing this while it is reducing the turn to zero. This could be one of the advantages to be derived from a 'rolling' start in sprinting (which, of course, is not permitted by the rules). It could result in the application of a greater horizontal component of force. The contrary twisting of hips and shoulders in running is another example. (See also pages 130–3.)

Eccentric thrusts, as shown in Fig. 59b and c, are wasteful of energy. Assuming, for the moment, that the diver in Fig. 59 projects his Centre of Gravity to the same height in all three dives; in Fig. 59a the point of application of the thrust moves through the same distance and acquires the same velocity as his Centre of Gravity; but when the same take-off impulse is directed eccentrically (Fig. 59b and c) this point moves through a greater distance than his Centre of Gravity.

As the expenditure of energy is measured by the work done (see page 40) this in Fig. 59b is greater than in Fig. 59a—and even more so in Fig. 59c. Thus, an impulse exerted through the Centre of Gravity changes a body's linear kinetic energy while an equal impulse exerted 'off centre' changes the body's linear kinetic energy by the same amount, *but also* imparts rotational kinetic energy. Hence, unless rotation is required, eccentric thrust is wasteful of energy.

In our illustration[1] the diver's rotation off the board is brought about by a single couple; the reaction to his leg thrust and the sweep of his arms, i.e. the force of the springboard, acts vertically upward and the force of his weight, acting through his Centre of Gravity, pulls vertically downward. He obtains this eccentric or sideways thrust about the Centre of Gravity by bringing his head and arms (i.e. just under a fifth of his total body mass) forward beforehand and, in bad diving, by bending forward markedly from his hips (Fig. 60).

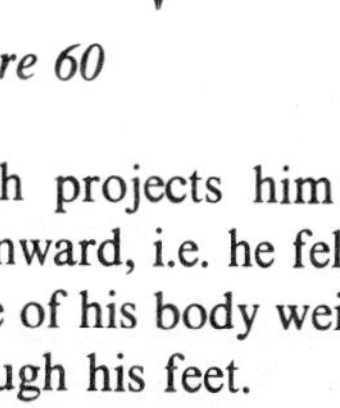

We have seen that the forces of a couple must be equal and yet, in diving from the springboard, the force of the upward vertical thrust actually exceeds the downward pull on the man's body. The forces turning him are indeed equal, but it is the excess of force from the board which projects him into the air. If his Centre of Gravity moved downward, i.e. he fell off the board, then the reverse would apply: the force of his body weight would then be greater than that which passed through his feet.

Figure 60

As Orner[2] has written, 'If a competitor performs a well-executed dive, it will be good because the direction, height and rotation imparted to his body through the diving-board are a close approximation to his exact needs for the correct number of somersaults in the particular position intended and his control in the air will be quite marginal.

[1] There are other ways of originating rotation at take-off (see pages 93–100).
[2] W. Orner, 'Rebuilding a champion's armour', *World Sports*, (August 1964).

'The picture of a diver jumping from the board steeply without rotation then circling deliberately for a spin, finally halting his rotation completely to dart vertically into the water is pure illusion—and the diver's art! The illusion is most effectively shattered when a diver errs on take-off by taking too much turning force, and is unable to maintain the impression of "stopped" rotation near the water.

'Unfortunately, many divers and coaches believe in the possibility of controlling dives fully in the air and are taken in by the illusion. The inevitable result is that they concern themselves mainly with the dive; that is the effects, rather than with the take-off, in which errors showing in the dive originate in a proportion of at least 90 per cent.'

Levers

The muscle forces of the human body are applied through a system of levers (bones rotating about their joints) to which the principle of moments, discussed earlier, is fundamental. In analysing movement in sport it is sometimes convenient to regard large segments of an athlete, e.g. an arm, leg or trunk, as a simple lever, in the same way as the use of a piece of apparatus may be analysed in terms of leverage.

The three types of levers (Figs. 61, 66 and 70) are classified according to the arrangement of the *fulcrum* (axis), the *force* and the *resistance*. The fulcra (A) are the joints and through muscle-contraction, force is applied at the points where the tendons are attached to the bones (F).

The resistance (R) may be merely the weight of the lever itself or the combined weight of the lever plus a load, like a shoe or throwing implement (Fig. 63). However, if (and this would be unusual in track and field athletics) the lever acts in a purely horizontal plane, *then the resistance in this plane will be due only to inertia*, resistance to change in motion, the pull of gravity being vertical. This resistance might also be a force acting within, or externally against, the body.

First class levers. With this type of lever the fulcrum is situated, 'see-saw' fashion, between the applied force and the resistance, both acting in the same direction (Fig. 61). The arms (i.e. the distance between force and fulcrum on the one hand and resistance and fulcrum on the other) may be equal or unequal; but if the force arm is longer the lever will favour

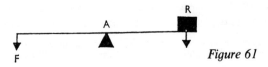

Figure 61

effective force, and if it is shorter it will gain in speed and range at the expense of force. Hence 'all that is lost in force is gained in distance, and vice versa'.

In both our examples of first class levers (Figs. 62 and 63) the resistance arm is much longer than the force arm, favouring speed and range but not force. This applies to most levers of the body. If, for example, in Fig. 63 the resistance arm is twelve times longer than the force arm, a triceps force of 96 lb exerts only 8 lb of force on the shot (96 ÷ 12). Or a force of 48 kg exerts 4 kg (48 ÷ 12). But such an arrangement has its compensations, since the muscles shorten slowly, developing very high tension.

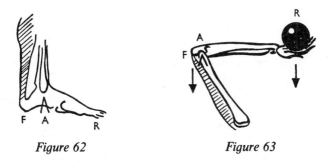

Figure 62   *Figure 63*

The interdependence of speed and range of action is illustrated in Fig. 64, where a short lever, AB is superimposed on a longer one, AC, both moving with equal angular velocity. The linear velocity of the lever ends is proportional to their radii; therefore, if AC is twice as long as AB, its end will travel twice the distance in a given time, i.e. it will have twice the linear velocity.

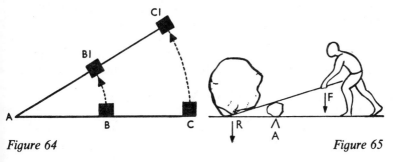

Figure 64   *Figure 65*

Fig. 64 shows another first class lever, where a heavy stone is raised by means of a crowbar; and, to take an example from athletics, when a pole vaulter adopts the 'carry' position, the downward force he has to exert with his rear hand is many times greater than the force of gravity pulling on the pole in front of his other hand, the fulcrum.

Second class levers. With levers of this class both force and resistance act on the same side of the fulcrum, but in opposite directions and with a longer force arm (Fig. 66). It therefore favours force, at the expense of speed and range: a wheelbarrow is another example of a second class lever (Fig. 67). But levers of this type are not common in track and field athletics.

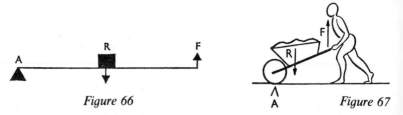

Figure 66   Figure 67

As an important exception, however, the foot is used as a second class lever in rising on the toes (Fig. 68). When the calf muscles pull on the heels, the body rises. Thus the toes become the fulcrum and the body weight lies between it and the point where force is applied, i.e. the heels, providing one of the few instances where the body's musculature works at a mechanical advantage. (If the applied force is vertically upward it will evoke a vertically downward reaction which must be added to body weight and be supported by the toes.) (See also pages 21–3, Newton's Third Law.)

This is exemplified in progressively loading the calf muscles by rising on the toes, with weights (Fig. 69). In this particular exercise the pull of

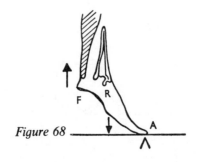

Figure 68

the calf muscles through the heel bone (with the toes as the fixed point) enables a relatively large load to be manipulated easily; for the line of action (through the common Centre of Gravity of body and barbell) is arranged so that it falls close to the fulcrum, viz. the toes (Fig. 69b).

Figure 69

The closer this line is to the fulcrum, the shorter is the weight arm and the smaller the muscular force required in lifting, and vice versa. This can be demonstrated most effectively by asking a person to stand with the front of their body close against the edge of an open door with their feet either side of the door and then suggesting that they rise onto their toes. To their surprise they will find this quite impossible to do, the reason being that the door prevents the line of gravity moving forward over the toes as it normally does in this movement. The result is that the weight arm is kept long and the advantage of this second order lever to lift load is consequently greatly reduced. The technique of weight *lifting* (where the aim is to lift the heaviest possible load) therefore requires that the weight arm shall be as short as possible; while the weight *trainer* (who is primarily concerned with the strengthening effect of the exercise) might attempt to lengthen it, *although this could lead to an unstable and even dangerous position.*[1]

However, when in the exercise (Fig. 69b) the person leans forward sufficiently to move the common Centre of Gravity *in front of* the toes, or when the toes and heel are free to move around the ankle joint (Fig. 62) the calf muscles can then operate the foot as a first class lever. This illustrates how the levers of the body can sometimes be used in more than one way; how, by a change in position, fulcra and points of resistance can be altered. (The muscular effect of this exercise is doubled, of course, when the full body weight is taken by only one leg.)

Third class levers. These are by far the most common of body levers. Here the fulcrum is at one end and the resistance at the other, with the

[1]G. T. Adamson, 'Some facts and fallacies on fitness training'. Amateur Athletic Association, England, *A. A. A. Coaching Newsletter*, No. 15 (July 1960), page 3.

force in between. Force and resistance work in opposing directions (Fig. 70). Third class levers lack great force of action. When, for example, a 16 lb (7.26 kg) shot is supported in the hand (Fig. 71*b*), the flexor muscles of the upper arm must exert a force of about 160 lb (72.6 kg), because the force arm is approximately ten times shorter than the resistance arm. Most of the muscles of the body are inserted near the joint in this fashion, with the resistance at the far end of the bone lever. A weak, long-levered athlete is therefore at a distinct disadvantage, for he can employ his levers against only very light resistances.

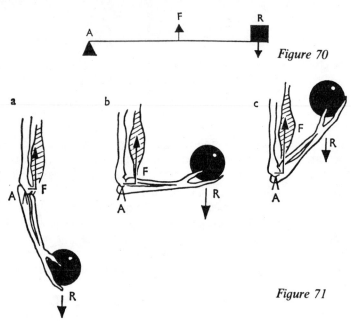

Figure 70

Figure 71

Examples of third class leverage are numerous in athletics. Taking, as illustration, movement in the horizontal plane: in the delivery phases of all the throwing events, force is applied between the athlete's fulcrum (i.e. his axis) and the resistance (the implement) (Fig. 72). Because of the short lever-arm such movements require great force of muscle action, even where the missile is comparatively light.

Force arms and resistance arms can alter with body movement; e.g. Fig. 71 (*a* and *b*) illustrate how, with the humerus held in a vertical position, both arms increase as the elbow bends—keeping the ratio between them (and, therefore, the degree of lifting difficulty) ap-

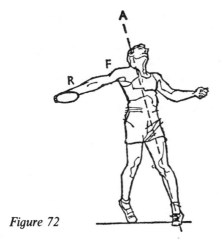

Figure 72

proximately constant. Again, when the forearm is raised from the horizontal (Fig. 71c) both force arm and resistance arm decrease.

In discussing the three classes of lever it has been convenient to assume that force is always applied at right angles, but in the action of muscles on the bone levers this is the exception rather than the rule. In fact, many muscles of the body never pull at an angle exceeding 20 deg.

The more acute the angle of muscle-pull, the farther and faster will a given degree of contraction move the bone, but this, again, is balanced by loss of effective force. Resolving the muscle-pull into two component forces: one, acting at right angles to the bone lever, is beneficial, moving the lever about its fulcrum, the joint (Fig. 73); but the other, acting along the line of the lever towards the joint, stabilises the joint by increasing friction, but makes no contribution to lever motion (Fig. 73). Usually, the stabilising component is much larger than the rotary component. Under

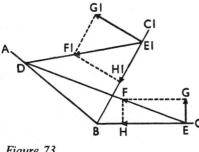

Figure 73

(From *Kinesiology and Applied Anatomy*, by Philip J. Rasch, Ph.D., and Roger K. Burke, Ph.D. (Henry Kimpton))

In Fig. 73, the line AB represents a stationary bone, and BC a moving one. When the muscle DE pulls at an angle DEB, the force contributing to motion (as represented by the line EG) is considerably less than when the bone lever is moved to BC1, where the effective force is represented by the line E1G1. This is because as the muscle's angle of pull changes, so do the sides of the parallelogram.

these circumstances it is fortunate, indeed, that muscles exert their maximum force when stretched, pulling at acute angles.

There is, therefore, an important distinction between mere force of muscle, and strength, which takes the application of force, leverage, also into account. Some athletes, fortunately endowed, possess muscular insertions that are farther from their joints than in the average person; and this, if true of one of their bone levers, appears to apply to them all! Only a very small difference is necessary to give considerable mechanical advantage.

Axes

The axis of a revolving body is a straight line, itself at rest in the body, about which all other parts rotate in a plane at right angles. We know that different parts of an athlete have their own axes, the joints, but here we shall consider the revolution of the *whole body mass*. Fig. 74 illustrates the three principal axes of rotation, and planes, of the human body in a normal standing position—with the mutually perpendicular axes passing through its Centre of Gravity.

Axes when in contact with the ground. There are countless instances in sport where athletes revolve in a vertical or near vertical plane about *para*-medial or *para*-transverse axes (i.e. axes parallel to those shown in Fig. 74) through their points of support. In a cartwheel, for example (Fig. 75), the gymnast turns about her hands and then about her feet—i.e. about a para-medial axis.

Likewise, take-off movements in long jumping (Fig. 150*a* and *b*) and the pivoting of the body on the supporting foot in running (Fig. 128*d–f*) can be thought of as rotations of the whole body about a para-transverse axis at a point where the foot meets the ground. Again, a pole vaulter (Fig. 156) swings about his hands immediately after take-off, or he and his pole, combined, can be thought of as a mass rotating about a para-transverse axis where the pole contacts the box—also applicable to a gymnast swinging by his hands on a horizontal bar (Fig. 56).

Nor need the extremities always be the point of support although, in track and field athletics, this is most common. In certain gymnastic exercises, for example, it is the head (in a headspring, Fig. 76), the shoulders (in a neckspring, Fig. 77), or the back or buttocks, as in certain tumbling movements.

Motion about a vertical or near-vertical axis is equally common in sport; and in track and field athletics the discus and hammer throwing events are good examples. With rotations of this type the body's axis

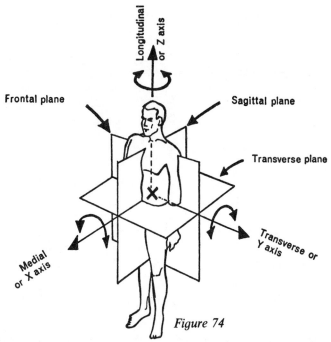

Figure 74

Principal Axes are those about which the human body will rotate without tending to force the axis into a different position. In an erect posture the longitudinal (Z) axis is vertical and the medial (X) and transverse (Y) axes are horizontal; but all three can have their positions relative to the ground changed with a change in body-attitude (see page 94). Where an athlete is in contact with the ground he may often be considered to rotate about axes parallel to those shown.

passes through (a) the base of support and (b) a point determined by the balancing about that base of the clockwise and counter-clockwise moments of *weight* and *centrifugal forces*. (Fig. 78).

When the athlete's posture is *symmetrical* (i.e. his or her position on

Figure 75

Figure 76

Figure 77

one side is a mirrored image of the position on the opposite side) this axis will always pass through the point of support and the common Centre of Gravity (which include clothing worn and any apparatus carried).

In the position shown in Fig. 79, therefore, the skater pirouettes about an axis which passes through the point of the skate in contact with the ice and, also, very close to her Centre of Gravity; for her position may be considered approximately symmetrical.

But where the position is markedly *asymmetrical* (as in the case of the rotating hammer thrower, Fig. 86) the axis, although still passing through the base, will not necessarily pass through the Centre of Gravity and the position will be markedly unstable.

In those activities (as in the shot, hammer, javelin and discus events) where some turning movements are made with both feet in contact with the ground, the support or base includes both feet and the intervening ground; so, in such cases, an axis can actually fall between the feet and move (as it must, in good throwing) from one point of the base to another (Fig. 80).

Most athletic events combine turning movements about both types of axes.

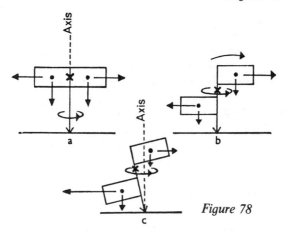

Figure 78

Fig. 78 is a simplified model representing an athlete twisting about a vertical axis.
(a) The two identical rectangular blocks are set symmetrically in relation to the point of support and their clockwise and counter-clockwise moments of weight and centrifugal force about the base balance. A stable condition is achieved temporarily, and the axis of rotation passes through the model's Centre of Gravity.
(b) With one block now lower than the other, their weights balance about the base but their moments of centrifugal force do not. The position is unstable.
(c) For balance, now, the figure must be tilted to equalise all moments about the base (corresponding to a change of posture in a rotating athlete); and a frictional force must be introduced there. In consequence, the figure's Centre of Gravity and its vertical axis will not coincide and the figure will remain unstable, requiring a continual shifting of its base.

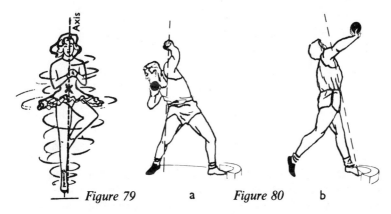

Figure 79   a   *Figure 80*   b

Axes in the air. For the purpose of analysing the movement of a body (e.g. an athlete or throwing implement) in the air (i.e. without contact with the ground, direct or indirect) it is convenient to consider the rotation about an *axis of momentum* passing through the Centre of

Gravity, because of the regularity of that point's flight path. The position of this axis relative to the ground depends upon turning movement (i.e. angular impulse) imparted to the body prior to breaking contact, but, unlike the body's principal axes, *it will remain fixed in direction throughout the jump or dive until contact is regained*, provided air resistance may be disregarded (see also page 91).

Thus, the diver (Fig. 81) rotates about an axis of momentum passing through his Centre of Gravity, and this maintains its direction relative to the ground and water until entry. In the air the high-jumper (Fig. 92) turns about an axis of momentum, while his principal axes (Fig. 74) are not fixed in relation to the ground because of his changing attitude in the air. But the axis of momentum of a spinning discus in flight (Fig. 127) can be shifted by air resistance. (See page 123.)

Figure 81

A body may sometimes be thought of as having rotation about an axis remote from the body itself. For example, a diver free in space (Fig. 81) can be considered to possess rotation about that point of the springboard where his feet were—a *fixed* axis (see pages 93–5). Again, through correct footwork and other techniques a thrower can increase the missile's radius of motion in turning, so that the path it describes may suggest a *moving* centre of rotation well beyond the circle.

In illustrating principles pertaining to the mechanics of athletics, the concept of a fixed, remote axis is sometimes useful, whereas that of a remote, moving axis is purely academic and of no practical value.

Moment of inertia

We have seen (page 18) that a body's inertia is its resistance to change in motion, and with linear movement mass is the sole measure of that inertia; the greater mass sets up the greater resistance and vice versa.

However, with angular motion the resistance offered to acceleration depends not only upon mass but also upon its distribution about the axis, i.e. the *moment of inertia* (symbolised, mathematically, as *I*);

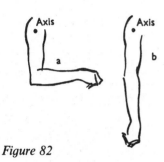

Figure 82

the closer the mass to the axis, the easier it is to turn. This principle, of great practical application in many problems of human locomotion, explains why one can rotate a limb much more easily about its longitudinal axis than a transverse axis of the same articulation.

In athletics, the distribution of mass can obviously be varied by changing position, by changing shape, about the different axes. For example, flexed or straight, the mass of the arm is the same in both positions in Fig. 82 and yet it is easier to move in the first position (*a*) for there its mass is closer to the shoulder-axis. Its moment of inertia is reduced. Likewise, the flexor muscles which pull the recovery leg forward and upward in running have an easier task with the leg bent than with a greater angle at the knee.

For the same reason the total body mass can be turned more easily about its longitudinal axis than a transverse one, and with most difficulty about a medial axis; all these axes pass through the Centre of Gravity (Fig. 83). Again, an athlete's resistance to rotation (i.e. his moment of inertia) in pole vaulting is greater with the body extended immediately after take off (Fig. 156*b*) than in the swing-up, where the legs are well flexed (Fig. 156*g*). And for this reason the correction of balance is easier the higher the athlete's Centre of Gravity above his base (see page 62).

Theoretically, to determine the moment of inertia of the body in any

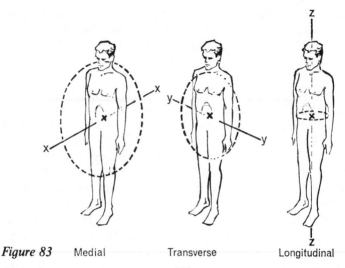

Figure 83   Medial   Transverse   Longitudinal

It is sometimes convenient to imagine the distribution of body mass about a principal axis as a ring (a 'circle of gyration') in which, *for the purpose of rotation only*, the mass can be considered concentrated—the sum of all the separate moments of inertia of its parts in a particular position. The moment of inertia is then MR^2, where M is the mass and R the 'radius of gyration'.

In an erect posture the moment of inertia of the body is greater about the medial (X) axis than about any other through its Centre of Gravity; least about a longitudinal (Z) axis.

position *about a given axis*,[1] it would be necessary to take each particle separately, multiplying its mass by the square of the distance (measured perpendicularly) to the axis, i.e. its radius; finally, all the separate results should be added together. This, however, is not practically feasible and the moment of inertia is determined experimentally in other ways. However, the theoretical suggestion is important because it tells us that the moment of inertia is dependant upon the *square* of mass distribution. In other words, if the mass of the body could be arranged so that it was twice the distance away from its axis of rotation, the moment of inertia would be increased four times. From this we can deduce that quite small adjustments of mass can make relatively large differences in the moment of inertia.

[1] The body's moment of inertia, unlike its mass, is not inherent to the body, for its value depends on the axis about which it is computed. In athletics it is usual to consider moments of inertia with respect to axes passing through Centres of Gravity, joints or points of support.

A person standing rigidly upright on a frictionless turntable with arms extended horizontally (Fig. 84*b*) has, about a vertical axis, very approximately two and a half times the moment of inertia of a position where the arms are held to the sides (Fig. 84*a*). In the first position he is two and a half times more difficult to turn; i.e. to produce an equal angular acceleration, and with the turning force applied at the same point in both positions, the impulse (force × time) must be two and a half times greater; or an equal impulse must be applied at two and a half times the distance to the axis.

In the *arabesque allongé* skating and dancing position (Fig. 84*c*) resistance to turning will be about six times greater than in Fig. 84*a*; when the body lies on the table horizontally (Fig. 84*d*), with the vertical axis passing through its Centre of Gravity, about ten times. In fact, relative to an axis passing through its Centre of Gravity, the moment of inertia of the body is least about a longitudinal axis, with the arms extended and close together above the head (Fig. 85*a*) and greatest when turning in a similar position about a medial axis (Fig. 85*b*) but with arms parallel. But it is greatest of all in a fully extended position with the hands as axis (Fig. 56) (when, usually, the moment of inertia of the *whole body* is found by adding (1) the moment of inertia of its mass, supposedly concentrated at its Centre of Gravity, about the main axis and (2) its moment of inertia about a parallel axis through its Centre of Gravity). *In*

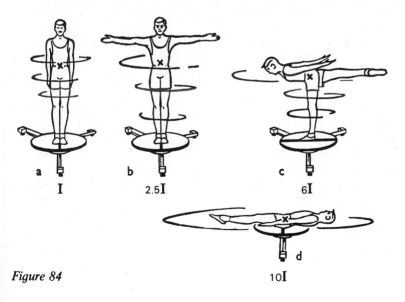

Figure 84

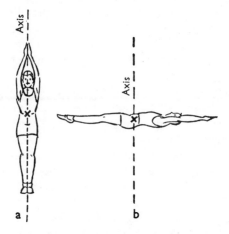

Figure 85   a   b

fact, the body's moment of inertia is always greater about an axis not passing through its Centre of Gravity than that about a parallel axis that does.

Angular velocity[1]

The angular velocity of a body moving uniformly is the angle through which it turns in a second. If, for example, an arm moves through a right angle in one second, its angular velocity about the shoulder axis is 90 deg. per second. Likewise, if the somersaulting diver (Fig. 81) turns completely (i.e. through 360 deg.) in two seconds, his angular velocity will be 180 deg. per second. Angular velocity may also be thought of in terms of revolutions[2] per second, and there are other units in which it can be measured.

Angular velocities, like velocities, are rarely uniform in athletic movement, but if we wish to determine the angular velocity of a body at a given instant of acceleration, we must assume it to be moving uniformly for a short time; the shorter the period, the more accurate the calculation will be.

When a turning force ceases to act then from Newton's First Law, the body to which it has given angular velocity will continue to revolve at a uniform rate, or, if brought to rest by force, the body will remain at rest.

---

[1] Symbolised by the Greek letter ω (called *omega*).

[2] Man can tolerate up to 90 revolutions per minute without undue physiological stress; but for comfort and absence of dizziness five revolutions per minute, or less, seem desirable.

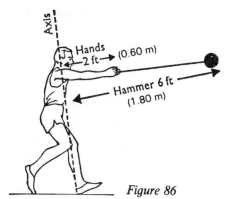

Figure 86

For example, the diver (Fig. 81) turns in the air as a result of forces applied on the springboard.

It follows, therefore, that an arm or leg can be moving relative to other parts of an athlete's body without force acting simultaneously. However, with the human body, because of internal resistances due to opposing muscle forces and the elastic tensions of fascia, ligaments and tendons, where there is motion of such a kind there is usually force acting also. These internal resistances must always be overcome before force can set the various body levers in motion.

As previously mentioned in connection with levers (page 72), the linear velocity of a point on a turning body is directly proportional to its distance from the axis. Hence (assuming the hammer thrower's hands to be 2 ft (0.60 m) from the axis passing through his base, and the hammer head 6 ft (1.80 m) away) the hands have only one-third of the linear velocity of the hammer (Fig. 86). Again, if two discus throwers turn with equal angular velocities, the athlete with the greater radius of discus movement gives greater speed to the missile.

When the body has angular velocity, its motion may be considered as the linear movement of any point, plus a turning about that point with the same angular velocity. For example; the angular velocity with which a long-jumper rotates about his jumping foot as it rests, momentarily, on the board (Fig. 150*a* and *b*) is equal to that with which he can be considered to turn during the take-off about his moving Centre of Gravity; if he does nothing to counteract it before leaving the ground (and maintains this position in the air), it will be the angular velocity with which he will continue to turn about his Centre of Gravity in flight.

As viewed from a fixed position, a rotating body may be observed as turning *clockwise* (i.e. in the same sense as the moving hands of a clock) or *counter-clockwise*.[1] We therefore speak of angular velocity as indicating not only angular speed but direction as well.

The conservation of angular momentum

The product of a turning body's moment of inertia and its angular velocity is called its *angular momentum*, which, like momentum, is a vector quantity possessing both magnitude and direction. *It bears the same relationship to angular impulse as does momentum to impulse* (see pages 32 and 65); for just as the impulse of a force is equal to the momentum of the mass moved by that force, so is angular impulse (the product of a torque and the time for which it acts) a measure of the angular momentum given to a body. It is a concept of great importance in analysing turning movement in sport.

According to the law of the conservation of angular momentum, a turning body isolated from external forces, i.e. left completely by itself, will have a constant angular momentum; that is to say, the product of moment of inertia and angular velocity about the axis of momentum is constant—a rotational analogue of Newton's First Law.

If it were possible to make a turntable with frictionless ball-bearings and a man standing on it were set in motion by a push, he would continue for ever to revolve with angular momentum, if we ignore air resistance. By the same token, the angular momenta of divers, high and long-jumpers, etc., whose body masses turn in the air, 'free' in space, may, for all practical purposes, be considered constant in magnitude and direction (for the force of gravity, which acts equally on all parts of a revolving body, can be ignored).

Under these conditions the total angular momentum is entirely unaffected by any rotational movements made with the legs, arms or some other part of an athlete. This will be discussed in more detail later (pages 91–123).

However, by changing the moment of inertia of the body during rotations it is possible, correspondingly, to speed up or slow down the turning rate. If, for example, the man standing on the revolving turntable (Fig. 84a) increases his resistance to turning two and a half times by stretching his arms sideways (Fig. 84b), then his angular velocity will be two and a half times slower, and if he resumes his first

---

[1] These are relative concepts; they depend on the position of the observer.

position (Fig. 84*a*) he will spin at the original rate; but total angular momentum throughout will be unchanged. (See also Appendix, demonstration A.)[1]

The principle is well exemplified in diving. Accepting that, in relation to a transverse axis passing through the Centre of Gravity, a 'straight' position (Fig. 87*a*) has approximately three and a half times the moment of inertia of a 'tuck' position (Fig. 87*b*), if the diver leaves the springboard with just sufficient angular momentum for a complete somersault in the 'straight' position it will enable him, should he so choose, to spin from two to two and a half times 'tucked'. Here allowance is made for the time it takes to adopt the more compact position after leaving the board and a final straightening out prior to entering the water.[2]

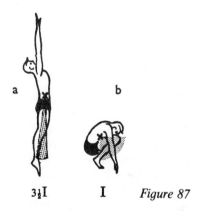

a   b

$3\frac{1}{2}I$ I *Figure 87*

Fig. 87 illustrates a geometrical interpretation of angular momentum, taking, as an example, the motion of a diver's ankles around his Centre of Gravity *in a given time*. If the angular momenta of positions a and b are equal, the areas swept out will also be equal. Note the ankle's increase in linear as well as angular velocity in the tucked position. (The angular momentum of a particle about a point is the product of twice the mass and the area swept out in a unit measure of time.)

[1] But energy is not conserved, for the centripetal force applied to draw in the arms does *work*; so that energy is greater when the rotation is rapid, less when the arms are extended.

[2] Once the surface of the water is broken, the hands or feet become the axis of body rotation. In a good dive, therefore, hands or feet enter just *before* the completion of the required number of somersaults and rotation will possibly continue under water in order to draw the body through the point of entry rather than rotating about this point which would substantially increase the entry splash.

This example from diving points to one way in which turning during flight can be controlled in long-jumping. Should the jumper leave the board rotating forward (as is the general tendency) and then 'jack' or 'tuck' prematurely (as is often the case), his angular velocity is markedly increased thereby and his feet are driven down and back in relation to his Centre of Gravity, for a poor landing. On the other hand, by keeping the body extended in the air, 'jacking' at the last moment, this can be averted (Fig. 153).

Taking another event, a pole vaulter swings slower with his body stretched out just after take-off than when tucked up at the end of the swing, in readiness for his pull-push action. Conversely, the pole and athlete together rotate more rapidly (relative to the planted end of the pole) as the athlete leaves the ground than when he moves his mass to the other end of the pole as he makes his bar clearance movements.

Ballet dancers and skaters frequently spin at very high speeds. While they are building up angular momentum their arms are stretched out and the free (non-supporting) leg is permitted to swing wide of the body's vertical axis (Fig. 88*a*) then, suddenly, the arms and leg are brought in with tremendous effect (Fig. 88*b*). A graceful finish and slowing down or stopping are then cunningly combined by again extending the arm and free leg masses (Fig. 88*c*).

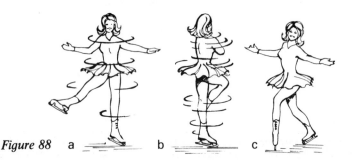

Figure 88   a   b   c

Hammer throwers, like the pirouetting dancers and skaters, keep the free leg close to the supporting leg during their turns, thus getting the hips and feet in position quickly, ahead of the rest of the body and the missile.

Again, maintaining balance on ice is the more difficult because of a tendency to rotate about the body's Centre of Gravity, as opposed to the feet—where, in the latter case, the moment of inertia is approximately four times greater.

Determining the axis of momentum

Reference has been made already to an axis of momentum, fixed in direction and about which jumpers, divers, etc., will possess unchanging angular momentum in the air. The position of this axis can be calculated provided the body's separate momenta about a vertical, transverse-horizontal and medial-horizontal axis (Fig. 89) at the instant of take-off are known. Here the principle is applied to a high-jump take-off.

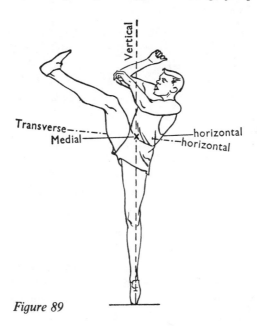

Figure 89

As angular momentum is a vector quantity, each of these three separate turns is represented by a straight line which, in length, is equal to the magnitude of the corresponding angular momentum; all three meet at the athlete's Centre of Gravity. It has been assumed, for this particular jump, that there is least angular momentum about the vertical axis and most about a medial-horizontal axis; with backward rotation, also, about a transverse-horizontal axis. However, the turning combinations will vary from style to style, and even from one jump to another by the same athlete.

For a resultant to be found, the direction of each separate turn must also be known. Conventionally, *positive direction is that which makes the*

turning look clockwise[1] and, therefore, each axis is looked along so that
this is so (Fig. 90), and arrow-heads are then added to point accordingly
(Fig. 91).

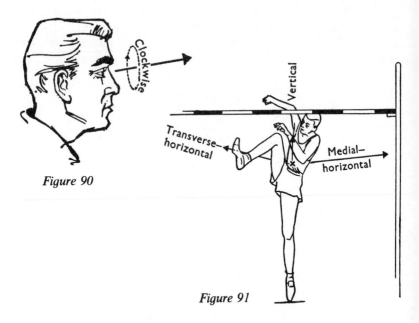

Figure 90

Figure 91

By using the parallelogram method in three dimensions (described in
connection with velocity and forces, pages 11 and 36) the magnitude and
direction of the total angular momentum and the position of the axis of
momentum can then be established. The latter, in the case of our high-
jumper, will be slightly at an angle to the horizontal and approximately
45 deg. to the crossbar, fixed in direction throughout the jump (Fig. 92).

In a somersault dive (Fig. 81) or long-jump (Fig. 150) where take-offs
are properly balanced, it is not difficult to estimate, from the movements
in the air, that the axis of momentum is horizontal. But in many other
activities, e.g. high-jumping, it is frequently not perceptible in any but a
purely theoretical sense and, in the air, the athlete appears to turn
separately, but simultaneously, about his longest and shortest axes; i.e.
his axes of minimum and maximum moment of inertia, respectively. In
theory it is possible to resolve an athlete's total angular momentum at

[1] This common method of associating a vector with angular momentum is often called
'the right-handed screw rule'.

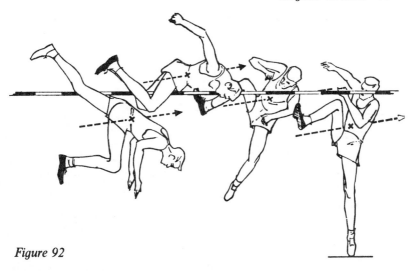

Figure 92

any time when he is in the air in space—about either the vertical or horizontal axes previously referred to (page 92) which remain fixed in direction, or *his body's* longitudinal, medial and transverse axes, which change their position relative to the ground as the athlete moves in the air. (See also page 117.)

As a matter of interest (for it does not arise in track or field events), given sufficient time the human body moving about a prescribed *fixed* axis will finally settle down to rotate with stable equilibrium, selecting its axis of greatest moment of inertia. This, apart perhaps from a small wobbling called *nutation* (lat. *nutare*, to nod, see page 119), then coincides with the axis of momentum.

An illustration of this principle can sometimes be seen in the circus or on the variety stage where one performer, suspended from a cord gripped by the teeth, is turned by a partner hanging upside down from a trapeze. At first the suspended person revolves rapidly about the body's long axis (Fig. 93*a*) but quickly (and automatically) assumes a horizontal position, turning about the body's '*preferred*' axis of greatest moment of inertia (Fig. 93*b*) which now coincides with the vertical axis prescribed by the cord.

Turns originating on the ground

A careful analysis of track and field techniques shows that, to greater or lesser degree, almost all athletes break contact with the ground during

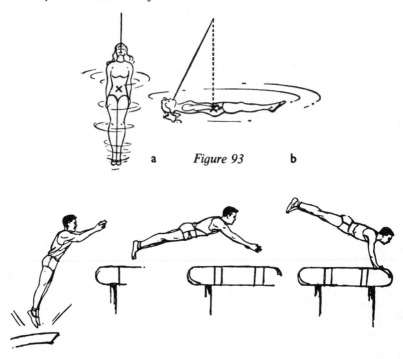

a   *Figure 93*   b

performance, turning momentarily about an axis of momentum. However, it by no means follows that they are always conscious of it, or should be so.

Imperceptible in good running, it nevertheless occurs on each stride and during high-hurdle clearances. More obviously it happens in the jumping events and in the pole vault, as the athlete rotates about the crossbar on releasing the pole.

There are few good hammer throwers whose two feet do not leave the ground, simultaneously, during the last turn, though doubtless this is something not attempted. In all three of the other throwing events, when well performed, the breaking of contact, with a turn in the air, is important at least to the regaining of balance after the throw if not to the throw itself.

Although, as we shall see later, some turns in athletic movement can originate in the air, nevertheless in track and field athletics most are built up while the runner, jumper or thrower is in contact with the ground, when (through exerting a torque) angular momentum can be acquired in the following three ways: *checking linear movement, transference* and *eccentric thrust.* Usually, at least two of these sources are combined.

Checking linear movement. When a body, moving in a straight path, is suddenly checked at an extremity, a *hinged moment* results and angular momentum is developed. For example:

1. In vaulting over a box (Fig. 94) the gymnast, after a preliminary run-up, fixes both feet momentarily at take-off, while the rest of his body rotates over and beyond. This turning continues in the air, bringing the head and shoulders down and feet up in relation to his Centre of Gravity. The clockwise body turn illustrated (Fig. 94) is then reversed when the hands strike the far end.

Figure 94

2. As a result of planting the pole at the end of his approach, the pole vaulter (Fig. 157) rotates simultaneously about his hands and the end of the pole in the box.

3. The diver's somersaults (Fig. 81) can in part be due to checking the feet at take-off on the springboard, as already described; or (a variation of checking) from a standing position on the edge of the springboard he can *topple* into a somersault. In a running dive (where more forward motion is emphasised at take-off) rotation on entry can increase slightly as hands or feet are checked; i.e. to the angular momentum of the diver's somersault can then be added a new angular momentum.

4. The three previous examples are concerned with angular motion about horizontal axes but, in point of fact, the principle holds for turning about all axes, and sometimes about more than one at a time.

In the javelin event, for example, a thrower checking with his front foot (Fig. 193) can turn, simultaneously, about a horizontal axis (at the point where this foot meets the ground) and a near-vertical axis (passing through the throwing base). This imparts considerable linear velocity to the throwing shoulder and, subsequently, to the javelin. (See also pages 206 and 242–3).

As the linear movement of a point on a turning body is directly proportional to its distance from the axis, height can be of particular advantage to a thrower. Assuming, for the moment, that after checking with the front foot (Fig. 193*e*) the thrower's Centre of Gravity continues at its previous linear velocity, then the shoulder above it must move considerably faster.

However, checking must cause some loss in forward speed and the more acute the angle between ground and body at the first instant of contact (or, in the pole vault, the smaller the angle between pole and ground) the greater the loss will be. The advantage must be weighed against the disadvantage, as so often in track and field techniques (this subject is discussed in greater detail in Chapter Ten).

In analysing athletic techniques it is usually more convenient to consider take-off angular momentum about the Centre of Gravity.

Transference. Momentum, linear or angular, can be transferred from one object to another and from a part of an athlete to his whole body.

An example of the transference of linear momentum is shown in Fig. 95. If a snooker ball, rolling without 'side'[1] strikes one end of a row of balls, its momentum is transferred to the ball at the far end; if two balls are used (Fig. 96) then, on impact, two balls roll at the other end.

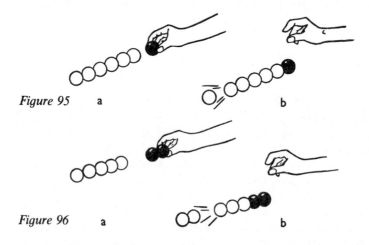

Figure 95   a   b

Figure 96   a   b

---

[1] 'English' to North Americans.

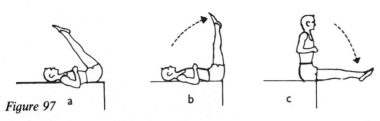

Figure 97

Transference of angular momentum from a part to the whole of the human body can be simply demonstrated (Fig. 97). From the position shown in Fig. 97*a* the legs are swung from the hips, unjacking the body (Fig. 97*b*) and when they are checked in their movement angular momentum transfers to the whole body, which then turns into a sitting position on the table (Fig. 97*c*). (See also Appendix, demonstrations B and C.)

The phenomenon is common to dancing and athletic movement where, often, angular momentum is first developed and stored 'locally' while in contact with the ground and used, later, to turn the whole body in the air. The following are examples:

Figure 98

(i) Fig. 98. In a *tour en l'air*, the ballet dancer first rotates the arms, shoulders and head in a horizontal plane, *with the feet firmly fixed on the floor*; for an effective build-up of twist in the body is possibly only when the lower parts cannot twist in an opposite direction. Then, as the legs drive him into the air, the effect transfers and his whole body twists.

(ii) A high-jumper's pronounced free leg swing at take-off can build up much of the angular momentum he will need subsequently for the lay-out over the crossbar (Fig. 142*k–w*).

(iii) On the springboard the diver develops angular momentum by swinging his arms (Fig. 99*a, b*). This helps to turn his body in the air (*Fig.* 99*c*).

Figure 99

a   b   c

'Local' angular momentum is best built up with the body part extended and accelerating through a considerable arc and about an axis coincident in direction with that of the turning effect required after transfer; for angular momentum, being a vector quantity, has direction as well as magnitude.[1] Maximum angular velocity should be developed before contact with the ground is broken. On transference, the effect on the whole body depends on the distance of the axis of 'localised' movement from the body's main axis, as well as the magnitude and direction of the 'local' angular momentum. In Fig. 99, for example, the turning effect of the arms on the body is all the more effective because of the distance between the shoulder line and the body's main axis passing through the diver's Centre of Gravity. For it is the arms' angular momentum about the main axis which is important. (See also page 112.)

Eccentric thrust. As, on successive take-offs, an athlete's line of thrust moves progressively farther, perpendicularly, from his Centre of Gravity, so will body rotation be easier and the projection of his Centre of Gravity be more difficult. (See *Moments*, page 65.) Thus, angular momentum can also be acquired by driving 'off centre', i.e. eccentrically.

In track and field athletics this type of thrust is usually applied to an athlete at a point where one foot is in contact with the ground—when its

---

[1] Foucault's experiment of 1851 (repeated dramatically at the entrance to the U.N. Building, New York), exemplifies the directional quality of angular momentum. A heavy ball, suspended, is set swinging to and fro over several hours. A large compass dial beneath *appears* to record a continual change of swing in a clockwise direction—due to the fact that, in the Northern Hemisphere, *the earth is rotating counter-clockwise.* (In New York the change is about 12° an hour; at either pole it would be 15°, i.e. 360° in 24 hours.) *In fact, the pendulum retains its plane of motion, regardless of the earth's rotation.*

line of action is often at a considerable perpendicular distance to his Centre of Gravity. However, the transmitting of a *large* force from the ground to the athlete can take place only when the thrust passes close to his hip, knee and ankle joint and to his Centre of Gravity (Fig. 100). Otherwise there is a tendency for these joints to collapse and the thrust develops angular momentum beyond the athlete's ability to control it. (See also *Impulse*, page 32.)

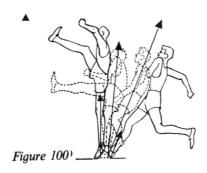

Figure 100

The following are examples of eccentric thrust:

(i) By bringing his head and arms forward, as a preliminary to his downward thrust against the springboard, the diver moves his Centre of Gravity slightly forward of his feet (Fig. 59*b*, *c*). In a good dive the required turning effect is combined with sufficient height off the board (see pages 70–2). (He need not 'break' or 'pike' at the hips (as in Fig. 60) to do this. He can also lean or topple, with body straight, before experiencing an upward thrust from the springboard—using different degrees of lean, depending on the dive—and so combine two methods of building rotation. Thus, a stick balanced as in Fig. 52*a* will not rotate when thrown directly upwards but it *will* do so when first angled to the vertical.)

(ii) Although not perceptible in good jumping, part of a high-jumper's lay-out over the crossbar is due to an eccentric leg thrust at take-off (Fig. 91). But the best jumpers sacrifice only a fraction of their upward spring to obtain sufficient rotation (Fig. 92). They gain more from their position at the high point than they lose in take-off velocity.

(iii) In a gainer (i.e. reverse) dive (Fig. 101) angular momentum is imparted to the body by means of a final foot thrust, often made with the toes gripping the end of the springboard. This is all the more effective because of its distance from the diver's Centre of Gravity.

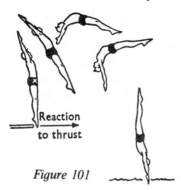

Reaction
to thrust

Figure 101

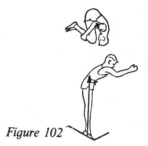

Figure 102

(iv) In initiating a front somersault, with no travel, on a trampoline the performer 'breaks' at the hips (Fig. 102). The reaction of the trampoline thus projects him vertically, with a forward somersault. (Here, the total horizontal momentum generated while the feet are in contact with the trampoline must be zero. This means that if, at this time, he imparts momentum forward to some part of his body, e.g., in toppling clockwise, he must give the rest of his body equal momentum backward, e.g., by shifting his hips horizontally in an opposite direction. Thus the trampoline will have exerted no residual force horizontally.)

(The checking of linear momentum is, in fact, caused by an eccentric thrust, whereas a transference of angular momentum produces such a thrust—because the rotational limb movement involved influences the direction of ground reaction.)

Turns originating in the air

Action and reaction. While Newton's Third Law applies to all motion, it is particularly important to an understanding of human and animal movement which begins in the air, 'free' in space. For whereas take-off surfaces can 'absorb' the reactions to turns originated on the ground, the body alone can do this when initiating movement in the air. (See also Appendix, demonstration D.)

By way of comparison and illustration, we will consider two phases of a pike dive (Fig. 103). When the diver drives down on the springboard it reacts with equal force by thrusting upward against his feet; when, as a result, his body is thrown into the air, its linear and angular momenta are equal but opposite to that given to the earth; for impulse and angular impulse are common to both; the motion of every object on the earth's surface produces its miniature *reverse* counterpart in the earth itself—although the latter's enormous mass precludes any measureable effect on either its position or its rotation.

But later, when the diver 'pikes' in the air (Figs. 44 and 103), the muscles pulling the trunk down and forward, clockwise, act simultaneously on the thighs, pulling the legs upward in a counter-clockwise direction. Expressed in terms of the contraction of a single muscle, the fibres exert their force equally on origin and insertion, producing rotations on either side of the hip joint that are equal but opposite in their angular momenta. The muscle forces required to stop these rotations are also equal and opposite.

Here are some other examples of this phenomenon. If, from the position shown in Fig. 104*a*, the outstretched arm is swung horizontally

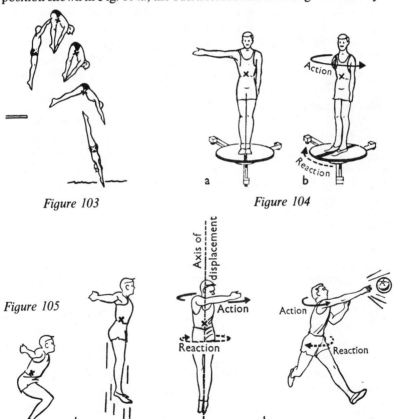

Figure 103   Figure 104

Figure 105

across the body (Fig. 104*b*), the reaction moves the turntable and the standing athlete towards the arm; when the same action is executed after an upward jump (Fig. 105*a, b*) the body's reaction is even more pronounced (Fig. 105*c*).

As the long-jumper brings his legs forward and upward for the landing (Fig. 150) the hip flexor and abdominal muscles pull his upper body forward and downward. When the hurdler pulls the rear leg across the hurdle rail (Fig. 120*a*) the contracting muscles simultaneously twist the trunk towards the trailing leg. And when the discus thrower, with both feet momentarily off the ground, twists his hips and legs in advance of his shoulders and the throwing arm (Fig. 190*d*), the acting muscles pull the upper parts of his body in an opposite direction.

With such 'contrary' movement, action and reaction occur in the same plane (e.g. Fig. 120*c*), or in planes that are parallel (e.g. Fig. 105*d* and Fig. 120*a*). They will be about an axis, an *axis of displacement* (displacement—a change in position), always at right angles and passing through the athlete's Centre of Gravity. Clockwise action produces counter-clockwise reaction, and vice versa, though certain very minor reactions to movement can be taken up internally and, therefore, invisibly.

The importance of action-reaction in swimming is stressed by Counsilman.[1] 'It is important to realise that, although a swimmer may swim in an almost straight line, his movements to accomplish this are all circular or rotary, or variations and combinations of this type of movement. When the swimmer is in the water he is suspended in a fluid, and any circular movement of his arm, either in the recovery or the pull of his arm, or in the movement of his legs, will tend to have a reaction which will distort his body alignment in the opposite direction.' (Fig. 106).

Relative moments of inertia. The angular velocity of the two moving body parts is inversely proportional to their moments of inertia about their common axis. Referring again to the pike dive (Figs. 44 and 103); assuming the moment of inertia of arms, head and trunk about the hips to be three times greater than that of the legs, the contracting muscles will impart angular velocities in the ratio of 1:3, i.e. while the trunk rotates through 30 deg. the legs describe a right angle.

If the man on the turntable adopts a sitting position (Fig. 107*a*) and then repeats the arm experiment, his rotation towards the extended arm

[1] James E. Counsilman, *The Science of Swimming* (Prentice Hall Inc., Englewood Cliffs, N.J., U.S.A., 1968), page 24.

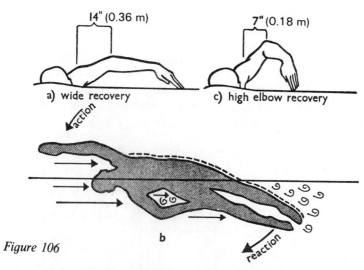

14" (0.36 m)

7" (0.18 m)

a) wide recovery

c) high elbow recovery

b

Figure 106

In the crawl, a poor arm recovery (due, usually, to insufficient shoulder flexibility) (Fig. 106*a*) can cause hips and legs to move in an opposite direction, increasing the swimmer's frontal and eddy resistance (Fig. 106*b*). This effect can be minimised by decreasing the arm's radius of rotation (Fig. 106*c*), i.e. by lifting the elbow and bringing the hand in. (After Figs. 1–4 and 1–3 of *The Science of Swimming*, James E. Counsilman, Prentice-Hall Inc., U.S.A.).

(Fig. 107*b*) is reduced in comparison with the previous example (Fig. 104) because of his body's greater moment of inertia about a vertical axis. By the same token, a high-hurdler's body is less affected by the movements of his trailing leg when he leans forward (Fig. 135). On the other hand, a long-jumper preparing for landing will get his heels higher, through quicker and with the minimum of trunk reaction by first bringing the legs forward flexed (Fig. 153*d*) before extending them

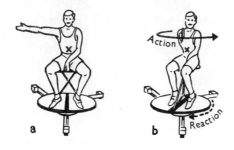

Figure 107   a   b

(Fig. 153*e*). It is therefore possible to control the angular range and speed of reaction to some extent.

We have seen that movement originated in the air cannot disturb an athlete's Centre of Gravity; thus, in piking (Figs. 44 and 103), when the upper body and arms and lower legs are brought forward in relation to the Centre of Gravity, the hips, lower trunk and upper parts of the thighs move back, and the product of the masses and their distances about the Centre of Gravity is unchanged.

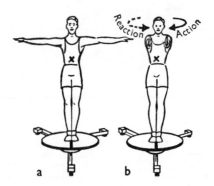

Figure 108   a   b

Control of reaction-location. Within certain limits an athlete can control the location of body reaction. We have seen how the turntable reacts to an arm movement in a horizontal plane; but when both arms are swung in opposite directions simultaneously (Fig. 108*a, b*), the reaction to the movement of one arm is 'absorbed' by the other and the turntable does not move.[1] A similar action of the arms after an upward jump (Fig. 109) will not affect the body. Again, a high-jumper's clockwise arm sweep (Fig. 110*a, b*) could produce a counter-clockwise reaction of the body, or it could be 'absorbed' by the other arm (Fig. 110*c*) or some other part.

When a hurdling rear leg movement is performed on a turntable, the reaction swings the table in an opposite direction (Fig. 111*a* and *b*); but if the arms are used correctly, they can absorb this reaction and the table remains still (*c*). In hurdling, this arm action keeps the trunk facing the front to the advantage of balance, direction and speed on landing.

Again, Counsilman claims that in swimming the crawl stroke with a wide, flat arm recovery (Fig. 112) the alignment of the hips (which,

[1] When it is then a matter of opinion as to which is the action and which the reaction! (See page 21).

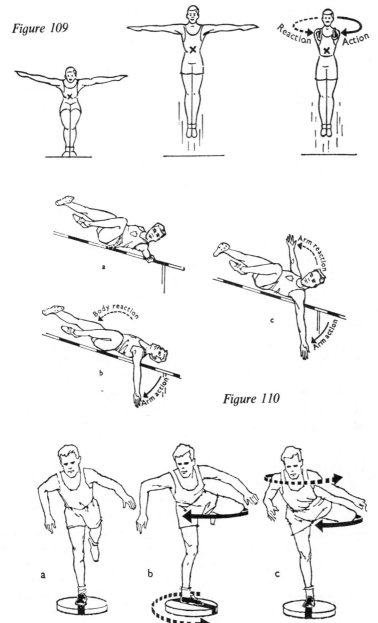

Figure 109

Figure 110

Figure 111

As the left arm recovers from position (a), the right leg is kicked horizontally (b) to absorb the reaction and then thrusts downward (c). Now the left leg has crossed over the right and is ready to kick sideways (e) as the right arm recovers (d). (After Fig. 11–18 of *The Science of Swimming*, James E. Counsilman, Prentice-Hall, Inc., U.S.A., page 32.)

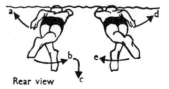

Rear view

Figure 112

otherwise, would swing laterally in reaction) can be cancelled out by a two-beat cross-over kick.

Illusions. While, doubtless, a working knowledge of the mechanics of movement improves what has been called 'the coaching eye', action and reaction in the air are often difficult for even an experienced person to detect because of rotation or spin developed at take-off. To explain: when a pike dive is well executed (Fig. 103) it appears that throughout the upward part of the flight the diver brings his upper body down towards fixed legs and then, keeping the arms, head and trunk still, throws the legs back on a fixed trunk to assume a straight position for entry (Fig. 103). Trunk and leg motions seem isolated and without reaction.

This is because the diver leaves the springboard with forward rotation. In piking, as we have seen, the legs are in fact pulled towards the trunk but, in a good dive, their angular velocity is approximately equal to the body's rotational speed in an opposite direction; thus the legs remain almost vertical as the trunk rotates down and forward.

Conversely, the trunk movement is the more pronounced during the upward flight because it blends with the body's overall forward rotation off the board. Later, in straightening out, the trunk rotates backward and the legs forward in an approximate ratio of 1:3, but the body's take-off rotation cancels out the trunk movement while greatly speeding up the movement of the legs (Fig. 103). *Thus, the diver's total angular momentum is first concentrated in the trunk and then in the legs.*

The pole vaulter's eccentric arm thrust at the top of the vault (Fig. 113*a*) imparts a rotation (clockwise in our illustration) to his whole body. But as he simultaneously 'jacks', pulling the trunk and legs in towards each other, the leg movement is the more apparent to an onlooker because it blends with the vaulter's overall clockwise rotation. But when, on releasing the pole, he 'unjacks' his body (Fig. 113*b*) overall rotation favours the lifting of the arms, head and chest, and the counter-clockwise leg reaction is hardly noticeable, or, perhaps, is completely nullified.

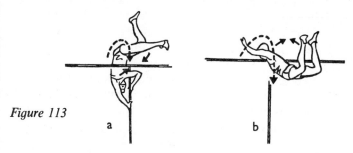

Figure 113

a   b

Similarly, the muscles pulling the hurdler's leading leg towards the ground also straighten up his trunk; at this stage of clearance he, too, 'unjacks' (Fig. 120*c*). But in the event of his taking off with forward rotation, his trunk maintains a forward lean for the landing and his leading leg sweeps down and back even more quickly. Likewise, in long-jumping, action and reaction in the air are sometimes difficult to discern and analyse through being 'superimposed' upon rotations of the whole body. Again, a Straddle high-jumper might the more easily clear his trailing leg by momentarily arresting the twist of his shoulders and trunk away from the bar in order to confine angular momentum to the lower parts of his body (see Fig. 142 s–w). And a gymnast executing a back somersault, taking off with arms extended above his head, could subsequently bring them to his sides (in a direction opposite to that of his overall rotation) and so increase the angular velocity of the rest of his body.

We have seen already (page 87) that an arm or leg can be moving relative to other parts of the body without force acting simultaneously. Theoretically, therefore, force can be applied to a limb while an athlete is in contact with the ground and, relative to the trunk, the limb will go on moving in the air without apparent reaction, for the reaction will have taken place on the ground. However, usually with body movement, where there is motion there is force also, because of the internal resistances which must be overcome.

Exploitation of relative moments of inertia. We know that movement originating in the air cannot change an athlete's total angular momentum about his axis of momentum (see page 97) because the action of one part of his body is 'cancelled out' by the reaction of another. Hence, it might appear that it is impossible to turn the whole body in the air without a *point d'appui*. However, the following examples will prove to the contrary:

(i) If a man, freely falling through space or standing on a frictionless turntable, extends his arms (Fig. 114*a*) and then swings them horizontally in, say, a clockwise direction, the lower parts of his body will then turn in a counter-clockwise direction (Fig. 114*b*). And when he lowers his arms and takes the twist out of his abdominal muscles by turning his shoulders counter-clockwise, a clockwise reaction is produced in his hips and legs. However, now that the moment of inertia of the shoulders and arms is so much smaller than when the arms were extended, the clockwise reaction of his lower body is slight. In consequence, the whole of his body has turned counter-clockwise (Fig. 114*c*).

Figure 114

(ii) This process—sometimes used at the completion of the twist, in a twisting somersault dive, to bring the hips and legs into line with the upper body—is similar to that which enables a cat or rabbit, dropped from an upside-down position, to twist in the air and land on its feet (Fig. 115). During the first stage of its fall the animal 'pikes' or bends in the middle and stretches out its hind

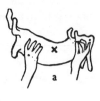

Figure 115a

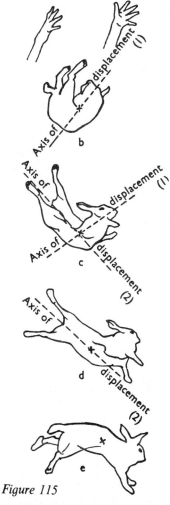

legs almost perpendicular to an axis passing through its trunk (Fig. 115*b*). It then twists the fore part of its body through 180 deg.; the head, fore legs and upper trunk are now ready for the landing. The hind parts react by being displaced through a much smaller angle, because of their much greater moment of inertia about this axis (Fig. 115*c*).

During the second stage of the animal's fall twisting takes place about a new axis approximately parallel with its hind legs (Fig. 115*c*), the twist being in the same direction as that of the head and trunk during the first phase. Therefore the hind legs now turn through the larger angle, for the moment of inertia of its upper body about this new axis is much greater (Fig. 115*d*). At the completion of this series of movements the animal's whole body is free from deformation and has turned through 180 deg. (Fig. 115*e*). In our illustration the rabbit turns about these two axes of displacement at different times. However, the movements can be—and usually are—made *simultaneously*.

Figure 115

Likewise, when a diver assumes a front-arch position, 'breaking' at the hips (Fig. 116), extended legs and hips can be used to rotate the trunk in an opposite direction. But to originate twists in the air by this 'contrary' method (and 450-deg. twists have been claimed for divers using a one metre board) the body must be neither too straight nor too 'piked'; and considerable spinal flexibility is required to continue the movement forward, laterally and backward.

(iii) An outstanding example of the use of this principle in sport is

a   b   c   d

e   f   g   h

i   j   k   l

(From *Manual of Diving*, Amateur Swimming Association, England)

Figure 116

seen in the half-twisting somersault, piked, dive (Fig. 117). The diver leaves the board with forward rotation (Fig. 117*a*) and then adopts a pike position (Fig. 117*b*). Now he twists his trunk through 90 deg. and *then* extends his arms sideways (Fig. 117*c*).

With the moment of inertia of the head, arms and trunk now greatly increased about the body's long axis, the legs are momentarily brought into line and twist taken out of the abdominal muscles (Fig. 117*c, d*); their twist continues until a pike position has again been assumed, but

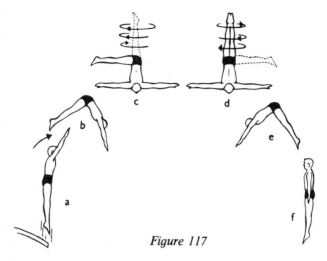

Figure 117

with the legs now on the side of the trunk farthest from take-off (Fig. 117*d*).

These leg movements produce no noticeable reaction or change of position in the rest of the diver's body because of (*a*) the latter's greater moment of inertia about the trunk's long axis, and (*b*) the illusion created by his forward rotation off the springboard—a rotation in the sagittal plane which tends to conceal his upper body's reaction to leg movement in that plane.

The diver has again assumed a pike position, but with his body still twisted (Fig. 117*d*). He then brings his arms back to their first position, stretched above his head, afterwards completing a 90-deg. trunk turn (Fig. 117*e*). Finally, now facing the springboard, he straightens out and enters the water (Fig. 117).[1]

Just as animals employ these movements without conscious analysis of the mechanics involved so, too, can athletes. And just as animals do not all conform precisely to the same movement pattern when faced with such problems of balance and safety so, too, in diving and other forms of athletic technique do methods of exploitation vary from one person to another. In originating twisting movement in the air, for example, there

---

[1] To allow time for the adoption of the correct entry position, most diving movement in the air is completed above the board. It must therefore begin quickly after take-off—*except* where the rules require a given position to be shown first. (See also page 10.)

are many variations of head, shoulder, trunk, arm, hip and leg movement available to the flexible, physically-clever performer. (Underwater experiments, with parts of the subject encased in a plaster cast to prevent movement, demonstrate that about three-quarters of twisting originating in the air is developed through the use of the spine; only about a quarter through hip movement. Head movement is important in so far as it influences the co-ordination of the body as a whole. The arms, although relatively weak in effecting rapid, *large* body counter-rotations, are none the less of great value in creating optimum conditions for movements of other parts of the body.)

To re-emphasise: these 'contrary' movements of the whole body in space always take place about axes of displacement which pass through the body's Centre of Gravity, but which, in most cases, are distinct from its axis of rotation and momentum (see also page 102). They cannot change total angular momentum.

Secondary axes. Another type of movement involving the exploitation of relative moments of inertia is concerned with motion of a part of an athlete about an axis at a distance from his Centre of Gravity—a 'local' or 'secondary' axis.

From Newton's Third Law it follows that when a man falling freely through space, or standing on a frictionless turntable, twirls an arm in a circle above his head so that its axis of movement corresponds with the body's longitudinal axis, the angular momentum thus developed is simultaneously compensated for by turning *the whole body mass in an opposite direction*. In such a circumstance the arm action possesses a constant turning effect on the rest of the body (Fig. 118a).

(*Note*. Whatever the shape of a body, it is always possible to find a radial distance from any given axis at which the mass of that body could be concentrated without altering its moment of inertia about that same axis. The arm's radius of gyration shown in Fig. 118 is therefore the horizontal distance between its axis and a point which represents the sum of all the separate moments of inertia of its many parts; a point where, *for the purpose of rotation only*, we can consider the mass of the arm to be concentrated. It is *not* the arm's Centre of Gravity. The circle traced out by this radius will be referred to as the *circle of gyration*, see Fig. 83).

When a similar movement is made slightly to the side, however, the turning effect is in proportion to the arm's distance from the axis of displacement (Fig. 118b). In reaction, greatest angular displacement is produced when the arm is farthest from this main axis, and least when

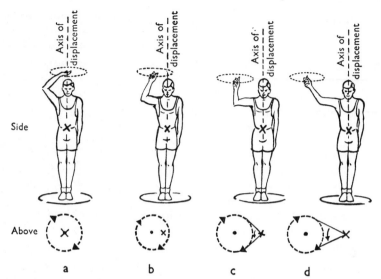

Figure 118

nearest, but the total rotational effect on the whole body (as a result of a 360-deg. arm movement) is the same as before.

Should the axis of arm action (now a *secondary axis*) be moved so far to the side that the arm's circle of gyration no longer 'embraces' the axis of displacement (Fig. 118*c*), then part of the arm movement produces a turning effect on the rest of the body *contrary* to that hitherto; for, relative to the axis of displacement, the arm moves through a sector of the circle of gyration in an opposite direction. However, when the arm is farthest from the body's main axis its turning effect exceeds that of our two previous examples *and, through a 360-deg. arm movement, the angular displacement of the whole body remains the same.*[1]

Fig. 118*d* shows how, with a further increase in distance between these two axes, the sector producing a contrary rotation is enlarged. By virtue of the greater distance between these axes it is also more powerful, but so, too, is the arm's turning effect in an opposite direction. Therefore, through 360 deg. of arm movement, the angular displacement of the whole body is the same as before.

---

[1] For the arm action described is due to a couple; and the odd fact about a couple is that its torque about an axis is independent of its distance from that axis—so a couple is specified by its *own* moment or torque. (See page 68).

It should be noted that the secondary axis of each rotating arm in Figs. 104, 105, 107, 108, 109 and 110 passes through the shoulder, the main axis passing through the man's Centre of Gravity. For the purpose of illustrating a principle, Fig. 118 has been over-simplified; for the movements of the arm are not shown to have an effect on the lateral displacement of the rest of the body, relative to its Centre of Gravity, as would be the case with a man falling freely through space.

Here it should be stressed that

(i)   while the arm movement continues the body can be turned horizontally through any required angle; but when the arm stops, the body stops also;

(ii) although the foregoing examples show motion in a horizontal plane, the phenomenon applies to motion in any plane;

(iii) such movement cannot change the body's total angular momentum about its axis of momentum.

In effect, therefore, it is the arm's angular momentum about the body's main axis (passing through the Centre of Gravity) which is significant.

Balance in the air. Movements which exploit relative moments of inertia are of particular importance to the maintenance of an athlete's balance in the air, for they can be used to counteract embarrassing rotations either originated at take-off or caused by air and wind resistance after contact with the ground has been broken. The following turntable experiment exemplifies this.

If angular momentum in *the same clockwise or counter-clockwise direction* is given to the man and turntable *before* he makes any of the arm movements described under *Secondary axes* (Fig. 118), the reaction to them will create an illusion of reducing total angular momentum or even of reversing its direction, depending upon the efficiency of the arm movements; but when the arm stops, the original angular momentum is again apparent. (See also Appendix demonstration E.)

Three examples taken from sport follow:

(i) A ski jumper with forward rotation in the air (movement hardly conducive to a safe landing!) can move his arms about his shoulders, in the same vertical plane and in the same direction as the embarrassing body rotation, and thus take up some of it, causing his body rotation to slow down. However, when the arm movement stops, the original body rotation again reveals itself (Fig. 119a).

Factors limiting the value of this action to the ski jumper are (a) working together in a sagittal plane, the arms cannot be swung with full

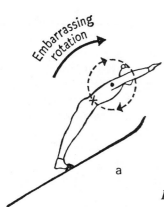

a   b

Figure 119

range behind the shoulders and (*b*) as they move past the trunk they could possibly *add* to the body's forward rotation (for the reason given under *Secondary axes*).

(ii) In the hitch-kick long-jumping technique (Fig. 150) the forward rotation of the arms and the movement of the legs have a forward angular momentum. This may be (*a*) less than, (*b*) equal to, or (*c*) greater than the forward angular momentum with which the jumper left the board, depending upon the take-off angular momentum and the efficiency of his arm and leg movements in the air.

In the first case (*a*) the arms and legs will take up some of his angular momentum, causing his forward rotation to slow down. In (*b*) they will take up all his angular momentum, and so his forward rotation will cease temporarily; and in (*c*) the trunk will automatically rotate backward about the body's Centre of Gravity, otherwise the jumper will have generated angular momentum in the air, which is impossible.

(iii) The long-jumper corrects lateral balance (i.e. his movement in a frontal plane) by the use of his arms (Fig. 119*b*). When they are moved about his head in that plane their influence on the rotation of his whole body is the more effective because of the distance between his shoulders (secondary axes) and his Centre of Gravity (through which must pass his axis of displacement). Depending upon its efficiency, the arm action slows down, stops or even reverses body rotation, yet without changing his total angular momentum; when the arms stop, the rotation of his whole body 'takes over' again.

It is sometimes convenient to 'break down' movement originating in the air into simultaneous rotation in several planes. Thus, a combination of rear leg recovery and front leg downward drive in hurdling may be considered as simultaneous body rotations and reactions in the three main planes, i.e. transverse, frontal and sagittal (Figs. 120*a*, *b* and *c*).

We have already seen (page 104) that, in a transverse plane, the action of the hurdler's lower limbs twists his upper body towards the trailing leg (Fig. 120*a*); in a frontal plane it also tilts it down in the direction of this leg (Fig. 120*b*); and in a sagittal plane the reaction rotates him backward, as in a hitch-kick (Fig. 120*c*). In all three planes, clockwise motion produces simultaneous counter-clockwise reaction, and vice versa; in each case angular momenta are equal but opposite. For this reason the movements of the rabbit described on page 109 are also responsible for a slight change in the *vertical plane* in which its body lies.

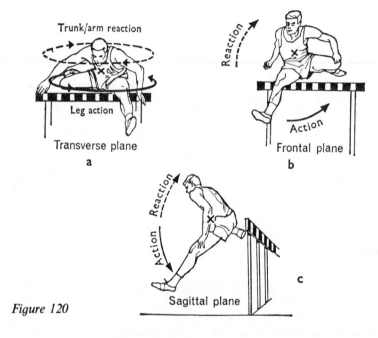

Figure 120

These principles of balance and reaction also apply to types of movement in contact with the ground. For example, a man walking along a beam, but losing balance to one side, might regain that balance by rotating extended arms *in his direction of falling*, as with the maintenance of lateral balance of the long-jumper in the air (Fig. 119*b*). But the difference would be that, on the beam, (1) his arm movements could, at the same time, displace his Centre of Gravity and (2) would need to be *accelerated*, not moving at uniform speed—as would be sufficient merely to *confine* angular momentum to the arms in the air. For whereas, in the air, angular momentum about his Centre of Gravity would be constant, through toppling on a beam it would be increasing throughout and, for balance, would have first to be reduced to zero and then reversed.

More spectacularly, when a tight-rope walker carries a long pole weighted at both ends (Fig. 121) its much greater moment of inertia (as compared with extended arms) ensures that:

Figure 121

(i) only a slight movement of the pole in the direction of falling is necessary to restore balance (i.e. clockwise pole movement evokes a counter-clockwise reaction in the acrobat's body) and

(ii) it is very much easier to keep the common Centre of Gravity (of acrobat and pole) directly above the rope;

(iii) much more time is available in which the performer can sense imbalance developing and make corrective movements.

In running, too, the alignment of the body (both on and off the ground) depends to some extent on such principles. In a frontal plane, for example, arm action (flexed in its forward swing, extended for part of its backward motion) serves as a compensation for the angular momentum developed by the legs in that plane.

Balance in motion in all sport is, to greater or lesser degree, influenced by the factors discussed both here and under *Forces* (2): *Balance in motion* on page 63 and *friction* on page 59.

Nutation and gyration

So far, we have generally assumed the total angular momentum of a rotating athlete (in contact with the ground or free in space) to be expressed in such a manner that the theoretical axis of momentum and his overt axis of rotation coincide, are unchanging in their relationship and are therefore fixed in direction. In Fig. 122 *a* the body's longitudinal axis and in *b* its medial axis are examples of such stable rotation—both being due to the imparting of an angular impulse about only *one* principal axis of the body. (For, in the posture shown, rotation about any other axis through the Centre of Gravity—*including the body's transverse axis*—will not possess this stability.)

The more marked the difference between the body's moments of inertia about its three principal axes, the easier it is to achieve conditions closely approximating to Fig. 122*a* and *b*; and, because the body's medial and transverse moments of inertia are so nearly equal, *b* could almost be regarded as rotation about *any* axis through the Centre of Gravity at right angles to the longitudinal axis. (Note: In the posture shown it happens that *a* and *b* show body-axes of minimum and maximum moments of inertia respectively. But with the athlete in a different position (piked, for example, Fig. 123) the transverse axis might be the one associated with maximum moment of inertia and it would be difficult to determine a longitudinal axis.)

Such movement as has been described above is, in fact, a rare phenomenon in athletics, for it is extremely difficult to impart rotation about only one principal axis—usually *some* rotation is developed about one or both of the other two principal axes, albeit inadvertently; in order to perform properly, an athlete has usually to develop angular momentum about his transverse axis or about more than one of his principal axes simultaneously. Under such a circumstance his motion can often be described in terms of *twisting about his longitudinal axis, together with a simultaneous "gyrating" of this axis (in the same sense) about the axis of momentum*—i.e. with these axes no longer coinciding.

Thus, the axis of momentum of a high-jumper leaving the ground with twist about his longitudinal axis while rotating forward about his transverse axis (Fig. 124*a*) (with their associated angular momenta, shown in Fig. 124*b* in the ratio of 1 : 2) will be fixed in direction at the angle illustrated, with its diagrammatic length appropriately pro-portioned. In the air the jumper will twist about his longitudinal axis which, at the same time, will commence to describe[1] a closed conical path (with its vertex at the Centre of Gravity) about his axis of momentum, so that if he originates no movement in the air, *this conical*

---

[1] In high jumping, a *complete* conical path is never traced out.

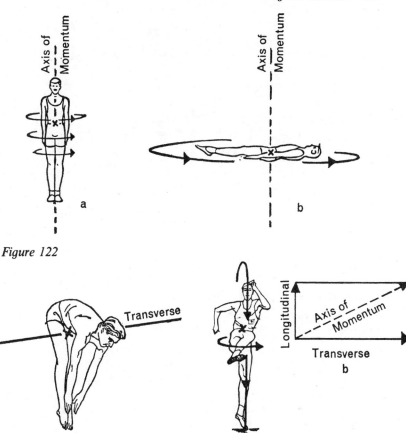

Figure 122

Figure 123

Figure 124

a

path will not vary and there will be no interchange of angular momentum between these two rotational motions (Fig. 125).

With different initial angular impulses about the principal axes (causing, therefore, different proportions of angular momenta) the closed path described will be changed in size. When that path is very small indeed (apparent only as a nodding or wobbling of the longitudinal axis as it moves around the axis of momentum) it is usually referred to as *nutation*; whereas a marked conical motion, too great to be regarded as mere nutation, may more conveniently be called *gyration*.

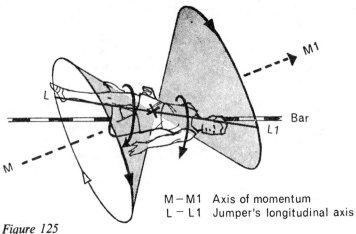

M — M1   Axis of momentum
L — L1   Jumper's longitudinal axis

Figure 125

The trading of angular momentum

Although, as we have seen (page 88), a freely-rotating athlete cannot change his total angular momentum and, under the conditions described above, will experience no interchange of angular momenta between gyration and twisting, *through action and reaction he can redispose body-mass, relative to his axis of momentum, and so alter the direction of his principal axes* to (a) rid himself of the complexities of multi-axial rotation by stabilizing his rotation about only one of them, or conversely (b) deliberately bring about gyration.

Thus, a gymnast somersaulting forward as he leaves the trampoline (i.e. rotating forward about a transverse axis) (Fig. 126a) can originate movement in the air (Fig. 126b–e) which causes a change of direction of his body's principal axes. In consequence, he absorbs some angular momentum by twisting about his longitudinal axis, simultaneously changing the initial somersaulting about the transverse axis into the motion illustrated (Fig. 126f–i). In this case, the size of the cone-angle described by the longitudinal axis will be fairly large, because his moment of inertia about this axis is comparatively small.

The initiation of a twisting about the longitudinal axis does not alter the *rate* at which the somersaulting takes place—providing there is no change in the body's moment of inertia about transverse and medial axes; the angular velocity of gyration about the axis of momentum

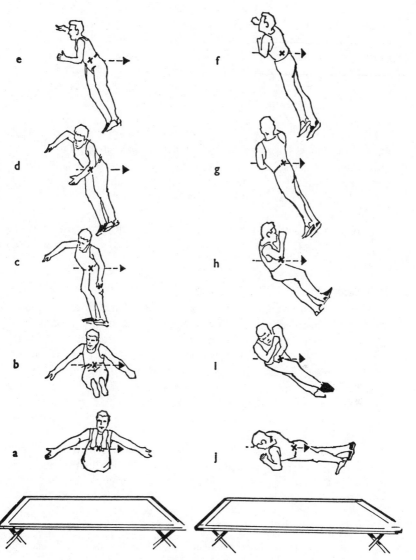

Figure 126

remains the same.[1] But, of course, if the twisting is rapid and the cone-angle therefore very much reduced, the motion will not *look* so much like a somersault. Likewise, by originating movement in the air (i.e. through action and reaction) a straddle high-jumper, for example, can bring his longitudinal axis more into line with his axis of momentum and so twist more rapidly away from the bar—more effective than the mere reduction of his moment of inertia about his longitudinal axis (as discussed on page 88); or, conversely, a Flop high-jumper could eliminate twist developed at take-off by bringing his transverse axis into line with his axis of momentum.

However, in Fig. 126, where, in the process of displacing his principal axes, the gymnast has *increased* his moment of inertia about his medial and transverse axes (changing from a piked to an extended position: compare *a* with *f–j*), the angular velocity of gyration *decreases*, as it does whenever the moment of inertia is increased.

Where—often for aesthetic reasons—twisting at take-off is to be avoided, trampolinists, divers, etc., derive it from somersaults, when angular momentum about a transverse axis can be used, later, for 'trading' around a longitudinal axis.

Precession

Whereas nutation and gyration involve no change in total angular momentum, *precession* does. Thus, a discus leaves the (right) hand with angular momentum primarily about its axis of greatest moment of inertia (Fig. 127*a*). (*Primarily*, because this axis will nutate about the axis of momentum). When a lifting component of force (i.e. a torque) acts to the left of this axis (as seen from a throwing position) the force has a clockwise turning effect on the spinning discus, imparting a new angular momentum to it in the same clockwise sense (Fig. 127*b*).

As a consequence of this constantly-applied turning effect, the axis of momentum changes direction (an effect called *precession*) and the discus automatically corrects its attitude to conform, tilting its forward edge upwards. As in all precession, *the spin axis moves in the direction of—* '*chases*'*—the torque axis.* (Fig. 127*c*; see also page 219, *The flight of the discus*).

---

[1] For the plane of the body's rotation in the somersault before the twist starts (i.e. the plane at right angles to the axis of momentum) changes slightly as the twist is originated, reducing the body's moment of inertia about this axis. (Compare Fig. 126*a* with *f*.)

With the same angular velocity about the axis of momentum but a smaller moment of inertia, the angular momentum due to the somersault is less than it was—the rest appearing in the form of a twist.

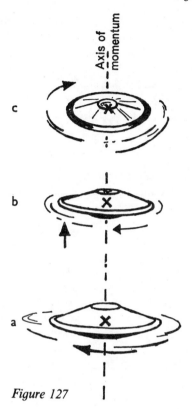

Figure 127

Precession also happens in hammer throwing where, as speed is gained from turn to turn, the path traced out by the hammer head steepens progressively (see page 231). There is also a tendency to tilt its axis through failure to keep the thrower's weight over his left, turning, foot (right handed athlete)—an imbalance which shifts the missile's low point from the most favourable delivery position. Although eccentrically-applied forces (and, therefore, precessional movements) are in operation in all track and field techniques, only in these two events are they apparent and of any real consequence.

Running

Running, 'the classical athletic sport',[1] can be considered both simple and difficult: simple, because it is an instinctive, natural skill performed at some time by all but the most unfortunate; difficult in its mechanical complexity.

No two athletes run in precisely the same way, for people vary in their anatomic structure and body proportion, in strength and flexibility, in posture (often influenced by characteristics of personality) and in their interpretation of some fundamental phase of running action. Moreover, the emphasis on particular aspects of form changes from one running event to another. The ancient Greeks were aware of this; Philostratus of Lemnos in his *Gymnasticus* speaks of sprinters 'moving their legs with their arms to achieve speed, as if winged by their hands'; and Aristotle analyses aspects of running and jumping in his *On the Gait of Animals*.

Yet all the many kinds of running, from the shortest sprint to races over the longest distances, share certain basic mechanical principles, a knowledge of which is helpful not only to an understanding of running itself, but in the analysis of other track and field events and sports. For many skills are derived from or are influenced by these innate running movements.

Running movement is brought about by a combination of forces: *internally*, muscular force, producing a change in ground reaction, as well as overcoming resistance due to muscle viscosity, the tensions of fascia, ligaments, tendons, etc.; *externally*, the force of gravity, the resistance of the air and the forces exerted by the ground on the runner's shoe (to ensure that the ground can exert a maximum forward force, the runner wears spiked shoes; see also page 59).

Compared with the locomotion of modern machines, human loco-motion is cumbersome and inefficient, for it depends upon the rotation

---

[1] J. Lindhard, *Theory of Gymnastics*, 2nd edition (Methuen, England, 1939), page 321.

of legs and arms, i.e. approximately 47 per cent of the body's total mass, and their moments of inertia necessitate the use of tremendous muscular force and expenditure of energy to start, retard, stop or reverse limb movement. In terms of effort economy a wheel mechanism is far better; but Nature uses only rods and levers, arms and legs.

The human body is designed for accuracy of control rather than mere mechanical efficiency, however, and its combined adaptiveness, elasticity and strength have never been equalled by machines. In particular, the three leg levers, articulated on the pelvis, adapt themselves admirably to an enormous variety of postures, efforts and movements, of which running is only one.[1]

Good running calls for a co-ordinated action of the entire body. However, for the purpose of movement analysis it is convenient to consider it in various parts and phases.

Leg action

Running speed is the product of *length* and *frequency* of stride, their ratio changing from one phase of a race to another and from athlete to athlete. Yet these two factors are always interdependent, and maximum running efficiency exists only when they are in correct proportion, depending, mainly on the weight, build, strength, flexibility and co-ordination of the runner.

In examining the performances of 56 Olympic class male sprinters, Hoffman[2] found that the average stride length over 100 m was 1.14 times an athlete's height or 2.11 times his length of leg (measured from the Greater Trochanter of the Femur to the sole of the foot); while, again on average, stride frequency diminished with an increase in height and leg length.

In a second study[3] of 23 female sprinters of similar calibre he found the average stride length over 100 m equal to 1.15 times the athlete's height and 2.16 times her length of leg; but when compared with male sprinters of the same class, height, length of leg and length of stride, female striding frequencies were markedly lower.

[1] Over difficult terrain, the locomotion of most running animals is unsurpassed by manmade vehicles. It is not only faster and more economical and reliable, but more adaptable to changing environment.

[2] K. Hoffman, 'The relationship between the length and frequency of stride, stature and leg length', *Sport* (Belgium), VIII, 3 (July 1965).

[3] K. Hoffman, 'The length and frequency of stride of the world's leading female sprinters', Treatises, texts and documents WSWF in Poznan Series (Poland), Treatise No. 17 (1967).

Fig. 128 represents the complete cycle of leg movement, i.e. over two strides. It divides naturally into phases of *recovery*, when the leg swings from the hip with its foot clear of the ground, and *drive*, when the foot is in contact with the ground. Both are finely co-ordinated and are, by far, the most energy-consuming movements.

Figure 128   a   b   c   d   e

f   g   h   i   j   k

Recovery phase. The instant the toes leave the ground the foot, which had been brought momentarily to rest, undergoes an acceleration, to approximately twice the speed of the body,[1] when the leg flexes at the hip, knee and ankle joints (Fig. 128 *a* to *e*). This appears to be the result of (i) a reflex mechanism which prevents over-extension and (ii) the forward motion of the thigh causing (iii) a transference of angular momentum to the foreleg. These flexions are marked, particularly, in sprinting.

In this way the mass of the leg is brought closer to the hip axis, reducing the leg's moment of inertia and increasing angular velocity. The work of pulling the leg mass forward and upward (mainly that of the

[1] Since a runner expends more energy with a weight attached to his foot than when the same weight is attached to his body, the barefooted distance runner would seem to gain an advantage equal to a significant decrease in body-weight.

hip flexors, supported by the abdominals) is also reduced because of the tapering of leg mass; for the arrangement of the muscles ensures that the comparatively light calf and foot, distant from the hip, are easier to accelerate (a principle which also applies to the arms).

The co-ordination of both legs is so timed that the flexion of the recovery leg is greatest, and its back-kick highest, fractionally after the front foot meets the ground (Fig. 128*d*). The swinging thigh then begins forward-upward movement of great importance to the runner's drive; the acceleration of this thigh increases the force exerted by the ground, thus increasing the speed with which the Centre of Gravity is moved away from the supporting foot.

At the limit of its forward swing (coinciding with the completion of rear leg drive, Fig. 128*f*) thigh movement is reversed, the leg extends from the knee joint and the foot accelerates first forward and then backward (Fig. 128*g* and *h*). The reversal of thigh movement (brought about primarily by the glutei and hamstring muscles) produces a transference of angular momentum and flail-like action in the fore leg; yet the movement is smooth and neuromuscularly controlled.

It is important to note that in efficient running the leading foot is never stretched grotesquely for a longer stride; *stride length is the product of a driving forward of the entire body.* For effective drive the ball of the foot should strike the ground at a point vertically below the shoulders.

The recovery phase is much more the result of muscular control than a pendulum action; for the leg is made to oscillate faster than it would under its own weight and length. It takes longer than the driving phase and for about half the time on each stride, when both feet are off the ground, the legs recover simultaneously. This is in contrast to a walking action, in which the legs swing for not more than half the stride duration, never more than one at a time and contact with the ground is unbroken (Fig. 129).

Driving phase. The foot lands:

(i) First, on the outside edge, and with the toes pointing slightly outward. It then takes the full weight of the body at a point which varies with the runner's speed; in sprinting, well up on the ball of the foot, almost flat-footed at very low speeds. As the body passes over the foot, the heel touches the ground lightly. These movements are an instinctive, *natural phenomenon.*

(ii) With its leg flexed at the knee joint, 'giving' on impact (Fig. 128*c, d*); knee and ankle axes are parallel.

(iii) Ideally, with a backward speed, relative to the runner's Centre of

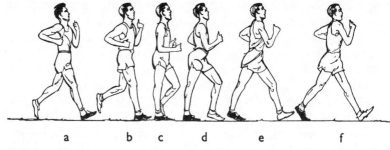

Figure 129

The Walking Action (a–f). Walking differs from running in that (1) contact with the ground is unbroken and, momentarily, both feet touch the ground simultaneously on each stride—in a period of "double-support". As a result (2) the supporting-driving phase of leg movement takes longer than the recovery phase, the legs swinging one at a time. Also (3) the body attains its greatest height as it passes over the supporting leg (c) and is lowest with the legs widespread (a, f); the hip action peculiar to race walking is used to eliminate this rise and fall on each stride. The backwards rotation of the hips also moves the apparent pivot of the legs upwards giving a virtual increase of effective leg length and allowing an increase in stride length without breaking ground contact. As the walking pace is increased (d, e, f), the period of double-support shortens, the strides lengthen and quicken and the hips assume a lower position as the front foot meets the ground (f). With an increase in walking speed, the legs swing with increased angular velocity, so that the time taken in recovery is almost constant. Force patterns[1] (as recorded on force platforms) almost invariably indicate the favouring of one leg over the other; and these are affected by walking speed, body build and age.

Gravity, at least equal to his forward speed over the ground (see page 59).

(iv) In front of the Centre of Gravity; the distance diminishes with an increase in speed.

The optimum position of the feet in running is one in which their inner borders fall approximately along a single straight line. When one foot is placed directly in front of the other, lateral balance is impaired. Too wide a spacing (sometimes due to large thighs or knock knees) encourages a 'weaving' running action.

Experts are not agreed on whether the leg's backward movement can be used to 'pull' the runner over the foot before the 'push' of the drive. Some say it is impossible, while others rate it purely incidental to grounding the foot quickly for another drive. Still others recommend a deliberate pulling action.

Mechanically, pulling and pushing forces are equally efficient: e.g. it is

[1] A. H. Ismail, J. W. Banang and K. R. Manning, *Assessment and Evaluation of Hemiplegic Gait* (Purdue University and Crossroads Rehabilitation Centre, U.S.A., August 1965).

all the same whether a railway engine pushes or pulls; but with the human machine pushing forces are much stronger. The formation of the leg is unsuited to a pulling force, for the resultant of (1) the ground's reaction to such a force and (2) the upthrust of the ground on the foot cannot pass through the runner's Centre of Gravity (see Fig. 133*a*, which shows a sprinter's eighth stride from the blocks). Hence, to attempt to accelerate the Centre of Gravity by this means is a waste of effort (page 71). Distance runners (who, in conserving a little energy on each stride, save a great deal over the full distance) should therefore reject the 'pulling' theory on grounds of effort economy.

As for sprinters (whose first concern must be high speed, not economy of effort), they can obtain and benefit from this second impulse *provided* the front foot has backward motion, relative to the ground, as touch-down occurs. Obviously, such a method of acceleration becomes progressively more difficult as the athlete gathers forward speed; and at top speed there can be little—if any—relative motion as this foot contacts the track. (See page 59). However, whereas the distance runner permits the lower leg to swing naturally as it approaches the ground, the sprinter's need for a rapid striding cadence (in good sprinting of about four and a half to five strides per second—it quickens *very* slightly with a progressive reduction in the stride-impulse and drops off slightly towards the end of a race) demands an emphasis on getting the front leg quickly under the body for a more immediate leg drive.

The 'push-pull' hypothesis was extensively employed by some sprints coaches in the late 1950s. The problem that it introduces lies in the fact that, for an effective 'pull', the foot must land well in front of the Centre of Gravity, with the knee extended. Thus, as the body passes over the supporting leg the knee must flex to prevent the Centre of Gravity from rising at each stride. The force generated by the hamstring muscles in assisting extension of the hip must therefore be increased to overcome the 'passive insufficiency' due to the knee flexion which brings the origin and insertion of the hamstrings nearer together. This increased force of contraction is an important factor in causing muscle injury. Indeed 'push-pull' action in sprinters is a direct cause of hamstring damage.

As the body moves over the foot (Fig. 128*i,j*) the thigh's backward motion (relative to the hips) is momentarily retarded, while flexion increases at the knee and ankle and the heel drops to touch the ground lightly. This gives the foot more time in which to apply force against the ground and stretches the extensor leg muscles. The lowering of body weight also reduces the athlete's moment of inertia about the supporting foot, making it easier and quicker to pivot over and beyond.

The supporting leg's accelerating effect on the runner increases progressively as he moves forward, and the leg is able to direct more of its driving force towards the body. However, the *forward force* (of which very little is required to maintain a constant speed, even in sprinting) reaches a maximum and then tapers off before contact with the ground is broken (Fig. 133). In good running, the *vertical component* of this force (approximately two and a half times body weight in sprinting) exceeds the horizontal component, even in acceleration, because (1) the runner's weight has to be cancelled out by an equal and upward force before he can start any movement from the ground; (2) his length of stride is dependent upon his being off the ground for a sufficient period of time; and (3) a predominantly horizontal thrust would have a line of action passing so far from his Centre of Gravity as to produce an unwanted and uncontrollable turning effect about that point.

The gluteus maximus, hamstring, quadricep, gastrocnemius and hallucis longus muscles bear the burden of the movement. Extension originates in the stronger but slower muscles surrounding the runner's Centre of Gravity, and is taken up at the knee, ankle and foot, in that order. All extensions end together with the foot well behind the body (Fig. 128k)—again pointing slightly outward, with the runner breaking contact with the *inside* front edge.

Eccentric movement. In a normal standing position, a man's Centre of Gravity is situated approximately at the level of the upper third of the sacrum and, with the raising of various parts of the body, in running at times it is even higher. Fig. 130 illustrates how, relative to the athlete's Centre of Gravity, leg movement is eccentric, i.e. 'Off centre' (see pages 71 and 99).

Thus, while the force of reaction to the leg drive translates, or projects, the body's Centre of Gravity, its upward thrust tends to lift, and its forward thrust pushes forward, the corresponding hip (Fig. 130 which, for simplicity, shows the line of thrust actually passing through the hips). Likewise, in recovery, the forward-upward swing encourages a retarding and dropping

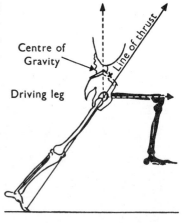

Figure 130

of the hip on the same side of the body. *In fact, hip action tends to reduce the thrust received from it or delivered to it.* The greater the effective leg drive, the more powerful these tendencies are; and as, in the course of the stride, the direction of the thrust or swing changes, so does the proportion of these horizontal and vertical reactions.

However, such hip movement is prevented by muscles and ligaments; e.g. as the body is first supported and then driven forward by one leg, the corresponding gluteus medius and minimus muscles prevent a sagging of the opposite hip. In the contrary, the hips *follow* the legs.

The reaction cannot be denied, however (see pages 21–3); *if the pelvis will not assimilate the by-product of eccentric leg thrust, then another part of the body, and/or the ground, must.*

Arm and shoulder action

Because of the muscular connections between the pelvis and the upper trunk (e.g. internal oblique and latissimus dorsi muscles) most of this reaction in running is absorbed by the upper body, which can be seen to twist rhythmically in opposition to the leg movement. However, a little is taken up internally and by the ground (upon which a torque is exerted), and is therefore not apparent.

We have seen (page 104) that the location of body reaction can be controlled to some limited extent. In different types of running the reaction to the eccentric leg thrust is absorbed by:

(i) vigorous, but properly directed, arm action (as used in good sprinting; Fig. 131);

(ii) the shoulders and arms twisting *en bloc*, without a pivoting of the arms about the shoulders. This action was exemplified in the style of Emil Zatopek;

(iii) a combination of (i) and (ii) above, as is most common to all but the short sprinting events (Fig. 128).

Sprinting. In sprinting the accelerations of leg movement required for a striding cadence of four and a half to five times per second (the frequency in top-class competition) and for a powerful leg thrust, are possible only when the shoulders are kept steady about the trunk's longitudinal axis; because the trunk, with its great inertia, cannot twist and untwist with sufficient rapidity.

In good sprinting the reaction to the horizontal (i.e. twisting) component of the leg thrust is absorbed by the more easily controlled arms, and the shoulders remain steady. However, to 'take up' this angular momentum, the arms have to operate with sufficient force and, primarily, in a sagittal (i.e. backward-forward) plane. Force of action is indicated by their radius and angular acceleration, while their range about the shoulders denotes the time/distance of force application. Arm action will tend to be more effective in absorbing 'twist' the greater its distance from the body's longitudinal axis.

Both forward and backward arm movements are part of a clockwise or counter-clockwise upper body twist; they work in sympathy with each other, not in opposition. During their forward swings they are flexed at about a right angle, giving great angular velocity and co-ordinating with the quick recovery action of the forward-swinging leg (Fig. 131*c, d, e*). *The forward arm movement* sets up a backward reaction on the corresponding shoulder, 'absorbing' the forward twisting which would otherwise ensue. Of particular importance here is the upper-arm movement in a sagittal plane; a slight cross-body swing of the lower arm is both natural and desirable.

Figure 131   **e**   **d**   **c**   **b**   **a**

The backward phase of arm action tends to thrust the corresponding shoulder forward. The arm's effect is at first strengthened and prolonged by a natural straightening at the elbow, corresponding with the longer leverage of the driving leg on the opposite side. But towards the end of its backward movement the arm bends and speeds up again, to match the final, fast stages of leg drive (Fig. 131*e*).[1]

The range of arm movement in sprinting (as represented by the path of its Centre of Gravity) is about as much in front of as behind the shoulder axis. It varies with the individual (e.g. thin, small arms might

---

[1]The arms' varying length in swinging to and fro also prevents an undesirable rotation of the body in a frontal plane (see page 117).

move through a greater arc) and, to a certain extent, from one phase of a sprint to another (emphasised, especially at the start); but usually, the hands swing no higher than shoulder level to the front, nor more than a foot (0.3 m) behind the hip-line to the rear (Fig. 131).

While, in all forms of running, the primary function of the upper body is to 'take up' reaction to the eccentric leg drive, 'counter-balancing' and 'following' leg action, in sprinting particularly, the arms may be used to spur on the legs, which speed up and consequently add to their horizontal component of drive; for (as mentioned on page 21) action and reaction are interchangeable factors.

Since both arms accelerate upwards and downwards simultaneously their subsequent downward retardation[1] and upward movement add to the vertical component of drive; and their downward acceleration, coinciding with touch down, lessens the impact between the ground and front foot—being most effective, in each case, when the arms are carried close to the trunk.

Moreover, by losing upward speed fractionally before the completion of leg drive, the arms ease the compression of the thrusting leg—and so permit more forceful and freer use of its foot and ankle. Hopper[2] writes: 'It is in this connection that the vital importance of timing becomes obvious; and one wonders how many pulled muscles and other troubles are due to temporary lack of exact co-ordination between leg and arm action.' *So the arms can be accelerated either upwards or downwards at appropriate times—to increase the force between the supporting leg and the ground, or to reduce it.*

Longer distances. While wishing to maintain as high a speed as possible, those who run longer distances must conserve energy by reducing their effort and frequency of striding. Their weaker leg drive and slower leg swing in recovery develop less twisting angular momentum than in sprinting, and a reduced striding frequency (of somewhere in the order of three strides per second) gives the trunk time to take up the reaction to this angular momentum without recourse to forceful and tiring arm movement. Arm action is 'quieter' and does not fully compensate; hence the relaxed flowing shoulder-twist and gentle arm movement typical of the distance runner. However, excessive cross body arm action is associated with splay-footed gait due to excessive body twist.

[1] Which *constitutes an upward acceleration.*
[2] B. J. Hopper, 'Mechanics of arm action in running', *Track Technique*, U.S.A., No. 17 (September, 1964).

Trunk and head positions

Running movement can give maximum efficiency only when the athlete is properly balanced, which depends considerably upon the correct angling of the trunk. The following are relevant factors:

The force of the leg drive and the proportion of its horizontal and vertical components. As previously maintained (see pages 63, 67 and 68), for balanced running the moments of the vertical and horizontal components of drive must be adjusted about the runner's Centre of Gravity, and at uniform speed, can be considered constant: posture is almost erect though; when a good runner is viewed from the side, there is an illusion of a pronounced forward trunk lean when his driving leg is fully extended[1] (Figs. 128*a* and 131*a*); a fairer view is obtained when he is in mid-stride (Figs. 128*d* and 131*d*).

However, in acceleration (i.e. in the gaining or losing of speed) the problem of balance is complicated because of variation in the horizontal component of leg drive. In positive acceleration, for example, the faster a man runs the more difficult it is for him to exert a large force against the ground which, to him, seems to be receding rapidly; he is unable to move his feet fast enough. Thus, the force he exerts and its duration (i.e. impulse) are successively reduced (see pages 32 and 33).

[2](On leaving the blocks a sprinter will be in contact with the ground for approximately twice as long as when both feet are off the ground. After about ten strides the times will be equal; and, thereafter, will attain a ratio of between 1 : 1.3 and 1 : 1.5. At a maximum or near-maximum speed, while he is in contact with the ground in one unit of time he has to counteract the effect of gravity during 1.3 to 1.5 units—requiring an additional upward thrust of 1.3 to 1.5 times body weight. For, as we have seen (page 129), his vertical component of drive must at all times keep him off the ground for sufficient time to get his legs into position for the next stride; and the shorter the period of time for which he is in contact with the ground, the higher must be the value of that vertical component.)

For balance in varying accelerations a runner has constantly to alter the lever-arms of the force components by adjusting the position of his Centre of Gravity in relation to his supporting foot; this he achieves by changing the angle of his trunk (Fig. 132). In a phase of great positive

---

[1] As well as an impression of maximum forward thrust whereas, by then, all drive will have ceased.

[2] E. F. Housden. 'Mechanical analysis of the running movement'. 'Run, Run, Run' by Fred Wilt, *Track & Field News, Inc.*, U.S.A.

Figure 132

acceleration (the result of a large horizontal component of force), as in the first stride from the blocks (Fig. 132*b* and *c*), a sprinter needs a pronounced forward lean; hence the main justification for a crouched start. But later in his race, with a reduction in the force he can exert, he has to assume a more erect position to avoid toppling forward (Fig. 132*f*). (*Note:* Here it is a vertical component of leg-drive *in excess of body weight* on each stride which raises the sprinter's Centre of Gravity progressively towards a normal running position).

By the same token, balanced negative acceleration (as, for example, when sprinters slow down after breasting the tape) calls for a backward lean. An exaggerated lean either way reduces the stride length and places an unnecessary strain on the muscles of the trunk.

Rotation in a sagittal plane. So far, in considering the angling of the trunk, it has been convenient to assume the line of thrust from the ground reaction on each stride *always* to pass through a runner's Centre of Gravity. Certainly, the effect is as if it did so, and this approach to balance in running is recommended as most practical.

As Hopper[1] has shown, however, ground reaction, besides support-

[1] B. J. Hopper. 'Rotation—a vital factor in athletic technique' *Track Technique*, U.S.A., No. 10, December 1962 and March 1963 *Track & Field News*.

ing and propelling the runner, may be considered to create angular momentum in a sagittal plane (Fig. 133), for when the foot first meets the track both vertical and horizontal components of reaction act in front of his Centre of Gravity, tending to rotate him *backwards* (Fig. 133*a*). Later, when a large vertical component acts behind his Centre of Gravity, the tendency is for the trunk to be rotated *forward* (Fig. 133*c–d*), and (particularly in acceleration), to be rotated *backward again* just before the foot breaks contact, when the vertical component has greatly diminished (Fig. 133*f*).

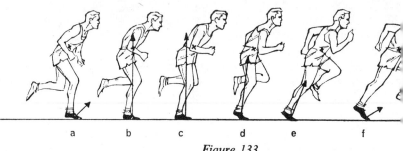

a   b   c   d   e   f

Figure 133

Hopper suggests that, to maintain the trunk in an efficient running position, the legs and arms 'take up' these angular momenta. Thus, with the line of thrust from the ground in front of the runner's Centre of Gravity, foreleg and forearm movements possess a counter clockwise angular momentum; and with ground reaction behind, their effect is reversed. Finally, this 'absorbing' process is reversed yet again.

But Hopper says, ' . . . the transmission of a big force from the ground to the body of the athlete will take place only when the line of its action passes close to both hip and the man's Centre of Gravity: so it is not surprising that the maximum ground reaction developed . . . in running does not occur until these conditions are fulfilled.'[1]

It seems likely that balance in running is dependent upon both methods, i.e. on the 'taking up' of embarrassing angular momenta, and on the adjustment of the position of the Centre of Gravity to the force and direction of ground reaction.

Posture, a product of heredity, environment and self-expression, is acceptable in an athlete if it permits the proper functioning of respiration, circulation, etc., and involves no unnecessary tensions or

---

[1] Conversely, the rotary motion of the forearms, feet and lower legs may be considered *responsible* for the direction of ground reaction.

restrictions. In considering its relation to running efficiency these should be the only criteria.

Static posture will, inevitably, influence both dynamic posture and technique. In defining this it can be said that four points—the tip of the Mastoid Process, the Greater Tuberosity of the Humerus, the Greater Trochanter of the Femur, and a point $1\frac{1}{2}$ in. (4 cm) in front of the Lateral Malleolus—should all lie on the same vertical plane. For in this way, the minimum muscular effort will be required to maintain an erect posture.

The posture of the hips is the key to that of the whole body, in that it (a) determines the inclination of the pelvis—the foundation upon which the spinal column is erected, and (b) influences the movements of the legs and, therefore, the posture of the feet.[1]

Postural idiosyncrasies can give an illusory, as opposed to real, trunk angle. Round shoulders and a tendency to stoop create an appearance of forward lean in running (Fig. 134a), while pigeon-chested or hollow-backed athletes seem to run with an upright carriage (Fig. 134b). Hip mobility can be of special influence in determining the angle at which the trunk is held in running, because unusual flexibility in these joints enables an athlete to adjust his balance while maintaining a more upright position.

Air resistance. As an athlete runs the resistance of the air not only requires him to do work which, in consequence, restricts his speed; it can also impair his running position; in particular, at top sprinting speed or when running into a strong head wind (or even into a wind blowing *across* the track), air resistance tends to straighten the trunk. Under such circumstances, therefore, he maintains balance by shifting his Centre of Gravity sufficiently far forward to counteract the tendency to rotate backwards. He leans well forward into a strong head wind and is more upright with a following wind. The need for greater emphasis on horizontal force when air resistance is increased has been mentioned already (page 37) and is illustrated diagrammatically (Fig. 30).

A wind in any direction has a slowing effect on a runner making a complete circuit of a track, for the opposing force it offers on one side is greater than the reduction experienced on the other; and more time must be spent in running against it. The wind's contrary impulse is therefore greater than its favourable one.[2]

---

[1] P. Wiles, *Essentials of Orthopaedics*, 4th edition, chapter 1 (J. & A. Churchill, 1965).
[2] For I.A.A.F. acceptance of world records up to and including 200 metres, and for the Long and Triple jumps, average wind speeds must not exceed 2 metres (6 ft 6¾ in.) per second (i.e. 4.473 m.p.h.) in the running direction—4 metres (13 ft 1½ in.) per second for Pentathlon and Decathlon records.

Head. By virtue of its weight (approximately a fourteenth of the total mass of the body in an adult) and position on the spine, movements of the head can have considerable effect on other parts of the body. Hence the expression 'The head is the rudder of the body'.

As a general rule it is better for the balance of the runner for the head to be kept in natural alignment with the shoulders, with the eyes directed to that end. However, a twisting of the head (i.e. in a transverse plane) need not upset balance and may even be necessary, sometimes, in middle and long-distance running.

The effects of a poor head position are often to be seen towards the end of a race, when runners are tiring; throwing it back straightens the trunk and shortens the stride.

Expenditure of energy

For practical coaching purposes the techniques of athletics are best studied through the concept of momentum (see also page 43), since accurate measurement of total mechanical work in athletics is always difficult and is fre-

Figure 134

quently impossible. For this reason, physiologists prefer to analyse in terms of energy, calculating directly from the amount of heat produced during exercise, or indirectly from oxygen consumption and carbon dioxide elimination. Although physiological techniques do not fall within the scope of this book, none the less they are closely related to the mechanics of running; the following information should be useful to coaches and teachers as a background to their study of man, the running machine.

In *aerobic* exercise, where an athlete's power is limited by the extent to which he can absorb and use oxygen—i.e. through the oxidation of glucose—a very good runner can perhaps increase his oxygen uptake to as much as 5.5 litres per minute.[1] Therefore, because a consumption of 1 litre (about a quart) of oxygen per minute corresponds approximately to a power output of 75 w, a good long-distance runner would be limited to about 300 to 400 w.

---

[1] Because, in general, the bigger the person the larger the oxygen uptake, it is usual to express the latter in millilitres of oxygen per minute per kilogram of body weight—an exceptional 84 ml if our runner weighed 65 kg (143 lb).

But muscles contain stored chemical substances from which energy can be obtained, and this *anaerobic* source (derived from the hydrolysis of glucose) provides an additional 450 w (about 0.6 horsepower) for one minute—extra power to be used as circumstances demand.

This second source might be expected to yield more, since both Hill[1] and Wilkie[2] have assessed maximum oxygen debt at 20 litres—'Enough to keep a man at rest going for an hour' (Hill). But according to Wilkie, only about a third of this is actually obtained as external mechanical work, though he says the reason, as yet, is not clear.

In sprinting, therefore, power output is not limited by oxygen consumption, but, rather, by the amount of muscle which can be used and the efficiency with which it is used. (See also *Power*, page 43).

It can be said that an oxygen uptake of 5 litres per minute (good for an average middle-distance runner and undoubtedly well in excess of the average sprinter's) will allow energy expenditure equivalent to roughly 375 w (0.5 horsepower).[3] It would seem, then, that if a particular sprinter should possess an uptake of 5 litres per minute and can use a third of his oxygen debt (say, 6 litres) he should work to an equivalent of 11 litres of oxygen per minute, i.e. about 825 w (1.1 horsepower).

In all forms of running some energy is spent on working against air resistance; as a man runs he drives part of the air to one side, and either carries along or pushes more of it in front of him. This requires work, diminishing his kinetic energy and, therefore, his speed. The force of this air resistance varies as the square of the runner's speed and is therefore greatest in sprinting. It has been estimated that, in still air, at a speed of 35 ft (10.67 m) per second (the top speed of a good sprinter) the force of air resistance is about 3.58 lb (15.93 n).

When an athlete runs, his Centre of Gravity undulates continuously—at top sprinting speed with an overall vertical range (i.e. from the lowest point after touch-down to its highest after ground contact has been broken) of from $2\frac{1}{2}$ to 3 inches (6 to 8 cm). Off the ground it moves up and down, and while he is in contact energy is used to stop the downward movement of the Centre of Gravity and to give it upward movement again. Because the foot makes contact with the

---

[1] A. V. Hill, *Living Machinery* (Bell, 1939).

[2] D. R. Wilkie, ibid.

[3] Assuming a conversion efficiency of 20 to 25 per cent, figures which compare favourably with man-made machines. (The efficiency of muscle is measured by the ratio of the mechanical work it can do to the energy of the fuel—i.e. foodstuffs—with which it is provided.)

ground almost directly below the Centre of Gravity, the retardation of downward movement can be expected to exceed the following upward acceleration, which occurs when the Centre of Gravity is in front of the foot. If this is so, the time spent in retardation is less than that of acceleration.

When the athlete is not in contact with the ground the vertical movement of his Centre of Gravity is, of course, regulated by the force of gravity. Here, again, the periods spent in upward and downward movement are most probably unequal.

Much more total energy is expended in producing and destroying the kinetic energy in the limbs. Each foot is brought to rest about every fifteen feet (4.5 m) and the remainder of each leg is slowed down and speeded up in a continuous cycle of movement. In addition, as the movement is mainly rotary, the direction is continually changing. This means that there is a continual change in the momentum of the legs, and this also applies to the arms.

While the athlete has contact with the ground, part of this total change in momentum is produced by the work done by the driving leg, and accounts for much of the energy expended by this leg. However, when there is no contact with the ground, all change is produced by the transference of momentum from one part of the body to another, at the expense of energy; for there is always a loss of energy in any transference of momentum, because some is transformed into heat.

In consequence, if the work done by the driving leg is not equal to the expenditure of energy during all the movements of a running stride, the runner will slow down. *This should serve to emphasise the danger of wasting energy through unnecessary movement and lack of proper relaxation.*

At very high running speeds, especially, muscle movement is uneconomical. By its very nature, human locomotion is wasteful.[1] Yet, through superior balance, relaxation and timing, trained runners can undoubtedly conserve energy and transfer momentum from one part of the body to another, so improving their efficiency. Indeed, the skill accomplished in many sports consists largely of concentrating momen-

---

[1] But Margaria et al., who obtained values of 40 to 50 per cent and even higher, regarded the efficiency of running as exceptionally high—attributing this to elastic energy stored, momentarily, on landing (i.e. eccentric contraction of muscle) used as an additional source of energy in the driving phase. This requires further study. (Cavagna, Sabiene and Margaria, 'Mechanical work in running', *Journal of Applied Physiology* (1964).

tum where it is wanted without unnecessary waste of kinetic ɛ

In contradiction to Professor A. V. Hill's original hypothesis[1] tl fastest time for a given middle or long distance could be attainɪ running at a constant speed, some physiologists[2] have since suggeᴗɪed that the second half of such races should be run faster than the first, with the athlete conserving his anaerobic (i.e. oxygen debt)[3] reserves until comparatively late in the race.

This latter opinion appears to have been substantiated, practically, in the running of many 1500 m/mile races so far. But world records have been established with slower and faster first halves; and, quite often, an athlete has achieved good results either way on different occasions. The present inconsistent pace-pattern over these middle distances is not easily explained.

In all other men's running events, however, clear patterns have become established. Thus, all great 400 metres races of recent years have been run at near-maximum pace, with the first half within 1.0 sec. of the athlete's best 200 metres time; yet without his slowing down by more than 1.0–1.5 sec over the remaining distance. In general, today's fastest 800 metres races are being achieved with the first half 5.0–7.0 sec slower than the runner's best-ever 400 metres time, and with the second half of the race, usually some 2.0–4.0 sec slower than the first.

Again—and almost without exception—fast 5000 metres races are now run with the first half 2.0–5.0 sec faster; with a very gradual, even, slackening of pace from beginning to end. And the pattern for 10,000 metres events is much the same, with the first half 10.0–20 sec faster than the second.

The writer thinks it probable that Professor Hill's conclusion is still valid; that running with a uniformly accumulating load of oxygen debt is preferable to the husbanding of anaerobic reserves; for an efficient use of energy a distance athlete should run his fastest race having (a) exercised to his maximum oxygen uptake throughout, while (b) gradually and evenly creating a full oxygen debt.

---

[1] A. V. Hill, *Muscular Activity* (Williams and Wilkins, Baltimore, USA, 1925).

[2] S. Robinson, 'Physiological considerations of pace in running middle distance races', *International Track and Field Digest*, U.S.A. (1956), pages 219–24.

[3] When energy requirements exceed that which can be supplied through a normal oxygen uptake, extra energy is obtained by breaking down glucose through hydrolysis, with the formation of lactic acid. This acid (which cannot be eliminated and of which the body can tolerate only a limited quantity) is subsequently changed back to glucose, the oxygen needed for the conversion being the *oxygen debt*.

It is said that, once the body has begun to accumulate an oxygen debt, *it starts to pay it back even before the exercise has finished,* so the *available* oxygen per minute is reduced. Thus a 5000 m runner with a maximum uptake of, say, 5 litres per minute, who in the course of his race begins to pay back at a rate of 0.5 litres per minute, can then call upon only 4.5 litres of aerobic capacity per minute.

If this hypothesis is correct, it would seem that the chemical consequences of running with an even distribution of energy can be responsible for a slight dropping off of pace over the second half of these races.

We can be certain that, as world records improve, few if any runners will be allowed to have 'something left' at the end of a record run—perhaps the chief reason why tactics calling for a faster first half will prevail among would-be record breakers.

CHAPTER SEVEN

Hurdling and Steeplechasing

It is impossible to excel in hurdling and steeplechasing events without basic sprinting or middle-distance running ability. For these races are won mainly on the ground, and therefore the best method of clearing a hurdle or water jump is that which returns the athlete quickly to the track with a rhythm and effort akin to a running action. Hurdling and water jump techniques are therefore modifications of running form.

Hurdling

To avoid jumping—which checks forward momentum and interrupts the running action—good performers at these events clear the hurdles by using a running step-over action of the front leg, combined with a sideways-swinging rear leg movement. In clearing low hurdles (as in the women's 400 m hurdles) neither movement is greatly emphasised; but in the men's 110 metres race, where the barriers are 3 ft 6 in. (1.067 m), even a tall, long-legged athlete has to exaggerate them (Fig. 135). The technique of the male 400 metres (3 ft (0.914 m)) hurdler (who, if taking an even number of strides between obstacles, will need to hurdle from either foot) falls between these two extremes.

The expert hurdler therefore runs over the obstacles mainly by 'making room' with his legs, and in the process raises his Centre of Gravity only a little more than in taking a running stride. Thus, in comparison with their times on the flat, champion high (3 ft 6 in., 1.067 m) hurdlers need no more than about 2.0 secs to clear ten barriers—an average of 0.2 sec per hurdle. Indeed, a few exceptional hurdlers have taken even less time.

Clearance: the flight-path of the Centre of Gravity. The fastest hurdle clearances are those where the athlete's Centre of Gravity is raised only slightly more than in taking a running stride—theoretically, with the high point directly above the obstacle and with take-off and landing distances almost equal (Fig. 136a). (Note that even in a running stride

Figure 135

the take-off exceeds the landing distance, i.e. relative to the high point of the Centre of Gravity.)

However, in negotiating the obstacles, hurdlers are compelled to raise their Centres of Gravity even higher, and take-off distances are greater because:

(i) their approach speeds do not permit the close take-off shown in Fig. 136a; they need more distance in which to raise the leading leg; and by taking off farther away, in consequence, must spring higher to avoid dropping on to the hurdle. The Centre of Gravity therefore attains a higher point, in front of the obstacle (Fig. 136b);

(ii) although even 3 ft 6 in. (1.067 m) hurdles can be cleared with the upper body and hips no higher than in running, this can be achieved only through a higher raising of the hurdler's Centre of Gravity; for, with the raising of the legs, the hips drop in relation to the Centre of Gravity (see page 57). If the Centre of Gravity were not so raised, the athlete would hit the obstacle.

Of necessity, therefore, even a highly-efficient clearance takes longer than a normal running stride. The distance it covers is also greater, and this, with the take-off to landing ratio, varies from athlete to athlete and, for any one hurdler, from one clearance to another. Distances and ratios are dependent upon:

(i) *economy of the clearance position.* In efficient high hurdling, a pronounced forward trunk lean and correctly timed arm and leg movement provide a 'lay-out' of extreme economy (Fig. 137a). Here the Centre of Gravity is as near to the hurdle as possible for a quick return to the ground. Conversely, a poor 'lay-out' (Fig. 137b) wastes time in the air;

(ii) *height of the athlete in relation to the height of the hurdle.* Compared with a taller athlete (where both are built proportionately and are equal in all other respects), the Centre of Gravity of a short hurdler moves greater vertical distances and therefore takes more time to rise and fall. In consequence his take-off and landing distances are greater.

He will not be at this disadvantage, however, if (e.g. through abnormally long legs) his Centre of Gravity is the same height above the ground at take-off. Using the same approach speed in both instances, an athlete should cover less ground in clearing a low hurdle than a high one;

(iii) *approach speed.* Theoretically an increase in sprinting speed lengthens both take-off and landing measurements. In fact, however, as a hurdler gathers speed over the first few flights so, successively, are increases in take-off distance matched approximately by landing reductions; ratios change, but the overall distance is constant to within a few inches or centimetres.

Conversely, as speed is lost (as usually happens towards the end of a race) take-offs shorten and landings lengthen. All this suggests that greater approach speed, with the concomitant lengthening of the take-off measurement, permits a more horizontal drive and a lower, faster clearance;

(iv) *leading leg action.* The faster the pick-up of the leading leg, the closer can the athlete get to the hurdle and the quicker his clearance can be. (This assumes a set speed of approach.) Accomplished hurdlers use a very fast, high leading leg action; flexion at knee and ankle reduces its moment of inertia about the hip joint, allowing maximum angular velocity; and its quick, high movement imparts speed to the hurdler's Centre of Gravity (Fig. 135*a*).

Through the sluggish action of a longer, heavier leading leg, tall hurdlers sometimes squander their height advantage; their take-off is too far back, with the Centre of Gravity raised too much in consequence. Tall men have the edge in these events, yet, through quicker, more exaggerated movements, athletes of a mere 5 ft 8 in. (1.73 m) have demonstrated exceptional efficiency in clearing even high (3 ft 6 in. (1.067 m)) hurdles. Often, the short hurdler's difficulty lies much more in having to stride unnaturally between the obstacles.[1] Recently more attention has been paid to the speed with which the leading leg comes down after the hurdle clearance. The longer the hurdler is in the air the greater will be his deceleration, the sooner he can regain contact with the ground again the sooner he will be able to resume his drive. Modern American hurdlers use a bent leading leg to achieve faster touch-down times. To counteract this faster leading leg action the leading arm is also bent, the hurdler 'leads with his elbow', rather than with the classic straight arm.

A combination of fast, high leading leg action, forward lean (marked in high hurdling, but not so emphasised in women's events) and powerful thrust from the take-off leg gives speed to the Centre of Gravity in a more forward direction; the efficient hurdler drives *at* the obstacles. In this way, athletes of only fair sprinting ability often maintain good average speeds throughout their races;

(v) *attaining the correct point of take-off.* A hurdle can be cleared efficiently only when the point of take-off is commensurate with approach speed, the subsequent raising and lowering of the Centre of Gravity and quickness in front of the obstacle; and it must be reached without overstriding.

If too close (a common fault with beginners), the hurdler has to jump high to avoid the obstacle, getting his high point beyond it (Fig. 138*a*). If he is too far away (Fig. 138*b*) again he must jump high to avoid dropping on to it. Either way, he wastes time, is too erect, hurries the trailing leg, lands heavily and disturbs his sprinting rhythm.

Most experts believe that a slightly shortened stride before take-off encourages forward drive and body-lean, causing a desirable (if only

---

[1] But modern synthetic track surfaces have certainly helped shorter hurdlers with great sprinting speed, while adding to the difficulties of very tall, fast, long-striding athletes.

slight) forward rotation before leaving the ground. But Housden[1] speaks of an overall *backward* rotation.

'The fast rise of the thigh of the leading leg causes backward rotation of the whole body as soon as the thigh slows down', while a forward trunk lean is responsible for, 'a rotation in the opposite sense as soon as the dip is completed'. He suggests that these do not cancel out; the hurdler leaves the ground with backward rotation—but the faster and more pronounced his lean, the less this rotation is and the more efficient his hurdle clearance.

A hurdler running the 110 m event in 13.4 sec has an average speed of only 26.8 ft (8.17 m) per second (i.e. 18.2 m.p.h., 29.6 km.p.h) yet at top speed in the race he might clear some hurdles at as much as 32 ft (9.8 m) per second, i.e. 21.8 m.p.h. (35.3 km.p.h.).

The formula $d = \frac{1}{2}gt$ (see page 8) can be used to calculate the time taken for his Centre of Gravity to rise specific distances, i.e. from take-off to the high point, and on this basis to estimate its horizontal motion in that time. Thus:

at 32 ft per second,	raised 2 in.,	it covers 3.3 ft
	" 3 "	" 4.0 "
	" 4 "	" 4.6 "
	" 6 "	" 5.7 "
	" 8 "	" 6.5 "

at 9.8 m per second (not an exact conversion from the previous table),

	raised 5.0 cm,	it covers 1.00 m
	" 7.5 "	" 1.22 "
	" 10.0 "	r 1.40 "
	" 15.0 "	r 1.74 "
	" 20.0 "	" 1.98 "

But these figures do not represent take-off distances, for at the instant of leaving the ground the hurdler's driving foot is approximately 1 ft (0.3 m) behind his Centre of Gravity (measured horizontally), and his high point of clearance is in front of the obstacle.

In Fig. 139 it has been assumed that in raising his Centre of Gravity 6 in. (15 cm) at a clearance speed of 32 ft (9.8 m) per second, the high point is 1 ft (0.31 m) in front.

---

[1] E. F. Housden, 'Forward lean over the high hurdles', *Athletics Coach*, British Amateur Athletic Board, (December 1973).

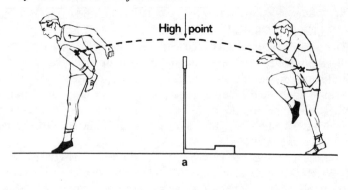

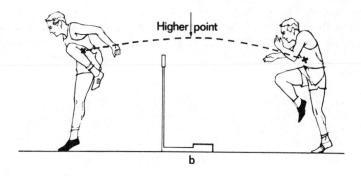

Figure 136

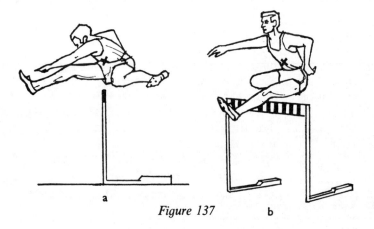

Figure 137

The take-off distance (A–D) is therefore 7.7 ft (2.35 m)—i.e. 5.7 ft (1.73 m) (B–C) plus 1 ft (0.31 m) (A–B) plus 1 ft (0.31 m) (C–D).

As to the landing (D–E): ignoring air resistance (i.e. assuming a constant clearance speed) this will be fractionally less than 4.7 ft (1.42 m)—i.e. 5.7 ft (1.73 m) (C–E) minus 1 ft (0.31 m) (C–D); for through a more erect landing and high rear leg position, his Centre of Gravity will not quite fall to its take-off level (Fig. 139).

To summarise: it is impracticable to lay down precise distances and ratios. In good hurdling:

(i) the Centre of Gravity's high point is as near, horizontally, to the hurdle as possible and is raised little above a normal running position. Controlling factors, here, are leading leg speed at take-off and the economy of clearance position. Thus, the hurdler spends the shortest possible time off the ground;

(ii) the hurdles are cleared at maximum horizontal speed. Therefore, provided condition (i) is fulfilled, the greater the distance between take-off and landing, the better. *In assessing clearance efficiency, time and distance should always be considered together.*

While hurdling events favour tall athletes,[1] short (5 ft 8 in. –5 ft 10 in., 1.73 m–1.78 m) skilful hurdlers lose less time in clearance than is often supposed, for, to some extent, they make up the disadvantage of an initially lower Centre of Gravity by using a closer take-off.

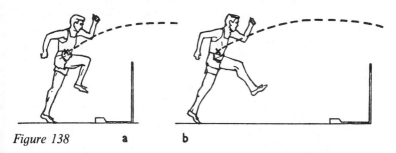

Figure 138   **a**   **b**

Clearance: other aspects. The following features of leg action are basic to all good hurdling:

(i) a pronounced *forward* take-off drive (Fig. 135*a–b*);

[1] The average height of the competitors in the 110 metres event in the 1968 Olympic Games was 6 ft (1.83 m). Given exceptional sprinting ability, it is still possible to be under this height and a hurdler of international calibre.

(ii) a wide separation of the legs immediately after take-off (greatly assisted by a fast lead leg and forward trunk lean (Fig. 135*b–c*));

(iii) a fast leg-pivot (i.e. the front leg's downward-backward motion co-ordinated with the lateral recovery of the rear leg, Fig. 135*d–f*);

(iv) a landing which flows smoothly into the first of the running strides. The hurdler 'comes down running' (Fig. 135*g*).

In all four phases, *front and rear leg movements should be regarded as components of a single action.* In this respect, the important points are:

Timing of leg action. Ideally, the legs should move fast and continuously throughout clearance, and should be so timed that the front toes land only slightly ahead of the Centre of Gravity (as in running) with the greatest possible backward speed relative to the hips (Fig. 135*f–g*). However, as the leg-pivot cannot begin until the front foot is clear of the hurdle, in high hurdling (and with short hurdlers particularly) there must be a split-second pause after take-off to allow the front foot to get into position for downward movement (Fig. 135*b–c*).

Pivot speed is influenced by horizontal speed, and the time spent off the ground. The greater the horizontal speed, the sooner can the front thigh begin its downward movement and the more delayed, relatively, can be the rear leg recovery. (In good high hurdling the rear knee and hips cross the rail at about the same time; in low hurdling, the trailing knee should be slightly ahead.) Other things being equal, an athlete with high clearance speed is capable of a better pivot timing than a slower hurdler—and obtains a smoother transition into the sprinting action.

A fast pivot, i.e. one related to the cadence of the running action, is the ideal, but this is possible only when the hurdler spends little time in

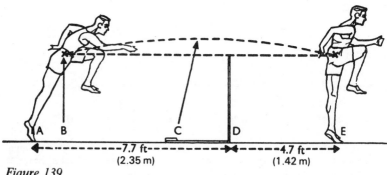

Figure 139

clearing the obstacles. However, the pivot must always be properly co-ordinated; if it is too fast for the rise and fall of the Centre of Gravity, the front foot lands too far behind the body and the athlete stumbles into a shortened first stride; if it is too slow, he may fail to clear the rear leg safely, or will land with the front foot too far ahead, checking his forward motion.

The correct timing of the trailing leg is important, since it determines the effectiveness of the second stride off the hurdle. From take-off the trailing leg should be pulled through in a continuous sweep. This will assist the downward movement of the leading leg; a conscious attempt to 'claw' with the leading foot should be avoided. The holding of a forward trunk lean encourages and simplifies this fast trailing leg action. The athlete should concentrate on 'running off the hurdle'.

Absorbing reaction. The leg movements of hurdling are the cause of greater upper body twisting reactions than in normal running. Yet, these reactions can be channelled and absorbed without upsetting balance and running continuity—a simpler problem for flexible athletes.

At take-off the reaction to leg movement is shared between the ground (which reacts by driving the hurdler forward and upward) and the upper body (which absorbs reaction to the eccentric leg thrust—i.e. in a transverse plane—by its forward lean and pronounced arm action). (The so-called 'double-arm action' is contrary to efficient body mechanics, and is not recommended. For the writer regards it as an unnecessary and difficult modification to natural arm-leg co-ordination which, despite the claims made for it and its use by some champions, is *not* essential to good balance and lay-out over the obstacles.)

However, the body alone can absorb reaction to leg movement originating in the air; and here, action and reaction are in parallel planes, and possess equal and opposite angular momenta about an axis (of displacement) passing through the hurdler's Centre of Gravity.

As the leading leg moves down and back and, simultaneously, the rear leg recovers laterally (Fig. 135*d–f*), reaction is absorbed:

(i) *In the transverse plane* (Fig. 120*a*), by holding a forward lean, to increase the horizontal distance between the axis of displacement and the secondary axes of the shoulders (see also page 111). Thus, the arms, swung wide of the body to increase their moments of inertia, take up more reaction than would otherwise be possible. This lean also increases the trunk's moment of inertia about the axis of displacement, enabling the upper body to absorb any further reaction without markedly twisting out of sprinting alignment.

(ii) *In the frontal plane* (Fig. 120*b*), by lowering an extended 'opposite arm' in its backward swing, whilst simultaneously raising the other, so preventing an exaggerated upper-body tilt towards the rear leg; reaction to counter-clockwise leg movement is absorbed by clockwise arm movement, and vice versa. (But this arm action does not always ensure lateral balance. Through a tilting of the pelvis—as the rear leg recovers and the leading leg moves down—some athletes (especially women) land *across* their line of running. Imbalance in this plane can also be due to an inward or outward lead-leg pick-up at take-off.)

(iii) *In the sagittal plane* (Fig. 120*c*) by a straightening of the upper body. In this plane the legs may be considered to work in opposition; the 'unjacking' of the body is caused only by the action of the front leg, for the other perhaps encourages a weak *contrary* rotation, weak because of the rear leg's smaller moment of inertia about the Centre of Gravity (through which the axis of displacement must pass).

Because of the trunk's greater moment of inertia about this axis, both range and angular velocity of the trunk are far less than those of the leading leg rotating in an opposite direction. Moreover, coaches who recommend forward rotation in a hurdle clearance (see page 146) claim that while the leading leg movement blends with and is quickened by it, this same rotation acts in opposition to the trunk's reaction; the trunk straightens a little yet maintains a forward inclination for balance and acceleration on landing.

Steeplechasing

In the course of running 3000 metres, clearing twenty-eight 3 ft (0.914 m) hurdles and seven water jumps, and in terms of energy expenditure, the steeplechaser cannot resort to the crisp, exaggerated hurdling movements of the shorter races; nor can he take a set number of strides between the obstacles. However, as steeplechasing standards improve, so does the general efficiency with which the hurdles are negotiated.

It must be emphasised that the proper hurdling of the twenty-eight 3 ft (0.914 m) hurdles is more efficient than clearances where the leading foot is placed on top of the hurdles. This latter method may be necessary for those who cannot hurdle, or whose approach has been miscalculated, but, since the athlete must raise his Centre of Gravity much too high and interrupt his running action, it is uneconomical. And it is slower, as is very obvious when a 'hurdler' and 'stepper' clear the last three or four hurdles in a close race. The would-be specialist steeplechaser should therefore master hurdling techniques—and from either foot.

In taking the water jump (Fig. 140) the skilled performer speeds up several strides before take-off and gauges this spot without chopping or changing stride (Fig. 140*a*). For it is essential to accelerate beyond average racing speed in order to negotiate this wide (12 ft, 3.66 m) obstacle.

Figure 140

He then springs on to the rail, meeting it just above the hollow of the front foot (Fig. 140*b*). Now, by maintaining a crouch position over a bent leg, he reduces the body's moment of inertia about the supporting foot, thus pivoting quickly and easily forward. The leg thrust (primarily horizontal) is powerfully yet smoothly co-ordinated (Fig. 140*c*). The trunk straightens, the rear leg is kept trailing momentarily and the arms are raised laterally for balance correction (Fig. 140*d*). The landing (about 2 ft (0.6 m) from the water's edge) is made on one foot (Fig. 140*e*) and the first stride is taken on to dry land (Fig. 140*f*).

Experience proves that although, in the early laps, it is possible to clear the water in one leap from the rail, this becomes increasingly costly in terms of energy as the race proceeds. It is therefore more economical to negotiate the obstacle in the manner described, and to do this throughout the race.

CHAPTER EIGHT

Jumping (High, Long and Triple)

The laws of mechanics are the basis of a complete understanding of all modern jumping techniques and a knowledge of these laws is an essential foundation of ability to coach these events.

High-jumping

Standing height, spring and lay-out are the key factors in this event.

In good high-jumping,[1] the running approach improves vertical spring and provides horizontal motion for crossing the bar. The take-off movements impart, of first importance, vertical speed to the jumper's Centre of Gravity; secondly, they initiate most of the rotation required for lay-out. The greater his effective spring, the higher will a jumper raise his Centre of Gravity; but he must so combine horizontal and vertical movement, and adjust his point of take-off, that the high point of the Centre of Gravity's path is directly over the bar (Fig. 12).

Since the use of weights is not permitted by the rules, the modern high-jumper does nothing to disturb the flight curve of his Centre of Gravity (see pages 16 and 57); but by changing position in relation to it he can clear a higher bar. However, in the best jumps the Centre of Gravity's high point above the bar and the completion of lay-out coincide; and, of course, the athlete gets into and out of his lay-out without knocking the bar down.

Spring and lay-out are key factors—yet maximum efficiency in one can be obtained only at the expense of the other. All good high-jumping, is therefore a compromise; to obtain economy of lay-out (though never *absolute* economy) good jumpers drive eccentrically at take-off (see pages 70 and 99), slightly reducing their effective spring, but in the

---

[1] There was a dramatic improvement in the general standard of high-jumping in the 1972 Olympic Games. Whereas, in Mexico in 1968, only 7 men cleared 2.15 m (7 ft 1½ in.), 19 men qualified at that height in Munich, 14 jumping it again in the final. Only one woman jumped 1.82 m (5 ft 11½ in.) in the Olympic Games in Mexico; 15 did so four years later.

process gaining more through their position over the bar. By contrast, poor high-jumpers, anticipating their movements in the air, sacrifice too much spring for their lay-out, or cross the bar in poor positions.

In this event most faults at take-off are the result of anticipating movement in the air. Indeed, many errors in all forms of motor-learning are errors of anticipation. Good high-jumpers are therefore 'take-off' conscious; poor ones often over-anxious to cross the bar.

APPROACH. (1) *Direction*. The direction of approach can greatly influence the component rotations at take-off, and their proportions about the vertical, transverse-horizontal and medial-horizontal axes (see pages 78 and 91). Indeed, the approach is so bound up with the jumper's take-off and subsequent movement in the air that, once habitual, any drastic change to it can mar performance.

An angled approach (i.e. from the side) can be advantageous to all high-jumpers, regardless of style, because (i) it facilitates a greater range of free leg swing at take-off (for the bar is not then at right angles to the jumper's line of approach), and (ii) it makes possible the throwing of some part of the body over and below the bar before the Centre of Gravity reaches its high point, of particular importance to jumpers employing a fast approach, who therefore need more *time* in which to clear the crossbar correctly.

However, when the angle is too acute, the athlete travels too much along the bar, at greater heights knocking it off at one point despite clearing it at another. An additional danger is that the lay-out will be anticipated at take-off, exaggerating the lean towards the bar and reducing effective spring. The recommended angle is one of approximately 20–30 deg.

One seldom sees a completely frontal (i.e. 90 deg. angled) approach, though many fine jumpers commence from the front before curving in to the bar on the last few strides—done naturally to direct the free leg at take-off and initiate rotational movements required for lay-out. Jumpers who employ a more frontal approach tend to attain the high point of their jump in front of the bar; often too, their free leg action has to be restricted or modified.

(2) *Speed*. The importance of approach speed increases with (i) the raising of the bar, and (ii) a sharpening of the run-up angle (for then the jumper is inclined to be longer over the bar); it is greater in those styles in which the athlete (as distinct from his Centre of Gravity) crosses at an angle—as, for example, in an Eastern Cut-off (Fig. 141), or Fosbury Flop (Fig. 149).

Figure 141

In the sense that a ball, rolling horizontally, changes direction on an inclined plane, run-up speed in high-jumping cannot be converted vertically; nor, in this respect, should the take-off leg be likened to a stiff pole. For although, initially, the take-off leg straightens, with its foot well in front of the hips, it flexes immediately strain is put upon it (Fig. 100). In fact, were it straight and stiff throughout, it could contribute little thrust, because knee joint extension would then be impossible, and the jar would be tremendous.

Yet the speed of a high-jumper's approach *does* have a definite material influence on his spring from the ground; for an increase, here, in controlled speed can contribute to an improvement in the *eccentric contraction* of the extensor muscles of the jumping leg (i.e. in the *speed* with which those muscles are *forced* to lengthen, momentarily), developing maximum tension and a greater pressure between the jumping foot and the ground (see also pages 27 and 28).

Dyatchkov[1] maintains that an increase of 0.1 m/sec linear speed increases the pressure on the jumping foot by 26–35 lb (11.80–15.90 kg) which (with a maintenance of the take-off angle) can improve jumping height by approximately 3.5 cm (1$\frac{3}{8}$ in.). He gives former world record-holder Valeriy Brumel's approach speed as 15.65 m.p.h. (25.18 km.p.h.) at the penultimate stride. (Hay,[2] in his study of former world record-holder Pat Matzdorf, estimated an approach speed of 16.36 m.p.h. (26.32 km.p.h.) at this stage.)

In all good jumping the take-off foot is placed in front of the athlete at a distance which gives his free leg (in particular) and arms *time* to assist the thrust from the supporting leg (Figs. 100 and 142*j*); with greater approach speed, this foot must be planted even farther forward.

This demands, initially, a backward lean, and a lower hip position; and (*provided the jumper is strong and fast enough to use it*) it leads to a more favourable pre-spring position.

This long-striding, low, preliminary position is best obtained as a result of either (a) a comparatively slow beginning, with the body pitched forward in a semi-crouch and with the hips and legs 'moving ahead' of a relaxed upper body on a marked quickening over the last three strides, or (b) a rapid increase in speed from the start, with less acceleration before take-off (Fig. 142).

The value of the run-up to spring, therefore, lies in contributing to range, force and speed beyond what is attainable in a standing high-jump. Jumpers should experiment to see if they can benefit from a faster run-up; yet each will possess a 'critical speed'[3] beyond which take-off efficiency will be impaired, varying greatly from jumper to jumper, largely because of variations in muscular strength, elasticity and intrinsic speed. Although, of recent years, the approach speed of top-class jumpers has increased, still, for most, a run of only seven to ten *effective*[4] strides suffices.

TAKE-OFF. Here, the jumper must (i) impart maximum vertical velocity to his Centre of Gravity commensurate with (ii) acquiring just

---

[1] V. M. Dyatchkov, *High Jumping* (Moscow, 1966).

[2] J. G. Hay, 'A kinematic analysis of the high-jump', *Track Technique*, U.S.A., No. 53 (September 1973).

[3] Which can be improved, by training. Since increases in strength involve changes in *timing*, skill practice should accompany physiological modifications; skill-training and strength-training should go hand in hand.

[4] i.e. not counting the walking or jogging strides which often precede the approach proper.

Figure 142

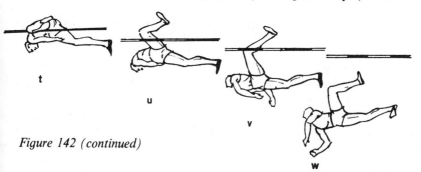

Figure 142 (continued)

sufficient body rotation (i.e. total angular momentum) for his lay-out subsequently.

(1) *Attaining maximum vertical velocity.* A jumper projects himself into the air by moving his limbs so that he exerts a force against the ground larger than that supporting his weight; and the reaction to this additional force accelerates him upwards. His vertical velocity also depends upon the *time* this extra force is applied, i.e. the *impulse* (see page 32); the greater the impulse, the greater the velocity.

In athletics, the use of greater muscular force usually results in faster limb extension—but increases in force are often effectively greater than decreases in time, so total impulse is improved (see page 32). This is so in good high-jumping where, *for a given athlete and his jumping form*, the higher the jump, the shorter the take-off time.

Also important is the method by which take-off impulse and rotational movements are developed; for whereas, in a Straddle jump, they are the result of a pronounced initial backward lean followed by emphasised free leg and arm movements, in a Fosbury Flop they are brought about by a faster approach and a smaller range of free limb movement.

Thus, in general, the take-off period for Flop jumpers is shorter than that of Straddle jumpers—respectively, 0.13–0.15 sec and 0.17–0.24 sec.

In a high-jump take-off, the free leg and both arms are first accelerated upwards against the support of the jumping leg (and, therefore, against the resistance of the ground). Then, with the Centre of Gravity over the jumping foot and already moving upward, an additional impulse is applied through vigorous extension of the trunk and the take-off leg (Figs. 100 and 142). The important points, here, are:

(i) By bracing his take-off leg, initially, the jumper develops extremely powerful, if short-lived, tensions in the extensor muscles of the jumping leg—*eccentric contractions*. And he must possess great strength in that leg—otherwise it will tend to collapse in reaction to the abrupt checking of his forward movement and the acceleration of the free leg and arms.

(ii) It is the *vertical acceleration* of the free leg and arms (*not* the mere fact of their upward movement) which invokes an upthrust from the ground. Here again, it is the athlete who makes the effort to change velocity and the ground which provides the reaction to the change.[1]

(iii) Fig. 143 illustrates the importance of *early* free leg speed. When a line drawn through the Centre of Gravity (1) the thigh and (2) the foreleg and foot (and, therefore, of the Centre of Gravity common to both) makes a 30 deg. angle with the downward vertical (Fig. 143*a*) the *vertical component* of its velocity is already 50 per cent of its actual velocity; as much as 71 per cent of its actual value when that angle is 45 deg.! (Fig. 143*b*). Through its downwardly-directed centrifugal effect, early free leg speed can also add to the pressure on the jumping foot.

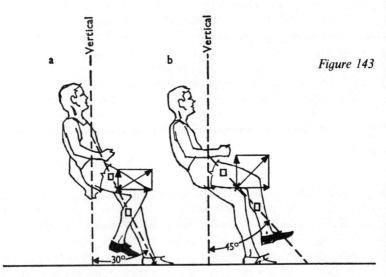

Figure 143

◻   Centres of gravity of (1) thigh and (2) foreleg and foot

✗   Centres of gravity of right leg

[1] E. F. Housden. 'A study in velocities; an analysis of the effects of the acceleration of the free leg in various athletic events', *Coaching Review*, Royal Canadian Legion (March 1966).

(iv) Ideally, the free leg and arms should be moving at their maximum vertical velocity at the instant of take-off; for their acceleration afterwards cannot add to the athlete's velocity (see pages 14 and 57). (Hopper[1] suggests, however, that in a good straddle the swinging leg ends its upward acceleration when horizontal. It then slows down, changing a downward thrust against the ground into an upward pull. He affirms: 'The fact seems to be that the proficient jumper is able to time the extension at hip, knee and ankle with the changing upward acceleration of the free limbs, so as to develop at all times the maximum ground reaction that each muscle-group of the take-off leg can handle in turn.') *This points to the need for great strength in the extremity of the take-off leg, and in those muscles (rarely strengthened sufficiently) which might enable the free leg to accelerate beyond the horizontal* (see also page 34).

(v) The movements must occur as simultaneously as possible; otherwise the take-off impulse suffers (see page 34).

(vi) Maximum vertical velocity can be built up only when the accelerations of the different parts of the athlete's body take place over sufficient range of movement; this applies particularly to the actions of the legs.

(vii) The jumper's Centre of Gravity should be projected from the greatest possible height commensurate with his (a) physique, and (b) jumping style. (Compare the final take-off positions of the Straddle (Figs. 100 and 142) and Fosbury Flop (Fig. 149)). In his study, Hay[2] found that this height tended to increase slightly with the raising of the bar. (See Fig. 144.)

(viii) To attain maximum vertical velocity, the up-thrust from the ground must pass through the athlete's Centre of Gravity. Because of the need to initiate rotation at take-off, however, a *slightly* eccentric thrust is essential (see pages 70–71).

(ix) Throughout their rapid extension, the trunk and take-off leg must continue to exert the greatest possible effective force against the ground despite the upward movement of the rest of the jumper's body (see page 33).

(x) Too fast an approach gives insufficient time for the application of the various forces against the ground; vertical velocity is then reduced, as is the take-off angle.

[1] B. J. Hopper, 'Comment', A.A.A. *Coaching Newsletter*, Amateur Athletic Association, England, No. 21 (April 1962), page 8.
[2] J. G. Hay, 'A kinematic analysis of the high jump', *Track Technique*, No. 53 (September 1973), *Track & Field News*.

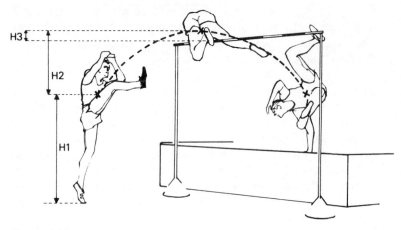

Figure 144

H^1:   The height of the jumper's Centre of Gravity at the instant of take-off. Hay suggests an index (H^1 Standing height × 100%) which could be useful for evaluating any jumper's take-off position (68.0%).

H^2:   The height to which the Centre of Gravity is lifted during the jump (37.0%).

H^3:   The difference between the Centre of Gravity's high point and the height of the bar—a negative quantity where the latter is below the Centre of Gravity, as is usual (−5%).

The percentages represent, very approximately, the contributions of these three parameters to the total height in a good Straddle jump. The value of standing height in this event will be obvious.

(xi) The take-off surface must be firm, or the effect of the various body impulses will be reduced.

Fig. 145 shows the effect of ground reaction on a high-jumper's Centre of Gravity (moving in a vertical plane). Here, the curve **AB** represents the low last stride before take-off (low, because of the importance of not wasting vertical impulse later (at **B**) in overcoming a dropping of body weight). **BC** denotes the path of the jumper's Centre of Gravity as this is influenced by a series of ground reactions while the jumping foot is on the ground. The arrows indicate the relative magnitudes and directions of these *residual* (i.e. ground reaction less body weight) forces at intervals of $\frac{1}{64}$ second.

In Fig. 145*a* ground reaction—through a series of controlled impulses—is always exerted at right angles to the direction in which the Centre of Gravity is moving, the effect being to change the latter's direction without changing its speed developed in the approach—excepting of course, a loss due to the rise against gravity. This, though ideal (postulating a jump much higher than the existing World record), is impractical.

Fig. 145*b* shows what actually happens in a good jump, where the need is to build up one very large impulse in a very short time. Now, by means of a braced jumping leg and acceleration of free leg and arms (transmitted impulses) (see page 32) the Centre of Gravity is driven upwards by an average thrust of four times body weight. However, this is only achieved at the expense of Centre of Gravity speed (which, in this case[1], dropped from 18.2 ft to 14.8 ft per second) (5.55 m to 4.51 m per second). In fact, the direction of ground reaction is unfavourable to the speed of the Centre of Gravity until point X is reached—when the forces of this reaction are rapidly diminishing.

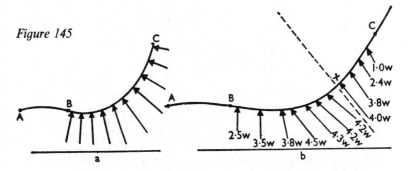

Figure 145

So it is impossible to impart the most favourable parabolic path to the Centre of Gravity without some loss of forward speed. The high-jumper has to accept a compromise between the beneficial effect of a big checking force at take-off and the detrimental consequence of its backwardly-inclined direction.

(2) *Acquiring rotation.* In even the best high-jumps the time between the instant of take-off and the moment when the body's Centre of Gravity reaches its high point is too short to permit an origin of lay-out in the air; it must begin on the ground.

For a given style of lay-out, however, the greater the jumper's spring, the less rotation he requires, for his rotation then acts for a longer period of time. For example, he will need less than when projecting his Centre

[1] B. J. Hopper, 'Rotation—a vital factor in athletic technique', *Track Technique*, U.S.A., No. 15 (March 1964).

of Gravity 2.5 ft vertically (0.395 sec) than in raising it only 1.0 ft (0.25 sec); or 0.85 m vertically (0.416 sec) than in raising it only 0.25 m (0.226 sec). (See following tables.)

Vertical Velocity (ft. p.s.)	Height (ft)	Time (sec)
5.66	0.5	0.177
8.0	1.0	0.25
9.8	1.5	0.306
11.31	2.0	0.354
12.65	2.5	0.395
13.86	3.0	0.433
14.97	3.5	0.468
16.0	4.0	0.5
(m.p.s.)	(m)	(sec)
1.40	0.10	0.143
2.21	0.25	0.226
2.80	0.40	0.286
3.28	0.55	0.335
3.70	0.70	0.378
4.08	0.85	0.416
4.43	1.00	0.452
4.74	1.15	0.484
5.04	1.30	0.514

(The metric table is *not* a direct conversion from the other.)

All three methods of acquiring rotation on the ground are combined in good high-jumping (see page 94). By checking linear motion (through momentarily fixing the take-off foot), transferring angular momentum (from the arms and free leg) and by thrusting eccentrically to the Centre of Gravity (with the jumping leg) a constant total angular momentum—in magnitude and direction appropriate to the style of crossing the bar—is developed on each jump. This can be resolved in terms of angular momenta about vertical, transverse-horizontal and medial-horizontal axes, which pass through the jumper's Centre of Gravity, at the instant of take-off. (Figs. 89, 91 and 92. See pages 81 and 91).

With one exception, rotations about each of these axes can be acquired in all three methods. Thus, a high-jumper's free leg swing can impart backward rotation about a transverse-horizontal axis, rotate about a medial-horizontal axis, or twist about a vertical one; or, as usually happens, it can combine all three (Figs. 89 and 91). Arm action can produce similar effects; granted that the mass and length of an arm are considerably less than that of a leg—but many good high-jumpers swing *both* arms, and their rotational influence on the body is enhanced by virtue of the distance between their axis, the shoulders, and the body's main axis.

Again, depending upon timing, direction and emphasis, the thrust from the jumping leg can develop rotations about all three axes, or no rotation at all; and by momentarily fixing the take-off foot (i.e. by checking linear movement) a jumper can turn about a transverse-horizontal and/or a vertical axis (though, by this method, rotation about a medial-horizontal axis is not possible).

In building technique, the aim should be to select from the various alternatives according to (*a*) lay-out requirements, (*b*) angle and speed of approach and (*c*) the physique and powers of co-ordination of the athlete. For reasons of initiating rotations, Roll and Straddle jumpers spring from the leg nearer the bar, Scissor, Flop and Eastern Cut-off exponents from the outside leg. Each good jumper adjusts his run-up, to suit his particular interpretation of high-jumping form, his strength, speed, flexibility and neuromuscular co-ordination.

A second important principle in the building of technique is to rely as much as possible upon the checking of linear movement for the rotational transfer required for lay-out; for it would seem to be the one kind of eccentric thrust (or torque) which can produce rotation without a loss of vertical speed. The high-jumper then relies less upon (although he can never be entirely independent of) the other methods, *viz* transference of angular momentum and jumping leg drive—both of which invoke off-centre ground up-thrusts.

In good jumping the approach angle is largely determined by the need for this and other forms of tranfer—an angle of approximately 20–35 deg. for Scissor (Fig. 146*a*), Osborn Roll (Fig. 146*b*), Straddle (Fig. 142), Arch-straddle (Fig. 46) and Flop (Fig. 145) lay-outs, but somewhat greater (40–45 deg.) for most Eastern Cut-offs (Fig. 141). To develop maximum angular momentum, the free leg swings comparatively straight and accelerates through a wide range (Figs. 100 and 142); but the knee is not kept locked (against a natural tendency to bend) once past a horizontal position.

High-jumpers who use a flexed free-leg swing (Fig. 139) are more dependent upon eccentric leg thrust and/or the checking of linear movement for their lay-out. For although a leg can swing with greater angular velocity flexed than straight, experience seems to prove that it

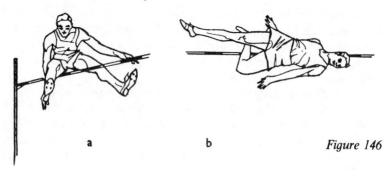

a   b   *Figure 146*

cannot do so to the point of developing as much angular momentum, because of its reduced moment of inertia about the hip joint. (Nor, possibly, can it accelerate the jumper's Centre of Gravity over as great a vertical distance, keep him as long over his jumping leg nor provide as high a position of his Centre of Gravity at the instant of take-off).

On the other hand, it would seem that a flexed free leg can the more easily be combined with a fast approach; and since (through a principle of neuro-muscular compensation which is said to operate through the entire range of human motion) the flexing of one limb may encourage a simultaneous extension of its opposite, many high jumpers may react instinctively to this natural tendency.[1]

Those who can derive as large an upward impulse from the ground by this means as others do using a straighter free leg must be able to hold their body rigid enough, momentarily, to transmit a large force in a very short time—a principle which applies, also, in long and triple jumping.

Fig. 147 (a reproduction of film tracings) exemplifies the rotational origins and take-off patterns, in 1964, of Olympic finalist Diane Gerace (Canada), as viewed from the rear.

CLEARANCE. Once contact with the ground has been broken, the high-jumper (who is not permitted the use of weights) does nothing to disturb the flight path of his Centre of Gravity, the parabola of which has been determined previously by his approach speed and take-off spring. In the air, also, he possesses a constant total angular momentum about an axis of momentum (which passes through his Centre of Gravity) fixed in direction. This total angular momentum, usually, is

---

[1] This hypothesis requires more solid experimental evidence. The idea stems from physiological experiments on decerebrate cats and with human beings who have suffered gross spinal chord damage. We cannot be certain, as yet, that it operates in the intact human being.

a   b   c   d   e   f   *Figure 147*

Straddle Take-off (Rear) (a–f) At the beginning of the take-off stride (*a*) the toeing out of the right foot suggests anticipation of weight-transference to the left. (*b*) Rotation about medial and longitudinal axes begins—both in the direction of the bar; the Centre of Gravity is now slightly to the left of the line of thrust, as viewed from behind and should remain so from here onwards. (But an excessive lean to the left will reduce vertical speed and the height of the Centre of Gravity at the instant of take-off.) (*c* and *d*) Body rotation about both axes is checked temporarily as the free leg takes up this angular momentum. (*e* and *f*) Trunk rotation about a medial axis is renewed as the free leg loses speed; and the trunk also takes over twist about its long axis and some backward rotation about a transverse axis. At this stage, the position of the free leg suggests insufficient early acceleration—and/or lack of flexibility—for it should be higher.

expressed as (a) twist about his longitudinal axis with (b) gyration of that axis about his axis of momentum (see pages 117–22).

By altering the position of his body in relation to his Centre of Gravity, however, he can clear a higher bar; and by changing his body's moment of inertia about the axis of momentum (with or without an interchange of angular momentum between twist and gyration) he can reduce or increase angular velocity.

Movement he originates in the air must cause an equal and opposite reaction; clockwise action of one part of his body must produce a counter-clockwise reaction in some other part, and vice versa; but, within limits, the jumper can control the location of the reaction within his body.

The angular velocities of two moving parts of the body about their common axis, i.e. an axis of displacement (which also passes through the body's Centre of Gravity) are inversely proportional to their moments of inertia.

(For fuller details of the above-mentioned principles, see pages 1, 57, 80–123 and 154.)

(1) *Lay-out.* Fig. 148*b–j* illustrates a series of jumps (made from the left foot and observed from the pit side of the bar) taken by one athlete. The high point of his Centre of Gravity is the same each time[1] (and is, correctly, directly over the bar); but, through adopting increasingly more economical positions about it, he is able to jump higher and higher.

Progressively, he reduces the gap between his Centre of Gravity and the bar; his best clearances are those where the bar has been raised to the level of—theoretically, even above—his Centre of Gravity. Put another way, the lay-out efficiency on each jump can be assessed by the body mass above and below the bar at this instant; the more mass the jumper has above it, and the higher its position, the poorer is his lay-out.

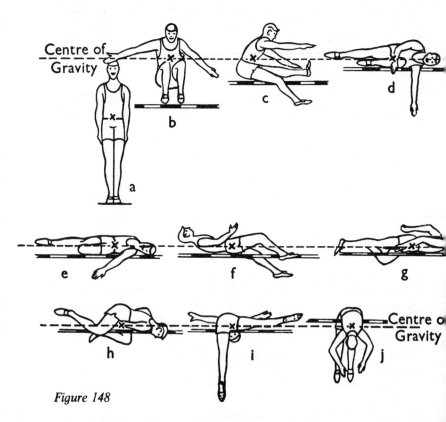

Figure 148

[1] i.e. assuming the same vertical impulse throughout.

Conversely, the more mass there is below the bar at the high point of the jump, and the nearer it is to the ground, the better is his lay-out *provided, of course, that all parts of his body eventually clear the crossbar.*

Clearly, Fig. 148*b* position is of little value in jumping for height; and although the Scissor technique (Fig. 148*c*) is a considerable improvement, there remains a gap of approximately twelve inches (0.305 m) between the bar and the jumper's Centre of Gravity; the upright trunk and raised legs force the seat down and there is little body mass below the bar.

By lying on his side at the high point of the jump an athlete using a Western Roll reduces the gap to approximately six inches (0.152 m) (Fig. 148*d*); but there is little mass below bar level, and therefore the space between his Centre of Gravity and the bar is greater than it otherwise would be. An Osborn Roll (Fig. 148*e*) (i.e. with the back to the bar) is fractionally better, but there remains little mass below the cross bar. (The many versions of the roll all possess at least some of the lay-out characteristics of these two main variations).

The bar can be moved even closer to the jumper's Centre of Gravity when he crosses on his back (Fig. 148*f*, Modified Scissors) or abdomen (Fig. 148*g*, Straddle); a complete lay-out in either style possibly saves as much as two inches (5 cm) on position Fig. 148*d*, but this lay-out has been unusual in a Modified Scissors jump.

When the trunk and limbs are curved round the bar, the gap is further reduced. Theoretically, such a position can be exaggerated to allow the jumper to pass over the bar while his Centre of Gravity passes beneath (Fig. 148*j*)—practicable in only exceptional high-jumping because, usually, it calls for the sacrifice of too much spring; and, of course, to 'jack' to the extent shown the athlete would have to be moving much too slowly, horizontally, to clear the bar.

Fig. 148*h* illustrates the Arch-straddle, which incorporates the draping effect and Fig. 148*i* shows a very good Eastern Cut-off lay-out which achieves much the same efficiency; at the high point, the jumper's hips and abdomen are raised in relation to his Centre of Gravity as a result of the low positions of the head, upper trunk, arms and free leg. In either position (Fig. 148*h–i*) it is conceivable that the bar could be raised to the level of the Centre of Gravity's high point.

The importance of, and difficulty in, reconciling the essential upward spring and lay-out have already been emphasised (see page 154). Scissor jumps give good take-offs; the free leg movement is efficient and the body is kept over the jumping leg, but the lay-out is usually poor

(Fig. 148*c*). A well-executed Eastern Cut-off combines the advantages of a Scissor take-off and an economical lay-out, but it requires exceptional control, suppleness and spring and is made even more difficult because the jumper must throw those parts of the body at take-off farthest away from the bar (i.e. his hips and legs) over first.

Hitherto, few athletes were happy in a Modified Scissor position (Fig. 148*f*), for control over the bar and safe landings[1] were difficult to achieve, though the style gives an excellent take-off. From this developed the form used by the 1968 Olympic Champion, Dick Fosbury, but with the bar crossed at approximately a right-angle (Fig. 149).

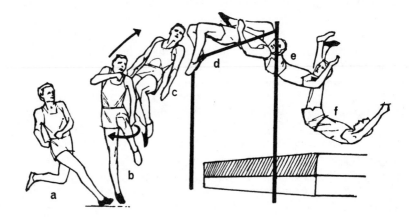

Figure 149

The Fosbury Flop. Lacking the deliberate free leg and arm movements of the orthodox Straddle style, the Flop take-off impulse is probably less eccentric and the athlete's rotation due more to a sudden checking at the end of a fast, curved approach.

(*a–b*) The take-off originates a pronounced clock-wise rotation towards the bar and some twist about the body's longitudinal axis. (*c*) The lowering and trailing of the free leg and arms advances the upper body relative to the jumper's Centre of Gravity for an effective lay-out; and (*d*), through action-reaction, these leg and arm movements can probably bring his transverse axis into line with his axis of momentum—so further twist is eliminated. (Where twisting continues, the arms can be stretched sideways, 'crucifix' fashion, to slow it down.) Bent knees and arched back improve the lay-out and quicken the rotation; at the high point the Centre of Gravity can be below bar level.

(*e–f*) Finally, the lower legs are cleared, and the landing made safer, by straightening and lifting the legs 'against' a contrary motion of the trunk and arms.

---

[1] The modern foam-rubber area makes landing much safer than it was, of course.

The Western Roll (Fig. 148*d*) provides a lay-out demanding no more than average co-ordination and flexibility; nor need it make exceptional demands on take-off spring. The Osborn Roll is better, but more difficult to control. A horizontal Straddle position (Fig. 148*g*) is better still, but take-off (i.e. rotational) difficulties are increased. An Arch-straddle (Fig. 148*h*) adds further to the problem of reconciling spring and rotation.

(2) *Movement originating in the air.* Even the best high-jumpers must originate most of the essential turning movement at take-off, for there is so little time to do it in the air (see also page 163). However, certain minor adjustments to lay-out can be originated after contact with the ground has been broken—*to the improvement of the jumper's take-off which, then, needs less of a rotational component.* Movement originated off the ground, however, has its equal and opposite reaction within the jumper's body (see pages 100–23).

An outstanding example of this action-reaction is to be found in a well-executed Eastern Cut-off jump (Fig. 141). At take-off, through an eccentric thrust from the jumping leg and free leg swing, the jumper rotates backwards mainly about a transverse axis and, simultaneously, twists about a vertical axis.

At this instant, also, torsion at the waist is caused by a twisting of the hips and shoulders in opposite directions about the body's long axis—movements not in parallel planes, however, for the trunk is stretched on the side of the jumping leg and is compressed on the other side by the action of the free leg (Fig. 141*a*).

These movements are reversed in the air; the shoulders now twist in the direction of take-off, the hips again moving in opposition; the stomach is turned towards the bar. The lateral stretching of the trunk is also reversed (Fig. 141*b–e*). Thus, the rotation of the hip girdle, turning 'against' the upper body, brings the jumping leg to its horizontal position (Fig. 141*e*).

Again, the free leg, thrusting towards the pit, now acts in opposition to the head and shoulders which are momentarily forced below bar level. As a result of all these movements, the jumper attains an arched lay-out over the bar; his hips are raised in relation to his Centre of Gravity because of the low positions of his free leg, head, upper-trunk and arms (Fig. 141*e*).

Finally, at great speed, the Cut-off jumper lifts his head, upper body and arms 'against' a backward kicking of his free leg (Fig. 141*f*); otherwise (because of his body's overall rotation) he would strike the bar with his face or chest. He lands on his jumping leg and now faces the crossbar.

By comparison, Straddle and Flop jumpers originate less turning movement in the air and the styles certainly make fewer demands on co-ordination, timing and flexibility.

In the Straddle (Fig. 142) take-off rotation is again developed by an eccentric thrust from the jumping leg and transference of free-leg and arm angular momenta; rotation about a medial axis is marked, with some twisting about a vertical axis, both in the direction of the crossbar.

In comparing the various interpretations of the Straddle style, however, it would seem that rotation about a transverse axis is of a less uniform pattern; for whereas, in some Straddles, the angular momentum generated by the free leg swing and arms is more than compensated by the jumper's forward rotation about his take-off foot, resulting in forward rotation about this transverse axis, this is not the case in others, and the athlete therefore leaves the ground with backward rotation about this axis or no rotation at all.

It is suggested, however, that (in the horizontal plane), in general, the axis of momentum in a Straddle jump is at an angle 30–40 deg. to the bar, inclined (because of rotation about a vertical axis) slightly towards the pit. Throughout the jump, therefore, it is at a considerable angle to the jumper's longitudinal axis (Figs. 92 and 142), i.e. the cone described by the jumper's longitudinal axis about the axis of momentum is large.

After take-off (Fig. 142p) the jumping leg hangs momentarily, keeping the hips high in relation to the Centre of Gravity and so helping to advance higher parts of the body quickly over and beyond the crossbar (*important in all the high-jumping styles*). Then, to displace the trunk, in reaction, and so bring it more into line with the axis of momentum, the leading leg is swung back to a position more parallel with the cross-bar; rotation and lay-out are thus speeded up.[1]

The head and chest barely clear the bar and drop rapidly below the main axis, while the hips and legs are raised above it (Fig. 142t). In addition, in some interpretations of the style, immediately after crossing the bar, the head and chest are forced even lower, against a downward thrusting of the free leg, to raise the hips and abdomen in relation to the Centre of Gravity and assist with the clearance of the rear (i.e. jumping) leg; this is then lifted and rotated (Fig. 142s–w).

The reaction to these leg and hip movements momentarily checks or, if

---

[1] An example of an inter-change of momentum, from gyration to twist.

sufficiently strong, even reverses the twisting of the upper body. Finally, with the jumping leg clear, the whole body rotates uniformly, the arms and upper body coming to earth before the legs.

LANDING. As the high-jumper drops towards the pit he develops kinetic energy, and the greater the distance of his fall, the greater is that energy (see page 41). To reduce risk of injury the fall should not be too great and, on landing, he should lose kinetic energy as gradually as possible—hence the need for built-up, soft landing areas.

Where the jumper lands on his feet he should flex his leg (or legs) under control: but where it has to be made in some other way (Fig. 142w and Fig. 149f) the impact can be lessened—the force of landing per square inch, or square centimetre, reduced—by increasing the area of body contact; and where the kinetic energy is the result of considerable horizontal motion, rolling in the pit (in the same direction as that motion) also reduces the impact of landing.

Long-jumping

Theoretically a jumper who could raise his Centre of Gravity 3 ft (0.91 m) at take-off (about the maximum achieved, so far, in high jumping) and combine this with horizontal speed of 36 ft (10.97 m) per second (near the top recorded sprinting speed) could long-jump 37.5 ft (11.43 m)—i.e. about 8.5 ft (2.60 m) farther than the existing men's world record. (The calculation is based on two assumptions: (1) that the jumper's Centre of Gravity would be $1\frac{1}{2}$ ft (43 cm) lower at the instant of landing than at take-off (so that it moves 34.67 ft (10.53 m) horizontally in flight), and (2) that he jumps 3 ft (92 cm) further because of his Centre of Gravity's distance in front of the board at take-off and its position behind the heels on landing.)

However, even the world's best long-jumpers take off at less than 30 ft (9.10 m) per second and raise their Centre of Gravity no more than 2–$2\frac{1}{2}$ ft (0.60–0.76 m). Even an athlete capable of a 7 ft high-jump and a 9.3 sec 100 yards sprint (or of a 2.13 m high-jump and a 100 m sprint time of 10.1 sec) would be compelled in long-jumping to take off at horizontal and vertical velocities much less than might be expected.

For experience indicates that about 6 per cent of his speed would be lost in preparation for take-off, and a further 10–15 per cent during his take-off movements. (Here again, it is impossible to impart the most favourable parabolic path to the Centre of Gravity without some loss of forward speed.) And despite this drastic reduction, his jumping foot could be in contact with the ground for only 0.11 sec—whereas a 7 ft

Vertical speed (ft per sec)	Rise of C. of G. (ft)	Time of flight (sec)	Horizontal speed (ft per second)					
			25.00	26.09	27.27	28.57	30.00	31.58

1. Assuming the Centre of Gravity of the jumper rises and falls equally

Vertical speed	Rise of C. of G.	Time of flight	25.00	26.09	27.27	28.57	30.00	31.58
5.66	0.5	0.354	8.85*	9.23*	9.65*	10.11*	10.62*	11.18*
8.00	1.0	0.500	12.50	13.04	13.63	14.28	15.00	15.79
9.80	1.5	0.612	15.30	15.96	16.69	17.48	18.36	19.32
11.31	2.0	0.708	17.70	18.47	19.30	20.22	21.24	22.35
12.65	2.5	0.790	19.75	20.61	21.54	22.57	23.70	24.95
13.86	3.0	0.866	21.65	22.59	23.62	24.74	25.98	27.35
14.97	3.5	0.936	23.40	24.42	25.53	26.74	28.08	29.56
16.00	4.0	1.000	25.00	26.09	27.27	28.57	30.00	31.58

2. Assuming the Centre of Gravity of the jumper 0.5 ft lower at the instant of landing than at take off

Vertical speed	Rise of C. of G.	Time of flight	25.00	26.09	27.27	28.57	30.00	31.58
5.66	0.5	0.427	10.67	11.14	11.64	12.20	12.81	13.48
8.00	1.0	0.556	13.90	14.50	15.16	15.88	16.68	17.56
9.80	1.5	0.660	16.50	17.22	18.00	18.85	19.80	20.84
11.31	2.0	0.749	18.72	19.54	20.42	21.40	22.47	23.65
12.65	2.5	0.828	20.70	21.60	22.58	23.65	24.84	26.14
13.86	3.0	0.901	22.52	23.51	24.57	25.74	27.03	28.45
14.97	3.5	0.968	24.20	25.25	26.40	27.66	29.04	30.57

3. Assuming the Centre of Gravity of the jumper 1.0 ft lower at the instant of landing than at take off

Vertical speed	Rise of C. of G.	Time of flight	25.00	26.09	27.27	28.57	30.00	31.58
5.66	0.5	0.483	12.07	12.60	13.17	13.80	14.49	15.25
8.00	1.0	0.604	15.10	15.76	16.47	17.25	18.12	19.07
9.80	1.5	0.701	17.52	18.29	19.11	20.05	21.03	22.15
11.31	2.0	0.787	19.67	20.53	21.46	22.48	23.61	24.85
12.65	2.5	0.863	21.58	22.52	23.54	24.65	25.89	27.26
13.86	3.0	0.933	23.32	24.34	25.45	26.66	27.99	29.46

4. Assuming the Centre of Gravity of the jumper 1.5 ft lower at the instant of landing than at take-off

Vertical speed	Rise of C. of G.	Time of flight	25.00	26.09	27.27	28.57	30.00	31.58
5.66	0.5	0.530	13.25	13.83	14.45	15.14	15.90	16.74
8.00	1.0	0.645	16.12	16.83	17.59	18.43	19.35	20.37
9.80	1.5	0.739	18.47	19.28	20.15	21.11	22.17	23.34
11.31	2.0	0.821	20.52	21.42	22.39	23.46	24.63	25.93
12.65	2.5	0.895	22.37	23.35	24.41	25.57	26.85	28.26
13.86	3.0	0.963	24.07	25.12	26.26	27.51	28.89	30.41

* Distance covered in feet

Vertical speed (m per second)	Rise of C. of G. (m)	Time of flight (sec)	Horizontal speed (metres per second)					

1. Assuming the Centre of Gravity of the jumper rises and falls equally

Vertical speed	Rise of C. of G.	Time of flight	Horizontal speed					
1.40	0.10	0.286	2.15*	2.29*	2.43*	2.57*	2.72*	2.86*
2.21	0.25	0.452	3.39	3.62	3.84	4.07	4.29	4.52
2.80	0.40	0.572	4.29	4.58	4.86	5.15	5.43	5.72
3.28	0.55	0.670	5.03	5.36	5.70	6.03	6.37	6.70
3.70	0.70	0.756	5.67	6.05	6.43	6.80	7.18	7.56
4.08	0.85	0.832	6.24	6.66	7.07	7.49	7.90	8.32
4.43	1.00	0.904	6.78	7.23	7.68	8.14	8.59	9.04
4.74	1.15	0.968	7.26	7.74	8.23	8.71	9.20	9.68
5.04	1.30	1.028	7.71	8.22	8.74	9.25	9.77	10.28

2. Assuming the Centre of Gravity of the jumper 0.1 m lower at the instant of landing than at take-off

Vertical speed	Rise of C. of G.	Time of flight	Horizontal speed					
1.40	0.10	0.345	2.59	2.76	2.93	3.11	3.28	3.45
2.21	0.25	0.493	3.70	3.94	4.19	4.44	4.68	4.93
2.80	0.40	0.605	4.54	4.84	5.14	5.45	5.75	6.05
3.28	0.55	0.700	5.25	5.60	5.95	6.30	6.65	7.00
3.70	0.70	0.783	5.87	6.26	6.66	7.05	7.44	7.83
4.08	0.85	0.856	6.42	6.85	7.28	7.70	8.13	8.56
4.43	1.00	0.927	6.95	7.42	7.88	8.34	8.81	9.27
4.74	1.15	0.988	7.41	7.90	8.40	8.89	9.39	9.88

3. Assuming the Centre of Gravity of the jumper 0.25 m lower at the instant of landing than at take-off

Vertical speed	Rise of C. of G.	Time of flight	Horizontal speed					
1.40	0.10	0.410	3.08	3.28	3.49	3.69	3.90	4.10
2.21	0.25	0.545	4.09	4.36	4.63	4.91	5.18	5.45
2.80	0.40	0.650	4.88	5.20	5.53	5.85	6.18	6.50
3.28	0.55	0.739	5.54	5.91	6.28	6.65	7.02	7.39
3.70	0.70	0.817	6.13	6.54	6.94	7.35	7.76	8.17
4.08	0.85	0.890	6.68	7.12	7.57	8.01	8.46	8.90
4.43	1.00	0.957	7.18	7.66	8.13	8.61	9.09	9.57

4. Assuming the Centre of Gravity of the jumper 0.40 m lower at the instant of landing than at take-off

Vertical speed	Rise of C. of G.	Time of flight	Horizontal speed					
1.40	0.10	0.462	3.47	3.70	3.93	4.16	4.39	4.62
2.21	0.25	0.590	4.43	4.72	5.02	5.31	5.61	5.90
2.80	0.40	0.690	5.18	5.52	5.87	6.21	6.56	6.90
3.28	0.55	0.774	5.81	6.19	6.58	6.97	7.35	7.74
3.70	0.70	0.851	6.38	6.81	7.23	7.66	8.08	8.51
4.08	0.85	0.921	6.91	7.37	7.83	8.29	8.75	9.21
4.43	1.00	0.987	7.40	7.90	8.39	8.88	9.38	9.87

* Distance covered in metres

high-jump would require 0.13–0.24 sec to impart the necessary vertical velocity of approximately 13 ft per second.

Efficient long-jumping, like good high-jumping, is therefore something of a compromise. In terms of a competent jumper's sprinting and high-jumping performances, neither speed nor spring are at a maximum: he reaches the board at a high, but not his top, speed, giving sufficient time for a great (but not his greatest) vertical impulse.

The tables on pages 174–5 (which do not allow for air resistance) give the horizontal distances travelled by the Centre of Gravity in flight for different combinations of horizontal and vertical velocity. Horizontally, the English measurements are based upon uniform sprinting speeds of 12.0 sec, 11.5 sec, 11.0 sec, 10.5 sec, 10 sec and 9.5 sec per 100 yards; vertically, upon the raising of the Centre of Gravity 0.5 ft, 1.0 ft, 1.5 ft, 2.0 ft, 2.5 ft, 3.0 ft, 3.5 ft and 4 ft.

In the metric table (*not* a direct conversion of the other) the figures are based upon uniform sprinting speeds of 13.3 sec, 12.5 sec, 11.8 sec, 11.1 sec, 10.5 sec and 10 sec per 100 m; vertically, upon the raising of the

Horizontal speed (ft per sec)	Height (ft)							
	0.5	1.0	1.5	2.0	2.5	3.0	3.5	4.0
25.00	12 45′	17 45′	21 24′	24 43′	26 51′	29 00′	30 55′	32 37′
26.09	12 14	17 03′	20 35′	23 48′	25 52′	27 59′	29 51′	31 31′
27.27	11 43′	16 21′	19 46′	22 53′	24 53′	26 57′	28 46′	30 24′
28.57	11 12′	15 39′	18 56′	21 57′	23 53′	25 53′	27 40′	29 15′
30.00	10 41′	13 30′	16 23′	18 45′	20 47′	22 35′	24 40′	25 39′
31.58	10 10′	14 13′	17 15′	20 01′	21 50′	23 42′	25 22′	26 52′

Horizontal speed (m.p.s.)	Height (metres)							
	0.1	0.25	0.40	0.55	0.70	0.85	1.00	1.15	1.30
7.5	10 34′	16 25′	20 28′	23 39′	26 15′	28 33′	30 34′	32 18′	33 54′
8.0	9 56′	15 27′	19 17′	22 18′	24 49′	27 01′	28 59′	30 39′	32 16′
8.5	9 21′	14 34′	18 14′	21 06′	23 31′	25 38′	27 31′	29 09′	30 40′
9.0	8 50′	13 48′	17 17′	20 01′	22 21′	24 23′	26 12′	27 46′	29 15′
9.5	8 23′	13 06′	16 25′	19 03′	21 17′	23 14′	25 00′	26 31′	27 57′
10.0	7 56′	12 28′	15 39′	18 09′	20 18′	22 12′	23 54′	25 22′	26 45′

(Among others, the formulae used in preparing these tables are:

$$h = \tfrac{1}{2}gt^2 \qquad v^2 = 2gh \quad \text{or} \quad v = gt)$$

Centre of Gravity 0.1 m, 0.25 m, 0.40 m, 0.55 m, 0.70 m, 0.85 m, 1.00 m, 1.15 m and 1.30 m. *In estimating the length of a jump from these figures, one must allow for the distance of the Centre of Gravity in front of the board at the instant of take-off, and its distance behind the heels at the instant of landing.*

The tables over show the take-off angle (to the horizontal) made by the flight path of the Centre of Gravity at the instant of leaving the board, for varying combinations of approach speed and height of jump. (Again, the metric table is *not* a direct conversion of the other.) The greatest practical angle must always be much less than 45 deg. (the angle sometimes recommended because it is generally known to give a projectile (*in vacuo*) maximum range). Indeed, it is impossible to jump at such an angle without using a very slow approach.

A jumper moving horizontally at 30 ft (9.14 m) per second could leave the board at an angle of 45 deg. only if his vertical velocity were also 30 ft (9.14 m) per second (see pages 13–17)—when his Centre of Gravity would be raised 14 ft (4.27 m) above its take-off height and the jump would measure approximately 56 ft (17.07 m). Again, even if he combined this take-off angle with the ability to raise his Centre of Gravity 4 ft (1.22 m) (i.e. at an initial velocity of 16 ft (4.88 m) per second), his jump would be only 16 ft (4.88 m).

APPROACH. Ideally, the length of the run-up in long-jumping should be determined by the athlete's ability to accelerate to top speed, taking an extra three or four strides to prepare for an upward leap from the board. Since research proves that, in making a maximum effort all the way, men sprinters attain this speed approximately 180 ft (55 m) from the start, ideally the approach should be over 200 ft (60 m). Indeed, since it can be argued that a long-jumper's maximum effort is required at the end of the run, not at the beginning, his initial acceleration might well be more gradual and his approach even longer.

In fact, the world's best long-jumpers to date have seldom exceeded 150 ft (45 m) in their approach; most have used from 120 ft to 140 ft (36 m to 42 m) and a few have barely exceeded 100 ft (30 m). In general, it can be said that they have attained, perhaps, no more than 90 per cent of their top sprinting speed.

TAKE-OFF. (1) *Attaining maximum vertical velocity.* The mechanical principles involved in long- and high-jump take-offs are identical; the emphasis at this stage should be on imparting maximum vertical velocity to the jumper's Centre of Gravity (see pages 154–64). However, in relation to high-jumping, there are the following differences:

(i) In this event the athlete attains a very much greater horizontal speed and does not accelerate into his final take-off stride. Therefore, although initially he places his jumping foot well ahead of his Centre of Gravity, he does not adopt the long, low final striding position of the good high-jumper, for to do so would result in too great a reduction of horizontal speed.

(ii) The long-jumper 'gathers' for his leap approximately three strides before reaching the board. He then adopts a more erect position (to enable his jumping foot to reach farther forward on take off) and on the penultimate stride lowers his hips slightly. Although the pattern throughout good long-jumping is by no means consistent, these preparatory movements usually lengthen the penultimate stride and shorten the final stride from three to nine inches.

(iii) At take-off, the free leg is swung well flexed at the knee, for speed of action (Fig. 150b). However, his more erect position here, and

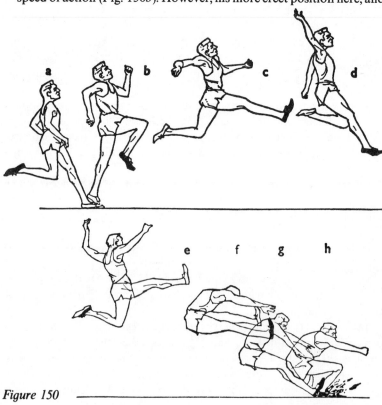

Figure 150

greater horizontal speed, give him a shorter time in contact with the board—and, therefore, a reduced impulse in comparison with the high-jumper.

The best long-jumping take-offs are those where resistance to forward motion is minimised and, within limits set by the athlete's horizontal speed, a maximum vertical impulse is directed through the Centre of Gravity; the flexed free leg, head, shoulders and arms are first accelerated upwards against a braced jumping leg before an additional vertical impulse is applied through a vigorous straightening of that leg (Fig. 150a–b).

(2) *Rotation.* Just as the reaction to the force of a runner's leg drive is directed eccentrically to his Centre of Gravity (i.e. in all three main planes, sagittal, frontal and transverse) so does this also apply to a long-jumper's take-off movements. And just as, for balance when running, clockwise and counter-clockwise moments about the athlete's Centre of Gravity in each plane must be equal (subject to the limitations mentioned on page 136), so is this true of take-off balance in this event.

Balance in the frontal and transverse planes presents fewer difficulties than balance in the sagittal plane, for the jumper finds the effects of eccentric thrust weaker and, therefore, so much easier to 'absorb' and control.

In the sagittal plane, however, there is a strong tendency to forward rotation due to the action of the legs in the run-ups, the checking of the jumping foot as it rests, momentarily, on the board, and the vertical component of the athlete's leg thrust as it acts behind the Centre of Gravity (Fig. 150a–b).

Backward rotation is encouraged by the horizontal component of the jumper's leg thrust, its vertical component when acting in front of his Centre of Gravity, and a transference of angular momentum from his free leg swing (Fig. 150a–b).

His emphasis on each of these constituent motions determines whether, in this sagittal plane, the jumper leaves the board with backward rotation, forward rotation or no rotation at all. It would seem that backward rotation can be obtained only by greatly exaggerating the length of the last stride, destroying essential horizontal speed. On the other hand, experience proves that a fast, efficient long-jump take-off produces either no rotation in this plane or—more often—some forward rotation.

FLIGHT. The mechanical principles governing the movements of athletes free in space have already been discussed in some detail (see pages 13, 57, 80–123, 167 and 168) and these apply equally to the flight of the long-jumper.

Without the use of weights (not permitted by the rules) he can do nothing to disturb the flight curve of his Centre of Gravity; both linear and angular momenta with which he leaves the ground remain constant in the air (ignoring air resistance). Obviously, therefore, the long-jumper cannot 'jet propel' himself in flight, and any movement he makes can be concerned only with the efficiency and safety of his landing.

(1) *Landing position.* The best landing position for a long-jumper is one which extends the flight path of his Centre of Gravity as far as possible and provides the greatest possible horizontal distance between his heels and Centre of Gravity, yet without causing him to fall backwards on landing.

To some extent, these factors are incompatible. A jumper adopting the best position for a delayed landing (Fig. 151*a*) fails to gain maximum horizontal distance with his heels, because, in this position, his hips have receded in relation to his Centre of Gravity. Again, a position giving maximum distance (Fig. 151*b*) hastens the landing, because the hips are now lower in relation to the Centre of Gravity; and falling backward in the pit is made more probable. Lastly, a position which presents no danger of falling back (Fig. 151*c*) reduces the distance gained by the heels and brings the jumper to the pit earlier.

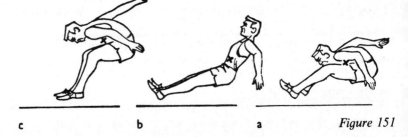

c   b   a   *Figure 151*

In practice, therefore, the best landing position in this event must always be a compromise; the legs are somewhat below the horizontal and the trunk leans slightly forward (Figs. 150*g* and 152); but the greater the jumper's horizontal speed, the more effective the position he can adopt without falling backwards.

It has been estimated that for every inch (2.5 cm) the heels are kept up, a jumper will gain about an inch and a half (3.75 cm); all jumpers are aware of the importance of keeping the legs up on landing, and yet in most good long-jumps the legs are dropped immediately prior to it, a fault usually attributed to abdominal weakness. However, since all parts of a jumper's body in the air are experiencing the same gravitational acceleration, this explanation cannot be correct; for here the legs are not being held up by muscles while other parts of the body are prevented from falling, as happens in hanging, with legs raised horizontally, from a beam or wall-bars; *when not in contact with the ground, the athlete can adopt and hold postures which would otherwise be more difficult* (page 51).

It is suggested that at this stage of the jump the legs are lowered for one or several of the following reasons: because (i) of forward rotation originated at take-off; (ii) the jumper modifies his position to avoid sitting back in the pit; (iii) by instinctively raising his head and straightening the trunk, dropping his legs in reaction, he *feels* he is delaying the moment of landing; and (iv) of the tension of the extensor muscles of the body, which may be too great for his hip flexor and abdominal muscles; only in this sense can the fault be attributed to muscular weakness (see page 51, *Weightlessness*).

Even in the best practical landing position, however, it is unlikely that the jumper's heels will contact the sand beyond an extension of the flight curve of his Centre of Gravity[1] (Fig. 152)—if, indeed, he can get them even *that* far in front of his body weight.

Figure 152

Landing efficiency is increased in long-jumping when, immediately before contacting the pit, the arms are behind the jumper (Fig. 152), for he then adds to the horizontal distance between his Centre of Gravity and heels (see page 57), and when he lands he can throw the arms vigorously forward to assist the forward pivoting of his body, transferring momentum.

[1] P. McIntosh and H. W. B. Hayley, 'An investigation into the running long jump', *Journal of Physical Education*, England (November 1952).

(2) *Movement in flight.* The foregoing analysis of the problems of landing and rotation off the board provide the key to the kind of movement in flight of greatest value to the long-jumper.

If he takes off with excessive backward rotation, he should extend his body—'hanging' (Fig. 153*b–c*)—to increase its moment of inertia about a transverse horizontal axis of momentum and so slow down this rotation. Then, immediately before landing, he should 'jack' at the hips and so increase his angular velocity, raising and extending his heels in relation to his Centre of Gravity (Fig. 153*d–e*).

a   b   c   d   e *Figure 153*

With either no rotation or forward rotation off the board about this same axis, however, he will profit from movements which will rotate the body backwards. If he leaves the board with no rotation, by cycling his legs forward, his trunk will automatically turn backwards, for he cannot change his total angular momentum in flight.

With forward rotation off the board, the angular momentum generated by the forward rotations of his legs (and, to lesser degree, his arms) should exceed his total angular momentum; the jumper's legs and arms must develop sufficient angular momentum not only to 'take up' these rotations, but also to turn the trunk and hips backwards in the sagittal plane. But when these arm and leg movements cease, the original body rotation (which cannot be destroyed in the air) reveals itself (see page 114).

A majority of athletes using this 'running-in-the-air' or 'hitch kick' style employ a single-stride technique (Fig. 150); yet it is open to doubt that this displaces body

Figure 154

weight sufficiently about the jumper's Centre of Gravity. Usually, he completes this single stride and attains his landing position too soon, rotating forward again before landing.

It would seem that an extra stride in the air would provide an even better landing position; two strides could give greater displacement, yet without bringing the jumper too quickly into his 'jacked' landing position. And, of course, theoretically, three strides would be better still, though no jumper has yet succeeded in completing three *full* strides in the short time between take-off and landing.

With forward rotation off the board, a 'sail' jumper (Fig. 154) speeds up the rotation; by 'jacking' quickly after take-off he reduces his moment of inertia about the axis of momentum and so increases his angular velocity. A 'hang' position (Fig. 153*b–c*) merely slows this forward rotation by increasing the body's moment of inertia. As in the case of the 'sail' jump, it does nothing to absorb or counteract rotation.

Because of their smaller moments of inertia the arms, even when fully extended, do not possess the turning effect of the legs. Yet, by virtue of the position of the shoulders—a secondary axis, in relation to the jumper's Centre of Gravity, the location of the main axis—the arms possess a considerable turning effect *above the head*, particularly where there is a maximum possible distance between the axes (Figs. 150*d–e* and 153*c–d*).

As the arms are lowered, however, their turning effect on the rest of the body weakens progressively; and if the athlete remains in a fully stretched position they might eventually encourage a forward body rotation. However, in practice, by the time the arms are nearing their lowest position the jumper has already 'jacked' in preparation for his landing; the sweep of each arm's radius of gyration therefore 'embraces' the main axis and continues its (now very weak) influence in favour of backward rotation of the whole body (see pages 112–7).

Certainly in the sagittal plane the legs are always the principal 'absorbers' of body-rotation in long-jumping; the arms—held wide of the body—have more to contribute to balance in the transverse and frontal planes.

The benefits of a hitch-kick can be exaggerated; men have jumped well without it. Yet, so far as is known, all the world's 26-ft (8.0 m) or better, long-jumpers, to date, have employed this technique, although it has sometimes been combined with a 'hang'.

Triple-jumping

The mechanical principles relating to high and long-jumping are also fundamental to the triple-jump (Fig. 155a–l) although, of course, the technique of this event differs.

The distance gained in a triple-jump is largely dependent upon the horizontal speed which can be developed in the approach and the extent to which this can be controlled, conserved and evenly apportioned over all three phases—hop, step and jump.

But, on each phase, the triple-jumper must also gain sufficient height at take-off and support his weight on landing. The movements required for this are responsible for opposing horizontal forces of a size which depends upon his mass, velocity, Centre of Gravity angles at take-off and landing and skill. The resistance of the air also reduces speed.

As he cannot change his weight, govern air resistance to any significant extent, nor produce a good jump without maximum (controlled) approach speed, he influences his overall jumping distance by controlling his angles of take-off and landing, by skilfully reducing the landing shock, and to a limited degree by driving horizontally on each take-off.

For the conservation of horizontal speed, ideally, the jumper needs a low-angled take-off and a steeply-angled landing, but these are incompatible: take-off and landing angles must always be approximately equal, particularly in the hop and step. Therefore, in the hop, for example, where a good jumper gains his distance mainly on approach speed, a comparatively low take-off angle favours conservation, while the acute angle at which he lands tends severely to check his forward movement.

To reduce this resistance, therefore, the expert triple-jumper moves his leading foot back quickly, in a 'pawing' action, immediately before landing to reduce its forward speed in relation to the ground (see page 59), lands with the greatest practicable angle between his leading foreleg and the ground, and then 'gives' at the hip, knee and ankle joints. Yet he must stress none of these movements at a cost, subsequently, of essential vertical speed. These principles apply equally to the step technique.

An analysis of slow-motion film showing twelve good triple-jumpers in action (some Olympic and world record-holders) has indicated a general pattern of technique for this event. In each of the phases average times of take-off and flight for these jumpers were:

Figure 155

Hop		Step		Jump		Totals		
Take-off	Flight	Take-off	Flight	Take-off	Flight	Take-offs	Flights	Total time
0.132	0.562	0.164	0.421	0.171	0.640	0.467	1.623	2.090

(seconds)

The analysis revealed that, without exception, all the jumpers were progressively longer in contact with the ground over the three phases—hop, step and jump—denoting a gradual reduction in horizontal speed. Again, without exception, in terms of time, all were longest in the air during the jump and shortest in the step. In fact, their jumping rhythms were never even. In our hypothetical average jump, for example, the jumper's Centre of Gravity would rise 15 in. (0.38 m) in the hop, only $8\frac{1}{2}$ in. (0.21 m) in the step and (assuming it 12 in. (0.30 m) lower on landing than at the instant of take-off) 14 in. (0.35 m) in the final phase. These figures also underline the difficulty of gaining height in the step and jump; for the average pressure of the foot on the ground after the hop would be 4 times that of the body weight; after the step, 3.8 times.

Yet this is not to suggest that coaches who advise an even rhythm— 'ta, ta, ta'—and a successively higher flight are wrong. For in coaching the triple-jump one must teach a higher, longer step than the athlete would do naturally and instil the idea of increased effort from phase to phase. Knowing what actually happens in a good jump a coach may yet correctly tell his athlete to attempt something different—the art, as opposed to the science, of coaching.

The basic principle in the triple-jump is that no one phase must be stressed to the detriment of the overall effort. But there can be no precise ratio of distance between the hop, step and jump because of the differences in athletes (in speed, spring, strength, weight, flexibility, proportions, etc., etc.). Certainly, no triple-jumper apportions his effort in exactly the same way from one jump to the next! However, a 10 : 7 : 10 ratio has been found suitable for beginners (e.g. 14 ft $9\frac{1}{2}$ in.: 10 ft 5 in.: 14 ft $9\frac{1}{2}$ in. for 40 ft—i.e. 4.51 m: 3.18 m: 4.51 m for 12.19 m), while international performances suggest a 10 : 8 : 9 ratio for the much more experienced athlete (e.g. 20 ft $9\frac{1}{2}$ in.: 16 ft $6\frac{1}{2}$ in.: 18 ft 8 in. for 56 ft (6.34 m: 5.04 m: 5.69 m for 17.07 m)—i.e. with greater emphasis on the Hop and Step).[1]

Hop. Because of the need to conserve horizontal speed, an expert triple-jumper gains hopping distance mainly on his approach speed; his jumping foot does not reach out as far ahead as in a long-jump take-off nor is his final leg thrust as vertical (Fig. 155*a–b*). He does not need the time in contact with the board to gain the impulse of the long-jumper. *He could hop higher and travel much farther in consequence, but only at tremendous cost to speed in the step and jump. In this first phase, in particular, restraint in the apportioning of height and distance (and, therefore, speed) is essential.*

[1] Eng Yoon Tan, 'Research into the hop, step and jump' (N. C. T. C. A: 29th Annual Meeting. Published by 'Champions on Film', $303\frac{1}{2}$ SO Main Street, Ann Arbor, Michigan, U.S.A.).

If he is to follow the hop with a balanced step of good length, the jumper must keep his body upright in this first phase, his head in natural alignment with the shoulders. To avoid a backward-rotating movement, some jumpers reverse their leg positions with approximately equal moments of inertia about the hips (Fig. 155 *c–d*), while others drop and straighten the free leg and markedly flex the jumping leg in flight to obtain a hitch-kicking effect. *To facilitate an 'active' landing on the hopping foot this reversing of leg position should be completed relatively late in flight*, with the thighs ranging through a wide arc, the hopping knee waist high and the legs moving continuously; for if the leading thigh is lowered prematurely the jumper's Centre of Gravity will pass quickly over and beyond the landing foot and his supporting leg will be too straight. In consequence, the step phase will be hurried, weakened and shortened.

A jumper who 'waits for the ground' lands in a slightly lower position and with greater leg flexion—both favourable to a 'cushioning' of the landing and a pronounced forward-upward drive in the step. At the instant of landing the Centre of Gravity should be approximately 1 foot (30 cm) behind the front foot, yet not so far back that the leg 'buckles' as a result of the backward thrust of the ground. In fact, the heel lands first, but a good jumper will not be conscious of it; the landing will feel flat-footed. The free leg trails at this stage (Fig. 155*e*).

The primary function of the arms is to absorb reaction to the powerful, eccentric leg thrust at take-off, to keep the trunk aligned properly. But in so far as action and reaction are interchangeable factors (see page 21), vigorous arm movement in a sagittal plane can also contribute to the horizontal component of leg thrust on each take-off; and, the upward acceleration of the arms on each occasion can augment vertical velocity (see page 159).

Ideally, therefore, the arms should be swung vigorously backwards and forwards in the hop, passing close to the trunk; and this applies also to the step take-off. However, where a jumper leaves the board unbalanced, rotating in a transverse and/or frontal plane, he must then extend his arms wide of the body in an attempt to produce counter-rotations (see pages 113–6); and, to the detriment of his step take-off, he must land with them in this sideways position at the end of the hop.

Step. The figure for the average pressure between foot and ground in landing from the hop in our hypothetical average jump for the twelve experts, gives some indication of the effort required to overcome that pressure and yet acquire new velocity and an optimum take-off angle for an adequate step. With beginners the step is used merely to recover from the hop; they put the next foot to the ground as quickly as they can, and this fault is accentuated when the hop has been too high or the landing foot has been placed too far in front of the body. On the other hand, world-class triple-jumpers rarely step shorter than 15 ft (4.50 m).

The key to developing a good step lies in the use of the free leg at take-off. Flexed, it should be swung vigorously until its knee is at least waist high; simultaneously, the other leg should drive hard down and back (Fig. 155*f*). Experience proves that in flight a jumper should 'float'; here again, he should 'wait for the ground to come up to him'; *keeping his front thigh at least waist level with a relaxed lower leg 'pawing' out and back for an 'active' landing.* The rear knee swings forward to a position beneath its hip (Fig. 155*g*).

It has often been suggested that this more vertical rear thigh position is easier than trailing it far behind between take-off and landing, for the reason that, otherwise, gravity 'pulls the leg down'. In flight, however, any body position relative to the Centre of Gravity can be difficult to maintain only by virtue of internal muscular tensions. Since gravity acts on all parts of the body with equal effect, there can be no other reason (see pages 7, 8, 53 and 181).

The step landing is the same as for the hop, except that some jumpers swing both arms to the rear before contacting the ground, in order to use a double arm movement in their jump take-off. This arm action is used, usually, with a hang technique. Too vigorous a backward movement of the arms, however, pitches the trunk too far forward for an effective jump; the athlete then falls, rather than springs, into the pit—with considerable forward rotation. *The trunk is best kept as erect as possible at this stage.*

Jump (Fig. 155*i–l*). Fundamentally, the technique in this final phase is that of the long-jumper, but in comparison, the triple-jumper is a shorter period of time in the air and has less horizontal speed on landing—if his hop and step have been executed correctly. Also, after the two previous phases the control of his jump is more difficult.

With less forward speed on landing, the triple-jumper is in greater danger of sitting back in the pit. Here, a little forward rotation (although never consciously developed in a good jump) might be to the jumper's advantage; he is also in greater need of movement which will help to pivot him forward over the fulcrum of his heels, i.e. an immediate and pronounced flexing of the legs on landing (reducing his moment of inertia about his heels) and a throwing forward of his arms, to build up and then transfer their momentum. (When momentum is transferred mass × velocity of the part equals mass × velocity of the whole (see pages 96–8.)

Sail and hang techniques are usually preferred to a hitch-kick, for the latter needs more time and control than are generally available. In both styles, the legs should be brought through well flexed at the knees before straightening, thereby reducing their moment of inertia about the jumper's Centre of Gravity, speeding up their movement and diminishing a trunk reaction which would otherwise mar the landing position (see page 102).

CHAPTER NINE

Pole Vaulting

An attempt to coach pole vaulting (Fig. 156) without an understanding
of the underlying mechanical principles has been likened to trying to
read without a knowledge of the alphabet. For by planting his pole the
vaulter creates a hinged moment which converts primarily linear motion
at take-off into angular motion (see page 93); and then, simultaneously
and interdependently, one pendulum (the athlete) swings from his hands
while the second pendulum (pole and athlete) pivots about the base of
the pole (Fig. 157).

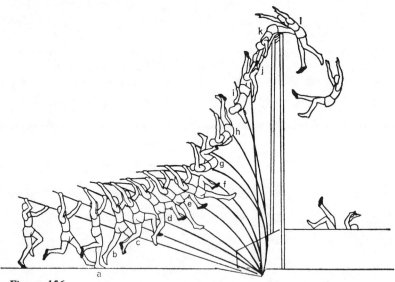

Figure 156

Adapted from Bill Falk, *Fibreglass Pole Vaulting* (M-F Athletic Company Inc., Rhode
Island, U. S. A.).

190

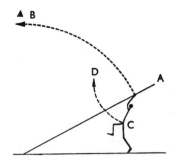

Figure 157

The good vaulter co-ordinates the timing of these two pendulums, projecting his Centre of Gravity high above his top hand just as the pole attains a near-vertical position (Fig. 156). However, in gaining height the expert does more than employ these two movements; he completes and improves the vault by executing a powerful, carefully-timed and well-directed pulling and pushing action, driving his hips and legs upwards (Fig. 156).

As Hopper has shown,[1] a vaulter's ability to clear a given height depends, first, upon his total angular momentum about a transverse axis through the point where the pole meets the box (Fig. 156). (In considering basic principles, the small mass of the pole and its moment of inertia will be ignored.) Second, it depends upon his skill in conserving and using that angular momentum properly.

The vaulter's total angular momentum consists of:

(a) his body's angular momentum about a transverse axis through his Centre of Gravity (due to the rotation of his forelegs in the run-up and, possibly, to rotational movement in the same forward sense in planting the pole), and

(b) the angular momentum of his Centre of Gravity, treated as a massive particle, about A (Fig. 158).

As shown previously angular momentum can *also* be expressed in linear quantities—better when dealing with an athlete's motion about an external point; as the product MVR where M is the athlete's mass (supposedly concentrated at his Centre of Gravity), V his velocity, and R the distance between his Centre of Gravity and the box, measured vertically at right angles to his running path (Fig. 159a).

---

[1] B. J. Hopper. 'Rotation—a vital factor in athletic technique' (*Track Technique*, U.S.A., No. 14, December 1964 (*Track and Field News*).

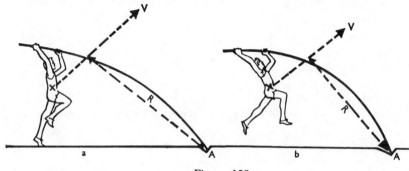

Figure 158

Assuming, for simplicity, uniform velocity in the approach and ignoring the slightly undulating path of his Centre of Gravity, then in equal times the latter moves through equal distances and its angular momentum about the box is constant. Geometrically, the areas swept out about A are also equal, each triangle having an area $\frac{1}{2}VR$ (Fig. 159b).

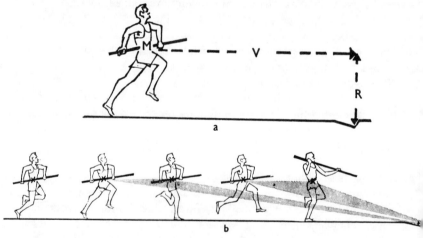

Figure 159

The vaulter can add to this angular momentum at take-off by springing off the ground, substantially increasing R by this means (Fig. 158a); but for this to be advantageous he must plant the pole in front of his body and jump without excessively checking his forward speed. (In all probability, all he can hope for is the *maintenance* of his run-up speed in the new direction.)

The vaulter's skill off the ground is the other basic factor. A successful clearance is largely dependent upon his ability to continue to move his Centre of Gravity forward and upward until it is vertically above A. After take-off, a large contrary turning moment (the product of his weight and its horizontal distance from the box) makes inevitable a gradual loss of angular momentum and tends to prevent this. It is therefore essential to reduce this horizontal distance as quickly as possible, particularly immediately after take-off.

The good vaulter achieves this by 'hanging' momentarily. He arches his body with the take-off leg almost straight (Figs. 158*b* and 156*b–d*)— a movement which (1) keeps his Centre of Gravity low and (2) permits it to move forward as rapidly as possible in a direction more horizontal than at the instant of take-off.

Thus, the low trajectory of his Centre of Gravity reduces the distance R in the product MVR, and so V, his speed, is maintained (Fig. 158*b*). (The 'metronome effect' is illustrated in Fig. 160.) And, momentarily, he avoids making any downward motion on the pole through an upward acceleration of his body; it has only to bear his weight.

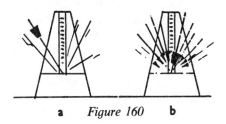

a   *Figure 160*   b

Just as the arm of a metronome oscillates more rapidly as its weight is moved closer to the fulcrum (Fig. 160*a–b*), so, on leaving the ground, does the expert in this event give speed to his pole by extending his body momentarily, keeping his Centre of Gravity close to the pole's base. This exemplifies the principle of the conservation of angular momentum (see page 88), for by reducing the moment of inertia, angular velocity is increased proportionately.

The immediate and pronounced bending of the fibre-glass pole assists both aims, reducing the shock of impact and loss of horizontal velocity. A wide grasp encourages this; it facilitates, simultaneously, a backward pulling action from a straightened upper arm and a forward thrust with the other—coupling movements which, while he is in contact with the ground, immediately establish the direction of pole-bend (Fig. 161) and,

Figure 161

during the initial stage of the pole-borne phase, keep his body away from the pole.

Now, if the pole is to continue to turn about point A, the force exerted on it by the hands (in the illustration at a point near the top hand; in fact it will be somewhere between the hands and will vary) must be directed slightly ahead of A so as to possess a beneficial turning effect (Fig. 162). The horizontal component of this force (HE) will be due to the equal and opposite checking (XB) of the vaulter's Centre of Gravity in this direction. The vertical component (HG) in the early stages of the vault should be little more than body-weight (Fig. 162a), for a marked upward acceleration at this time will increase the component and direct the resultant *behind* point A, slowing the pole down.

When the pole has moved more towards the vertical (Fig. 162b)—and with the vaulter's Centre of Gravity now approximately in line with the chord of the pole, i.e. an imaginary straight line between his upper grip and the bottom end (HA)—the direction of the force exerted through the hands (HF) will also have increased its inclination. Now, the horizontal (checking) force (XB) will be reduced, encouraging a premature straightening of the pole.

To avoid this, the vaulter begins an upward acceleration (i.e. his swing-up) without excessively reducing the pole's speed; the component (HG) is increased (Fig. 162b). And the more vertical the chord of the pole, subsequently, the smaller, progressively, will be the checking force and the better the position of the pole to support further upward accelerations.

In this swing-up the good vaulter 'breaks at the hips and knees', reducing the moment of inertia about his shoulders—so raising his body

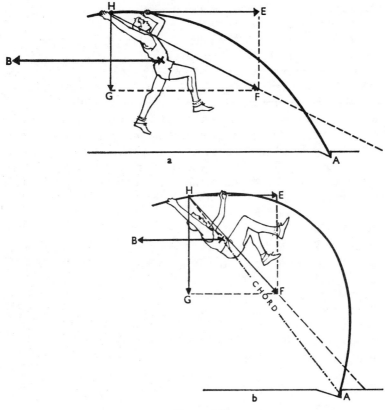

Figure 162

and increasing its rotational speed. This can be achieved with the free leg leading throughout (the jumping leg not catching up with it until the 'rock-back' position is reached) (Fig. 156*g*), or with emphasis on a 'hang' after take-off, when the swing-up and rock-back occur later and faster and with legs together. The swing-up reduces the speed of the pole-athlete pendulum, increasing the distance between the base of the pole (the fulcrum) and the Centre of Gravity common to pole and man.

From a position in which the hips and legs are close to and parallel with the pole (Fig. 156*h*) the good vaulter pulls *as the pole recoils*; for their simultaneous action can thus increase the impulse propelling him into the air (see pages 34–5). His body spirals upwards about a near-vertical axis, close to the pole, with the legs driven vertically in front of the plane of the uprights (Fig. 156*h*–*k*). The push is merely a continuation of the pulling action.

In these final moments the vaulter has not only to impart maximum vertical speed to his body; he has also to rotate it to raise parts of it still below the crossbar on releasing the pole (Fig. 156*j*–*l*). This he achieves partly by a transference of angular momentum acquired in dropping the legs *very slightly*, 'breaking at the hips' to assume an arched position at the high point (Fig. 156*k*). It is due mainly, however, to a couple (see page 68) created by the reaction to his thrust on the pole (acting vertically upwards) and the force of his weight (acting vertically downwards) (Fig. 58*b*). In efficient vaulting the force of the pole's upward thrust exceeds this downward pull; he releases the pole with his body rotating but still moving upwards (Fig. 156*j*–*k*).

Other aspects

Approach speed and height of grip. The following tables illustrate how, other things being equal, the height cleared in pole vaulting is proportional to the take-off speed.

The speeds, expressed in terms of a 'flying' 100 yards and 100 metres run at uniform speed, are common to the event. The heights are *those above the position of the vaulter's Centre of Gravity at take-off and take no account of the work he does in the later stages.* (The metric table is *not* a direct conversion from the other.)

Speed		Height (to nearest in.)	
Seconds per 100 yd	= ft per sec	ft	in
9.8	30.61	14	7
9.9	30.31	14	4
10.0	30.00	14	1
10.6	28.30	12	6
10.8	27.77	12	1
10.9	27.52	11	10
11.0	27.27	11	7
11.1	27.03	11	5
11.2	26.79	11	3
11.3	26.55	11	1
11.4	26.31	10	10
11.5	26.08	10	8

(These heights have been calculated from the formula

$$\tfrac{1}{2}mv^2 = mgh, \text{ i.e. } h = \frac{v^2}{64})$$

| Speed | | Height |
Seconds per 100 m	metres per second	in metres
10.7	9.35	4.46
10.8	9.26	4.37
10.9	9.17	4.29
11.0	9.09	4.22
11.2	8.93	4.07
11.5	8.70	3.86
11.7	8.55	3.73
11.9	8.40	3.60
12.0	8.33	3.54
12.1	8.26	3.48
12.2	8.20	3.43
12.3	8.13	3.37
12.4	8.06	3.32
12.5	8.00	3.26
12.6	7.94	3.22

(These heights have been calculated from the formula

$$\tfrac{1}{2}mv^2 = mgh, \quad \text{i.e.} h = \frac{v^2}{19.6})$$

It has been assumed that all the kinetic energy developed in the run-up can be used in raising the Centre of Gravity whereas, in fact, some must be dissipated by the impact of the pole with the box, some by the backward thrust of the ground on the athlete's take-off foot and some in energy losses associated with the bending of the pole. In addition, of course, the vaulter must retain sufficient horizontal speed to cross the bar. It is beyond the scope of this book to attempt to assess any of these factors.

Greater approach speed will enable the athlete to use a higher grip, provided he has the strength to control the resulting increased centrifugal force of his swing (see page 47); provided that any resulting increase in speed does not impair co-ordination. A flexible pole can be held higher than a stiff one; and his height, weight, spring, skill, the direction and strength of the wind, the run-up surface, his general fitness and motivation—all will influence the height of the vaulter's grasp on the pole.

A vaulter should aim for a maximum effective grip (i.e. the distance between the top of his higher hand and the ground when the pole is upright in the box) equal to twice his standing height plus at least 24 inches (0.60 m). This can be used with maximum controlled speed at each height (which is recommended) or the vaulter can lower his grip and run slower at easier heights, progressively raising his grip and increasing his speed throughout a competition.

The fibre-glass pole gives greater height in vaulting than tne female bamboo and metal poles used previously because it permits the use of a higher grasp and, in bending markedly, stores more energy; it provides an effective means of converting the vaulter's kinetic energy to potential energy. However, because this energy must be restored to the vaulter— and *quickly*—at the proper time, he must select a pole appropriate to his weight, hand-hold and speed.[1]

During the first decade of fibre-glass vaulting it was generally accepted that, because of the greater flexibility of the poles, good vaults could be made with the jumping foot within an area one foot (0.30 m) forward or backward of a position under the top hand. Today's improved vaulting and higher grips demand a greater precision—a return to the bamboo/metal pole concept whereby the foot should be *directly* beneath the top hand. For if it is further forward, or the plant too late, the modern vaulter—like the old—will be snatched prematurely off the ground (more than half the problems in vaulting are due to a faulty plant or take-off).

The vaulting technique with bamboo and metal poles required the lower hand to be shifted closer to the top hand in planting; for with the hands no more than 6 inches (0.15 m) apart the vaulter swung more effectively, was less likely to turn prematurely, divided the work of his arms more evenly and could raise his chest higher above his grip on release, than with the hands wide apart.

With fibre-glass, however, a much wider hand-spread is used in the approach to control the higher grip, and even with a shifting of the lower hand in the plant (as some vaulters still prefer) a $1-2\frac{1}{2}$ ft (0.30–0.75 m) spread helps quickly to establish the direction of pole-bend (as has already been mentioned), keeps the shoulders away from the pole during the swing, facilitates a fast raising of the legs in the swing-up and permits a more delicate adjustment of grip, as between one hand and the other; for slight changes in the suspension of body-weight can be made to control the degree of pole bend and its speed of straightening.

The swing. The 'hanging' movement (Fig. 156*b–d*) mentioned previously (page 193) is vital to bringing the pole to the vertical *only* when the highest grip is used commensurate with take-off velocity. With

---

[1] A common fault is for the pole to bend too much, recoiling too slowly.

a lower hand-hold there will be neither the necessity nor time for such an extended body position.

Nor should it be exaggerated beyond the athlete's ability, later, to raise and flex his legs against gravity and the centrifugal force tending to tear him away from his grip. This is particularly true of the tall, long-legged athlete whose Centre of Gravity will be low relative to his grasp; he will develop greater centrifugal force than a shorter man swinging with equal angular velocity and will therefore require more strength and speed.

The swing-up. In the process of reducing the horizontal distance between himself and the box, initially (page 195) the vaulter will have maintained a low position of his Centre of Gravity—it has little vertical speed (Fig. 156*b–e*); but now he must raise it quickly to retain, and even add to, the pole-bend and adopt a position from which he can benefit from its straightening and further increase his vertical speed by pulling and pushing. He lifts his legs viciously and rocks back, transmitting a large force through his hands into the pole (Fig. 156*g–h*); the hips should be above the head with, at first, knees flexed and tucked into the chest.

To adopt and hold the best position from which to use the released energy when the pole straightens, the vaulter 'stays on his back', holding his rock-back position until the pole is well into its recoil. This must be no passive pose, however, for as the pole pivots and recoils the tendency will be for the legs to be driven down; the vaulter must try to bring his feed further and further above his head.

The pull-push. The good vaulter pulls as the pole straightens—but *not early* in that process. Weaker, less co-ordinated athletes cannot pull against the pole's recoil and therefore delay their pull, doing less work and sacrificing height in the process. (See also 'Summation of forces', page 34.) The pull should be strong and fast, with the legs driven vertically in front of the plane of the uprights (Fig. 156*i*) and with the vaulter passing through the so-called 'L', 'J' and 'I' positions (Fig. 156*h–j*).

The turning of the body occurs partly as a result of a leg action whereby the original free leg is stretched vigorously upwards (vertically by some, and to the left of the pole, assuming a left-footed take-off, by others) while the take-off leg, flexed, cuts behind, turning the hips. It is also due to the unbalanced position of the hands, one above the other, which encourages a twisting of the shoulders in the direction of the grip. Turning (twisting) speed is related to pulling speed.

The push is merely a continuation of the pull.

The release. Ideally, all parts of the vaulter, and therefore his Centre of Gravity, should rise at maximum vertical speed until he has released the pole. Then he should 'jack' (i.e. flex markedly at the hips) to raise his abdomen in relation to his Centre of Gravity, improving his lay-out (Fig. 156*k*) (see page 57). Finally, with his hips clear of the bar, he should 'unjack' quickly to clear his head, chest and arms, depressing his abdomen and folding back his legs in reaction.

The more efficiently a vaulter converts horizontal to vertical movement, the greater the period of time for which he is over—and tending to drop on to—the bar, and the faster and more skilful must be his final movements.

CHAPTER TEN

Throwing

In all four throwing events the distance obtained is dependent upon the speed, the height and angle of release of the missile, and, in the discus and javelin events, on certain aerodynamic factors.

Speed

An efficient throwing technique is one in which the athlete exerts the forces of his entire body over the greatest range practicable (force × distance = work; see page 40) and, therefore, for the longest period of time (force × time = impulse; see page 32); for the speed of release in throwing is proportional to the average force exerted through the implement's Centre of Gravity. Other things being equal, the greater total body force produces the greater speed and the longer throw, since force = mass × acceleration (see pages 18–21 (Newton's First and Second Laws) and page 32).

The forces must be exerted against the missile in the proper direction, however—so far as practicable, in the direction of the ultimate throw; for the total effective force in throwing is the sum—the resultant—of all the components of the various body forces acting in that direction. As a general rule, in throwing, however, in the preliminary movements there is more horizontal drive than lift, and in the delivery more lift than horizontal drive. The eventual effect is to release the missile at an appropriate angle to the horizontal.

These two principles are fundamental to correct preliminary movement in throwing—in the run-up, glide or turns. In good throwing they are exemplified in the fast stretching and powerful recoiling of large muscle-groups; in the driving of body weight from one leg to another and (in the hammer and discus events in particular) in the use of maximum radius of movement in the turns.

In particular, by driving the pelvis ahead of the trunk, the good thrower creates torque between hips and shoulders; active trunk muscle is stretched rapidly in an *eccentric contraction* which exerts maximum tension. (See also pages 27 and 28).

The various forces of the body should be exerted in definite sequence and with proper timing; for the release speed in a good throw will be greater than in a bad one, even if the same effort has been expended and throws are equal in all other respects.

From a purely mechanical point of view it is immaterial in what order a given set of forces is applied, one by one or simultaneously; the final speed is the same. To accelerate a shot, discus, javelin or hammer, however, each body lever in turn must be capable of moving faster in a given direction than the missile is moving in the same direction; and the faster the lever can move the greater will be its effective force.

In a summation of throwing forces, therefore, the levers of the body should operate so that each can make a maximum, or very near-maximum, contribution to speed. Hence the use of slower but more forceful muscles and levers first (i.e. of the trunk and thighs); while the faster but relatively weaker joints (i.e. of the arms, hands, lower legs and feet) exert their forces after the missile has developed considerable speed. While the feet and hands *transmit* force during the earlier movements, therefore, their own smaller forces are *added* later (see *Impulse*, page 32).

However, there must be no undue delay in the application of the various forces because of forces which tend to retard the missile even before it leaves the thrower's hand, i.e. gravity (which tends to reduce upward motion) and the friction between the athlete and the ground at the instant of foot contact (which tends to slow the missile horizontally). Of major importance, also, is the need for maximum impulse. *All forces should therefore be applied as simultaneously as practicable.* (See pages 30 and 33, 72–5.)

Turns, glides and run-ups should be as fast as an athlete can use to good purpose; never so fast that he is unable to exert full body force subsequently in the delivery. In this respect, each athlete possesses his own 'critical', optimum speed of preliminary movement.[1]

For maximum speed of release the ground must provide adequate resistance to the thrower's movements, and for as long as he is in contact with the missile, for the force he can exert against it is limited, very largely, by the counter-thrust of the ground.

---

[1] Which can be improved by appropriate training.

Fig. 163*a* and *b* illustrate how force in a horizontal plane can be lost when both feet are off the ground. As the athlete on the turntable (Fig. 163*a*) attempts to put the shot, upper and lower parts of his body rotate in opposite directions (Fig. 163*b*); reaction to his movement in a horizontal plane must be absorbed by the turntable and his body, not by the ground. Likewise, force applied vertically in throwing is also dependent upon the resistance of the ground.

Figure 163 **a**   **b**

As Housden points out,[1] in developing angular momentum in discus throwing the athlete must have some part of each foot, or at least the whole of one foot, in contact with the ground. He recommends the following experiments; first, stand with both feet on the ground and with the right arm back behind the shoulder, swing the arm horizontally, and as it comes to the front of the body, raise the right foot and rise on the left toe. Through a transference of angular momentum from the arm, the body will then turn in the same direction. Then stand with only the left foot flat on the ground, repeat the arm movement and again rise on the toes. There is again a transference of angular momentum. (Here, in the first instance, a couple is derived from equal and opposite horizontally-directed forces exerted through the feet; in the second instance, these forces arise at the ball and heel of the one foot.)

[1] E. F. Housden, 'Mechanics applied to discus throwing', *Discobolus*, The Discus Circle Magazine, England, No. 8 (December 1959).

In a third experiment, stand with only the ball of the left foot in contact with the ground and repeat the arm movement. There will be no transference; (indeed, if the foot rests on a smooth surface, it will rotate towards the arm, in reaction, together with other parts of the body). From this, Housden concludes that a (right-handed) discus thrower *is unable to increase his angular momentum from the moment his right foot leaves the ground in the back of the circle until the instant his left foot lands in the front of the circle, and both feet are on the ground again.*

Certainly, a thrower can exert his greatest forces when both feet are firmly in contact with the ground (Fig. 183*h–k*). In the shot and javelin events in particular, however, effective contact by the rear leg is broken once it has completed its drive, and contact with the ground is maintained only by the leading foot (Fig. 192 and 193). It is important to consider the timing of the breaking of this rear leg contact in relation to the movement of the arm, to see how continued maximum horizontal force can be applied to the missile.

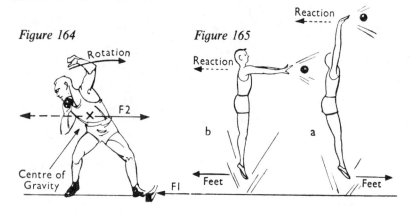

Figure 164

Figure 165

Taking shot putting as an example; when the front foot comes to the ground (Fig. 164) it loses speed. The horizontal force exerted by the ground has then a two-fold effect: it causes both athlete and shot to rotate about this foot, and reduces the forward speed of the Centre of Gravity common to athlete and shot. This is illustrated diagrammatically in Fig. 164, where the continuous straight lines show the couple causing rotation, and the dotted line represents the retarding force. (It should be noted that the two equal and opposite forces, F2, which balance and, consequently, do not affect the movement of the athlete, are used to clarify the illustration.) (See page 68.)

This sudden checking force causes an instantaneous change in speed at each point of the putter's body except one—below which all parts are slowed down, while all parts above this point are speeded up. It is important to realise that when the hand exerts a force on the missile, either above or below this special point, the reaction tends to move the feet forwards or backwards respectively. (When considering the movement of a rigid body, this point is known as the *centre of percussion* and its exact position can be calculated. (See Fig. 166.) As our shot putter is far from rigid, however, it can only be said that this point will be some distance above the Centre of Gravity.)

By way of illustrating this principle; when a man holds a shot with both hands at arms' length above his head and, after an upward jump, pushes the shot forward while he is off the ground, his feet should move forward (Fig. 165a); but when, under similar circumstances, he thrusts the shot forward at chest height, the reaction should then move them backwards (Fig. 165b). (By the same token, when the arm circling shown in Fig. 118 is executed at the level of the man's centre of percussion, his feet are unaffected and the movement invokes only the simplest of turntable reactions.)

In shot putting, correct technique requires the rear foot to be firmly in contact with the ground until the arm strikes (Fig. 192), permitting the ground to resist the tendency of the feet to move backwards. Once this rear leg has done its work and the arm strikes higher, however, the backward reaction on the hand tends to move the front foot forward and the ground reacts against it, allowing continued maximum force to be exerted.

Throwers who break contact with the ground before the missile leaves the hand may do so for lack of arm and shoulder strength; for a combination of the implement's inertia and accelerations developed by the legs and trunk may be too much for the arm—whose final action may have to be delayed until the accelerations have been reduced.

Or, again, contact could be broken prematurely to reduce the athlete's forward motion or to achieve greater height at the release. Or the feet may be too close together or otherwise incorrectly positioned. Or the arm could be striking too horizontally. (See also pages 34 and 239.) On the other hand, a Russian view[1] of discus throwing is that coaches deal

[1] USSR Higher Scientific Research Institute of Physical Culture, 1970, 'Final effort technique in the discus throw', reprinted in the *Yessis Review of Soviet Physical Education and Sports*, Vol. 5, No. 4 (December 1970).

with men, not machines; that athletes strong in the oblique musculature of the chest and abdomen, but relatively weak in the legs, should release with both feet in contact; whereas those whose legs possess a high speed-strength quality will *naturally*—and from a position where the legs are somewhat closer together—jump at this stage, releasing with both feet off the ground.

The difficulty of co-ordinating vertical and angular summations in discus throwing in particular has been mentioned (page 36)—a difficulty increased by the considerable moment of inertia of discus and arm about the body's longitudinal axis; the thrower breaks contact early because leg and trunk extensions are faster than the unwinding of hips, trunk, shoulders and arm. Clearly, keeping contact with the ground can be justified only if it adds to the total impulse, and circumstances will vary between throwers. Unacceptable, however, would be a premature 'jumping round' on delivery due to lack of strength, bad footwork, poor co-ordination, etc.

Maximum release speed in throwing (particularly in the shot, discus and javelin events) is influenced by the 'hinged moment' principle (see page 93), whereby, on attaining maximum, controlled (i.e. 'critical') speed at the end of the preliminary run-up, glide or turns, the front foot is checked (Figs. 191, 192, 193).

As we have seen, the checking force at the foot is one of two equal parallel forces acting in opposite directions, producing a couple—a forward rotation, a 'hinged moment'. This checking force also reduces the forward speed of the Centre of Gravity common to thrower and missile.

As the speed of a point on a turning body is directly proportional to its distance from the axis (which, in this case, is the athlete's front foot) the throwing shoulder will now possess more speed than the Centre of Gravity, but whether or not it is greater than the thrower's original linear speed depends upon the extent to which the Centre of Gravity slowed down. This, in turn, depends primarily upon the horizontal distance between the Centre of Gravity and the front foot as the latter comes to rest.

In javelin throwing, where this foot is far in advance of the Centre of Gravity (Fig. 193e), most—if not all—parts of the athlete lose speed at this instant. In so far as there is rotation about the foot, all parts of his body above the Centre of Gravity may move faster but not as fast, perhaps, as his linear speed immediately beforehand.

Such a sacrifice is still worth while to the javelin thrower, however;

indeed, it *has* to be made in good throwing. The front foot must be stretched well ahead of the body in order to provide an effective throwing position and, in view of the thrower's forward speed, to give sufficient *time* for the movements of throwing. The writer has seen no mathematical evidence to show that a javelin thrower's upper body improves its linear speed as a result of the front foot coming to the ground, but if that speed is retained, or is only slightly reduced, while the athlete adds his powerful throwing movements, it is obviously of great advantage, subsequently, to the speed of delivery (see also page 242).

In the shot and discus events, however, where (in comparison with the javelin thrower) at this instant the front foot is not excessively in advance of the Centre of Gravity (and where, therefore, there is less checking of forward speed), it seems very likely that there *is* a point which corresponds to a centre of percussion, (Fig. 166), with parts of the body above it speeded up; but this point will be changing constantly with changes in body position.

When the base of a rod (i.e. a thin, rigid, uniform rectilinear mass), moving horizontally in a vertical position, is brought to rest the speed of its Centre of Gravity drops by a quarter. If B is twice as far from A as the Centre of Gravity, it will move twice as fast as the Centre of Gravity; so the speed of B is improved by 50 per cent at the instant of checking. The centre of percussion in such a mass is always two-thirds AB from A. In a rigid non-uniform mass, however, the problem is much more difficult.

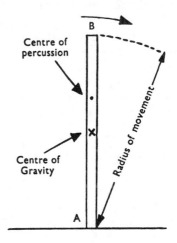

Figure 166

In throwing, the force exerted is to some extent dependent upon the athlete's mass. In discus throwing, for example, as the arm strikes (Fig. 190*e*–*h*) the tendency is for the rest of the athlete's body (especially the throwing shoulder) to move downward and backward in reaction, so reducing the effective force and time/range over which force can be applied.

In good throwing, the reaction to the vertical component of the arm's movement will be counteracted by the up-thrust of the ground, regardless of the thrower's weight; but the reaction to the horizontal component will cause the upper-body of a comparatively light athlete to move backward more than a heavier thrower, other things being equal. The heavier man can therefore exert more effective force over greater distance.

It follows that an athlete who breaks contact with the ground prematurely in shot putting will in all probability find the error more costly than when throwing a discus since, obviously, the reduction in delivery impulse involves the ratio of missile weight to body weight; i.e. the mass of the missile times *its* speed, equals the athlete's mass times *his* speed in an opposite direction. (See pages 22, 32, 204.) For this reason it has been argued that the reduction in delivery impulse due to breaking ground contact shortly before the discus leaves the hand is little more quantitatively significant than a gun's recoil as a shell is launched.

Sheer mass is also of value in increasing the radius of movement in discus and (particularly) hammer throwing, increasing the missile's speed; for the balancing of the moments of weight and centrifugal force (previously referred to on page 81) will be maintained by a closer approach of a massive athlete's body to an axis passing through his feet than in the case of a lighter athlete (compare Fig. 167a with b).

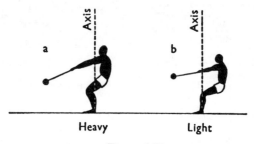

Figure 167

It can be shown, however, that an increase in mass for the purpose of increasing the missile's radius gives diminishing returns—a point is soon reached where minute gains in this regard are offset by other factors, e.g. lack of speed or agility.

Whitney[1] has suggested the importance of body mass in practical, day-to-day lifting. When this happens from a standing position, using

---

[1] R. J. Whitney, 'The strength of the lifting action in man', *Ergonomics*, Vol. 1, No. 2 (February 1958), page 101.

two hands, the feet are usually behind the frontal plane in which the lifting operation is attempted—*when the limiting factor is the maximum counter-balancing moment of the subject's weight, not his strength.*

When a steady[1] lifting force is applied, or in holding a load once it has been raised, the effort is proportional to body-weight, the moment of which about the feet then balances the opposing moment of the load (see Couples, pages 68–9). These moments can be changed by shifting the pivot between the ankles and balls of the feet; i.e. by extension or flexion of the feet about the ankles.

Strength becomes the limiting factor *only* when the toes fall in front of a frontal plane which includes the grasping axis—a situation attained, or closely approached, only in competitive weight lifting.

Angle of release

If a thrower is to obtain maximum distance, it will not be sufficient to give the missile maximum release speed; it must also be thrown at an appropriate angle.

When points of release and landing are level (and aerodynamic factors may be ignored) the optimum angle for the projection of a missile, regardless of its speed is one of 45 deg. (see page 16). In this case, vertical and horizontal component velocities are equal, and the missile also lands at a 45 deg. angle. (Here, distance is as the square of the velocity; so, for example, if the velocity increases by 10 per cent (from, say, 100 to 110 units) the distance will be increased by 21 per cent (from 100 to 121 units).)

It should be noted that the weight of a missile reduces the *resultant* vertically upward thrust delivered to it. To release, e.g. a shot at this angle, therefore, a thrower must exert a force *vertically* greater by the weight of the shot than the *horizontal* force.

However, in all four throwing events in field athletics the implement is thrown from a point above the ground and this affects the release angle. Then the optimum angle depends upon height and velocity of projection. In the shot and hammer events (where aerodynamic factors are of no account) the *optimum* release angle will be less than 45 deg. Theoretically, a missile thrown at this angle will land at an angle with the horizontal equal to the angle its release direction makes with the vertical. For example, a shot released at 41 deg. 40 min. will land at 48 deg 20 min. (Fig. 168) (released 7 ft (2.13 m) above the ground, at a velocity of 41.3 f.p.s.

---

[1] Whitney accepts a jerk mechanism as a natural method of *initiating* a lifting operation.

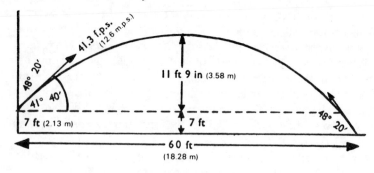

Figure 168

(12.6 m.p.s.) for a distance of 60 ft (18.28 m) measured horizontally from the point of release.)

Fig. 169 shows diagrammatically how, with just enough speed to attain a given distance from a specified height, the ideal angle can be found by bisecting the angle between a vertical line drawn through the thrower's hand at the instant of release, and a straight line joining this point and the point of landing. Fig. 15 shows that a low release speed requires a lowering of the release angle.

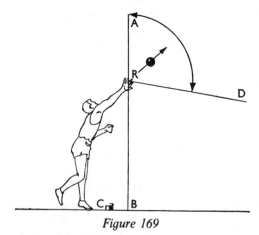

Figure 169

The optimum angles of projection for a put of 60 ft (18.28 m) (measured horizontally from the point of release to the point of landing, i.e. not allowing for the distance between the inside edge of the stop-board and the hand (approximately 1 ft, 0.3 m)), from release heights of

Height of Release in ft	Angle of Projection with horizontal (deg.)	Release Speed f.p.s.	Put in ft	in
8	45	44	67	8
		43	64	11
		42	62	2
8	40	44	68	0
		43	65	3
		42	62	7
8	35	44	66	7
		43	64	0
		42	61	5
8	30	44	63	9
		43	61	4
		42	58	11
7	45	44	66	10
		43	64	1
		42	61	5
7	40	44	67	0
		43	64	4
		42	61	8
7	35	44	65	6
		43	62	11
		42	60	4
7	30	44	62	7
		43	60	1
		42	57	9
6.5	45	44	66	5
		43	63	8
		42	60	11
6.5	40	44	66	7
		43	63	10
		42	61	2
6.5	35	44	65	0
		43	62	5
		42	59	10
6.5	30	44	61	11
		43	59	6
		42	57	1

Height of Release (metres)	Angle of Projection with horizontal (deg.)	Release Speed m.p.s.	Put in metres
2.44	45	14.3	23.08
		14.0	22.20
		13.7	20.76
2.44	40	14.3	23.15
		14.0	22.26
		13.7	21.45
2.44	35	14.3	22.63
		14.0	21.83
		13.7	20.99
2.44	30	14.3	21.63
		14.0	20.85
		13.7	20.08
2.13	45	14.3	22.82
		14.0	21.94
		13.7	21.09
2.13	40	14.3	22.86
		14.0	21.97
		13.7	21.16
2.13	35	14.3	22.29
		14.0	21.49
		13.7	20.65
2.13	30	14.3	21.24
		14.0	20.46
		13.7	19.70
1.98	45	14.3	22.69
		14.0	21.82
		13.7	20.96
1.98	40	14.3	22.70
		14.0	21.82
		13.7	21.02
1.98	35	14.3	22.12
		14.0	21.32
		13.7	20.48
1.98	30	14.3	21.05
		14.0	20.27
		13.7	19.51

8 ft, 7 ft and 6½ ft (2.44 m, 2.13 m and 1.98 m), will be 41 deg. 12 min., 41 deg. 40 min. and 41 deg. 54 min. respectively.

In hammer throwing the missile is released so close to the ground relative to the distance thrown that, for all practical purposes, 45 deg. can be assumed the proper angle of delivery. More accurately, however, its optimum angle is always slightly *less* than 45 deg. because it is released about 5 ft (1.5 m) above the ground. The precise angle can be calculated

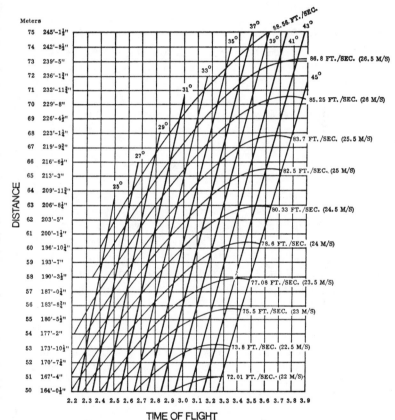

Figure 170

Relationship between distance thrown, time of flight, velocity and release angle.
After Fig. 2 of *Hammer Throwing*, Howard Payne, Amateur Athletic Association, England, 1969; and Toni Nett's graph in his *Die Technique beim Stop and Wurf*.

by first measuring the *distance thrown* and *time of flight* (to 0.1 sec) before referring to the graph (Fig. 170) on page 213.

If, for example, a throw of 60 m (196 ft 10¼ in) takes 3 sec, optimum conditions will not have been achieved. At the point where the vertical and horizontal lines (representing time and distance, respectively) meet, the sloping 35 deg. release-angle line and the 80.33 ft/sec (24.5 m.p.s.) release speed-curve also intersect. If the missile is released at this speed, yet at an angle of 43 deg. (follow the *curve* upward and to the right) it will reach 63 metres (206 ft 8¼ in.)

The forces exerted in throwing give greater release speed when they are directed nearer to the horizontal. In fact, a study of the dynamics of shot putting reveals that within certain limits speed of release is more important to an athlete than the use of an optimum angle.

In theory, a shot projected 60 ft (18.28 m) from a point 7 ft (2.13 m) above the ground must rise to a height of 18 ft 9 in (5.71 m) (Fig. 166). Yet most 60 ft (18 m) shot putters do not put so high and so do not release the shot at such optimum angles. It could be said, of course that by contriving to improve their elevation they could put even farther—and this could well be true of some. It seems likely, however, that at such levels of performance the factors responsible for maximum release speed conflict with those that give an optimum angle of delivery.

The tables on pages 211–2 illustrate the importance of release speed in these throwing events. The distances (to which, as we have seen, approximately 1 ft (0.3 m) should be added) have been estimated on the basis of three release heights (6½ ft, 7 ft and 8 ft, 1.98 m, 2.13 m and 2.44 m) and four angles (30 deg., 35 deg., 40 deg. and 45 deg.). They are based upon the facts of dynamics, irrespective of the launching mechanism, human or otherwise. Air resistance has been ignored. (The metric table, which caters for distances up to 23.15 m (75 ft 11½ in.) is *not* a direct conversion of the other.)

These figures, calculated to illustrate a point developed by Professor A. C. Aitken (University of Edinburgh), have been obtained from the following expression for the length of the put:

$$\frac{v^2 \sin 2\alpha}{64}\left\{1 + \sqrt{1 + \frac{64h}{v^2 \sin^2 \alpha}}\right\} \text{ft}$$

or

$$\frac{v^2 \sin 2\alpha}{19.6}\left\{1 + \sqrt{1 + \frac{19.6h}{v^2 \sin \alpha}}\right\} \text{m}$$

where v = release speed, α = angle of projection and h = height of release. The tables show that:

(i) 40 deg. is nearer the optimum angle than 45;

(ii) from 35 deg. upward comparatively little increase is made in putting, for the same velocity;

(iii) an increase in height of release from 6.5–7 ft (1.98–2.13 m) gives only an additional 5–8 in. (13–20 cm) in distance; from 7–8 ft (2.13–2.44 m) only 9–15 in. (26–38 cm);

(iv) relative increases in velocity very decidedly increase distance. For example, putting from a height of 7 ft (2.13 m) at an angle of 35 deg. at 42 ft.p.s. (12.80 m.p.s.), an athlete attains 60 ft 4 in. (18.39 m), but gains only 1 ft 4 in. (41 cm) by increasing his angle by 5 deg.; whereas, by returning to an angle of 35 deg. and increasing his speed by only 1 ft.p.s. (0.30 m.p.s.) he gains 2 ft 7 in. (78 cm) and as much as 5 ft 2 in. (1.575 m) for an increase of 2 ft.p.s. (0.61 m.p.s.).

The proper use of the strong leg and trunk muscles in throwing plays a vital part not only in releasing the missile at maximum speed, but also in projecting it at a correct angle; in particular, where the angle is too low, leg and trunk action—and not the arm or arms—is usually at fault.

In fact the emphasis on 'lifting' the missile with the legs and trunk during the actual throwing movements should be considerable, especially where comparatively great horizontal speed has first been developed in the run-up or movement across the circle; for the angle of projection will be the product of the preliminary and throwing movements (Fig. 171).

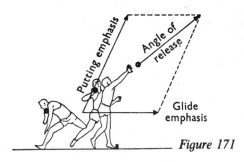

Figure 171

Aerodynamic factors

In discus and javelin throwing, distance depends upon speed, height and angle of release, as with the shot and hammer events, but by virtue of their size and shape, aerodynamic forces also influence the flight of discoi and javelins. These missiles do not describe simple parabolic curves.

As yet, the aerodynamics of discus and javelin throwing have not been worked out in every detail, for many unknown factors and variables (not the least variable of which is the thrower himself!) are involved. What follows is therefore no more than an outline of basic, relevant aerodynamic principles, with some comment as to their significance in these events.

General principles. In moving through the air a discus or javelin drives part of that air to the side and pushes some in front of it. This requires work and, therefore a reduction in kinetic energy and, therefore, speed. The air's resistance depends upon the shape and size of the missile; generally, the thinner and sharper it is at the front, the smaller is the resistance—which can be further reduced if its cross-section narrows gradually towards the rear, giving a 'streamlined' effect.

In front of the missile, therefore, there is a region of increased air pressure, and in its path another region where the air whirls irregularly, causing diminished pressure (Fig. 172). The kinetic energy of turbulent air movement in the wake of a discus or javelin accounts for much of the work needed to move it through the air; but the better the streamlining, the smaller will be this air disturbance. (Fig. 173; both bodies (*a* and *b*) present the same effective cross-section to the on-coming air yet, because of its streamlining, object *b* has 1/25 the specific resistance of *a*.)

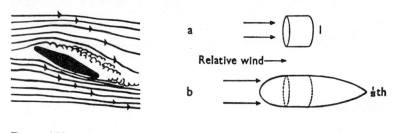

Figure 172   *Figure 173*

Air resistance is also dependent upon the speed of the discus or javelin, and is proportional to the square of the velocity.

When a missile is inclined at an angle to the wind (Fig. 174) the resultant of the forces exerted upon it by the air can then be resolved into vertical (*lift*) and horizontal (*drag*) components. The ratio between lift and drag depends upon the *angle of attack*, i.e. the acute angle between the plane of the discus or javelin and the direction of the relative wind (Fig. 175). Even small variations of this angle can sometimes produce abrupt alterations in the lift/drag ratio.

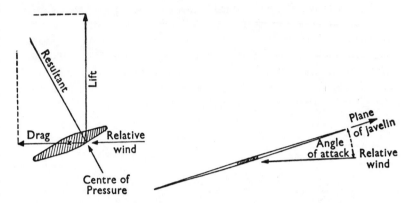

Figure 174   *Figure 175*

The term *relative wind* refers to the movement of the air in relation to the missile. *All motion is relative*; a discus or javelin can be suspended in an air-tunnel with the air flowing past, or it can be moving through still air. A following wind can therefore reduce the speed of the relative wind (lessening lift and drag) and a headwind can increase it (but must not be too strong to be of benefit in these two events).

A relative wind will not always directly oppose the flight-path of the missile's Centre of Gravity, however; usually, in throwing, air currents are continuously varying in both strength and direction. Nor, always, do the missile's flight-path and its plane coincide, an angle between being called the *angle of incidence*; this can be positive (i.e. above the angle of the flight path) or negative (i.e. below that angle) (Fig. 176). (In still air, a

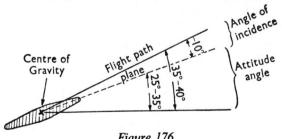

Figure 176

missile's angle of incidence and angle of attack coincide.) The angle between the plane of the missile and the horizontal is called the *attitude angle* (Fig. 176).

Fig. 177 shows diagrammatically how the sizes of the various lifting forces acting on a discus are dependent upon the angle of attack. When the angle is zero (Fig. 177*a*) the upward forces on the lower surface act only near its leading edge; but as the angle increases (Fig. 177*b*) these forces also increase, both above and below the discus. When the angle is of a certain size, however, air turbulence forms along the trailing edge and grows markedly with a further increase in angle.

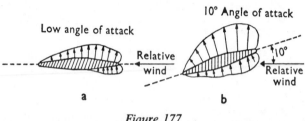

Figure 177

The shape of the discus or javelin and the angle it makes with the direction of the relative wind cause the speed of the air flowing over the missile's upper surface to be greater than that underneath. As a result, there is a diminished air pressure above the missile and the upward forces acting on it are greater than the downward forces (Figs 172 and 177*b*).

All the forces of the air acting on a discus or javelin may be added together to form a resultant (see page 37) which acts at a point called the *centre of pressure* (Fig. 174). This changes position with a change in the angle of attack; as this angle increases, the centre of pressure moves forward and the resultant force increases. There is a limit to which the angle of attack can be increased to advantage, and if that limit is exceeded turbulence behind the missile disturbs the smooth flow of air over its upper surface; the upward force (lift) almost disappears, drag increases and the missile stalls. This limiting angle is called the *stalling angle*.

The lifting force acting on a discus or javelin in flight therefore depends upon:

(i) its shape (which influences the nature of the air-flow past its upper and lower surfaces);

(ii) the angle of attack (within limits, the greater angle produces the greater lift);

(iii) the surface area (the greater the area, the bigger the total lifting force);

(iv) the square of the air speed (for example, lift is four times greater when a javelin is released at 50 m.p.h. (80.45 km.p.h.) than at 25 m.p.h. (40.225 km.p.h.));

(v) air density (the greater the density, the greater the lift).

The flight of the discus. A discus (which experts think a comparatively poor aerodynamic design) 'performs most efficiently as an air-foil between speeds of 69.8 and 80 feet per second' (or 21.27 and 24.38 m.p.s.) (Ganslen[1]), and its spin, in good throwing, provides some gyroscopic stability in flight, keeping the lift/drag ratio relatively constant.

Figure 178

For all its gyroscopic benefit, however, spin itself tends to increase the angle of attack (Housden[2])—a paradox which, perhaps again, shows how, in the analysis of athletic movement, advantages must be weighed against disadvantages. To illustrate: when a discus rotates in a clockwise direction (seen from above, Fig. 178) its left side meets the air at a greater speed than its right side; the former spins into the air, while the latter moves away from it. Therefore the upward force exerted by the air on the left side is greater and the centre of pressure is to the left. There is therefore a tendency for the discus to turn about the axis XOX' (Fig. 178) (clockwise, as seen from X).

This does not happen, however, because of its spin. Assuming an upward pressure exerted somewhere on OY (Fig. 178), this turns the discus about the axis OY (clockwise, as seen from Y); for each point on the missile is raised as it moves across OX and continues to rise until it reaches OX' (Fig. 178); every point on the discus is higher at X' than at X and, as a result, its front edge tilts upwards. Conversely, a downward force exerted at the centre of pressure will lower this front edge.

[1] R. V. Ganslen, *Aerodynamic Factors which Influence Discus Flight* (Research Report, College of Arts and Sciences, University of Arkansas, U.S.A., May 1958).

[2] E. F. Housden, 'Mechanics applied to discus throwing', *Discobolus*, The Discus Circle Magazine, England, No. 8 (December 1959).

The following figures (the S.I. tables *are* a direct conversion from the original American tables) show estimated distances a discus can be thrown for given initial speeds, using combinations of projection and attitude angles (Cooper, Dalzell and Silverman[1] (Purdue University) from wind-tunnel data supplied by Ganslen). Here it has been assumed that spin stabilises a discus, in good throwing, to the point of maintaining a constant attitude angle (the authors claiming that motion picture analysis indicates no appreciable change in this angle throughout flight).

The following conclusions may be drawn from these tables.

TABLE 1

INITIAL VELOCITY 70 f.p.s.

		Projection angle						
	15°	20°	25°	30°	35°	40°	45°	50°
10°	104	120	130	138	144	146	144	133
15°	110	124	136	144	150	150	148	136
20°	114	128	142	150	152	154	152	140
25°	114	128	144	150	156	154	152	144
30°	114	128	142	152	156	156	152	148
35°	112	128	140	148	154	154	152	144
40°	106	124	136	146	150	152	152	144
45°	104	120	134	142	146	146	146	140
50°	98	116	128	136	142	142	142	136

(Distances in feet)

INITIAL VELOCITY 21.34 m/s

		Projection angle						
	15°	20°	25°	30°	35°	40°	45°	50°
10°	31.70	36.58	39.62	42.06	43.89	44.50	43.89	40.54
15°	33.53	37.80	41.45	43.89	45.72	45.72	45.11	41.45
20°	34.75	39.01	43.28	45.72	46.33	46.94	46.33	42.67
25°	34.75	39.01	43.89	45.72	47.55	46.94	46.33	43.89
30°	34.75	39.01	43.28	46.33	47.55	47.55	46.33	45.11
35°	34.14	39.01	42.67	45.11	46.94	46.94	46.33	43.89
40°	32.31	37.80	41.45	44.50	45.72	46.33	46.33	43.89
45°	31.70	36.58	40.84	43.28	44.50	44.50	44.50	42.69
50°	29.87	35.36	39.01	41.45	43.28	43.28	43.28	41.45

(Distances in metres)

Attitude Angle (row axis label for both tables)

[1] L. Cooper D. Dalzell and E. Silverman, *Flight of the Discus* (Division of Engineering Science, Purdue University, Indiana, U.S.A., (May 1959).

(1) *Speed of release is the factor of greatest importance*, as emphasised previously (see pages 211–2, Shot Tables). A small increase in speed in discus throwing gives a comparatively larger increase in distance, however, because the lift on the missile is proportional to the square of its speed.

(2) *For a given speed, the most important variable is the angle of projection.* 150 to 200 ft (46 to 70 m) throwers should project at 35 deg. to 40 deg.; throwers of lesser ability should increase the angle slightly, but never above 45 deg. (With today's world-class velocities, the angle can be reduced to about 32 deg.)

TABLE 2

INITIAL VELOCITY 80 f.p.s.

Attitude Angle	Projection angle 15°	20°	25°	30°	35°	40°	45°	50°
10°	132	152	170	178	186	186	182	172
15°	148	164	180	188	194	194	186	174
20°	152	172	188	196	200	198	194	178
25°	154	174	190	200	204	202	198	184
30°	154	170	188	198	204	204	198	186
35°	150	168	184	192	200	202	196	184
40°	144	162	176	186	196	198	190	182
45°	134	150	172	180	186	190	184	180
50°	128	148	166	176	180	180	176	172

(Distances in feet)

INITIAL VELOCITY 24.38 m/s

Attitude Angle	Projection angle 15°	20°	25°	30°	35°	40°	45°	50°
10°	40.23	46.33	52.43	54.25	56.69	56.69	55.47	52.43
15°	45.11	49.99	54.86	57.30	59.13	59.15	56.69	53.04
20°	46.33	53.04	57.30	59.74	60.96	60.35	59.15	54.25
25°	46.94	52.43	57.91	60.96	62.18	61.57	60.35	56.08
30°	46.94	51.82	57.30	60.35	62.18	62.18	60.35	56.69
35°	45.72	51.21	56.08	58.52	60.96	61.57	59.74	56.08
40°	43.89	49.38	53.64	56.69	59.74	60.35	57.91	55.47
45°	40.84	45.72	53.04	54.86	56.69	57.91	56.08	54.86
50°	39.01	45.11	50.60	53.64	54.86	54.86	53.64	52.43

(Distances in metres)

(3) *The attitude angle should be between 25 deg, and 35 deg.* At the instant of release, therefore, there should be a negative angle of incidence of approximately 5 deg. to 10 deg. Although, at such an angle, air pressure will tend to depress the front edge of the discus, the ascending half of its flight-path automatically reduces the angle (Fig. 179). If the latter tendency is the greater, then the missile moves gradually into alignment with the tangent to the path of its Centre of Gravity—presenting a considerable surface-area to the ground during the descending half of the flight, benefiting by the cushioning effect of the air beneath and, therefore, gaining distance through a gliding motion (Fig. 179).

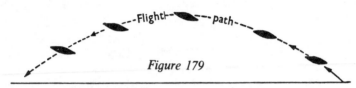

Figure 179

On the other hand, a positive angle of incidence upon release must increase as the discus moves forward and its flight-path curves towards the ground (Fig. 180). In addition, air pressure increases this angle, leading to a progressively stronger resistance to forward motion and, eventually, stalling. (The stalling angle for a discus is now said to be approximately 45 deg.)

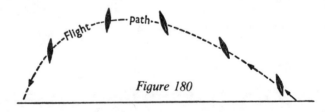

Figure 180

The greater the speed of the discus upon release, and the stronger the opposing wind, the smaller should be the attitude angle as the discus leaves the hand, to avail the throw of a more favourable lift/drag ratio. Practical experience proves that a discus can be thrown farthest into a wind blowing from front-right (right-handed athlete), and Pharaoh[1]

---

[1] M. Pharaoh, 'Observations on discus throwing' *A.A.A. Coaching Newsletter*, Amateur Athletic Association, England, No. 4 (April 1957), page 9.

(Great Britain; 4th, Discus, 1956 Olympic Games) maintained that the difference between throwing directly *into* a wind, and *with* that same wind, varied—for him—from about 5 ft (1.52 m) for a wind-speed of 7 m.p.h. (11.26 km.p.h.) to approximately 15 ft (4.57 m) at 20 m.p.h. (32.18 km.p.h.), the greater distance being thrown into the wind. Stronger headwinds reduce stability in flight and therefore shorten the distance.

Flight of the javelin. From 1955 to 1961 javelin throwing world records rose primarily through the use of implements of improved aerodynamic design, giving an increased stability and a better lift/drag ratio in flight. They were considered to add as much as 25 ft (7.62 m) to a good throw. These 'glider' javelins as they came to be called, were made in several different diameters to suit a thrower's ability and varying throwing conditions; they possessed a lighter spearhead, a more evenly-distributed surface-area and tapered less towards the tail than previously.

The year 1961 saw the end of this era of javelin throwing, however, because the International Amateur Athletic Federation further revised its specifications so as to limit these aerodynamic features and enforce a stricter uniformity as to the type of javelin used throughout the world. The javelin now permitted has a reduced diameter (a maximum of 30 mm as against the previous 35 mm) and its angle of taper and length of point are also specified. However, the regulations still permit some variation, for the javelin-diameter can vary from 25 mm to 30 mm and its Centre of Gravity can be between 90 cm and 110 cm from the point. Compared with the javelins used prior to 1955, in fact, the present implement remains 'aerodynamic'. There is still considerable disagreement, even among experts, as to the behaviour of an aerodynamic javelin in flight.

A Russian opinion, that of V. L. Kuznetsov,[1] assesses the optimum angle of release for the modern javelin at 28 deg. to 30 deg., ideally with the shaft at this instant in alignment with the tangent to the path of its Centre of Gravity (i.e. with a zero angle of incidence). When this improved javelin is released at much greater angles (e.g. at approximately 45 deg., as necessary in throwing the 'old' design) the tendency is to give it too great an angle of attack. It then rises and falls abruptly, for its centre of pressure is too far in front of its Centre of

[1] V. L. Kuznetsov, 'Mastery of Javelin Throwing Technique', *Track Technique*, U.S.A., No. 2, December 1960, (*Track and Field News*), page 46.

Gravity, creating backward rotation and stalling (Fig. 181*a*). (These two centres and the distance between them then create a couple whose turning effect is proportional to that distance (i.e. the arm of the couple).)

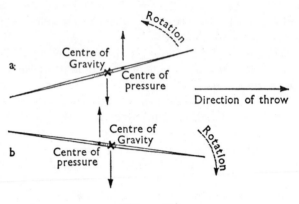

Figure 181

Some experts are of the opinion that the optimum release-angle of these aerodynamic javelins is nearer 40 deg., with an angle of incidence at this instant of approximately − 10 deg.; but they admit that an athlete must be very skilful to use it without creating too great an angle of attack, for in attempting to produce more 'lift' in the delivery, the tendency is to raise the head of the javelin. It is easier to control this angle when the delivery is more horizontal, and most athletes prefer to 'play safe' in this way.

In an aerodynamically well-designed object the centre of pressure remains comparatively stable in flight; the relatively even distribution of surface-area of the modern javelin is said to reduce the motion of its centre of pressure as it travels through the air. But, for best results, it must still meander. The desired flight is one in which the Centres of Pressure and Gravity approximately coincide throughout the early stages. As the flight proceeds, and the angle of incidence increases, the Centre of Pressure moves back and, just prior to landing, causes the point to drop rapidly into the required landing attitude. Throwers can select javelins according to their distance potential, a slower rotation of the javelin being required for a longer throw.

In the process of releasing a javelin a thrower automatically imparts spin about its long axis—the result of an outward rotation of his elbow and the sequence with which his fingers break contact during delivery (Fig. 182). This spin (clockwise, seen from behind, in the case of a right-handed thrower) can possibly give some gyroscopic stability in flight, provided it is of sufficient intensity. However, whereas some experts speak in terms of eight to thirty revolutions per second in a good throw, and regard this spin as important, others deny that much spin is ever developed or has any significance. (The ancient Greeks obviously thought it important; for they bound their lighter, elderwood, javelins with a leather thong—an *amentum*—looped over the first finger, or first two fingers, to impart this spin.)

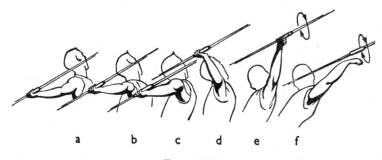

a   b   c   d   e   f

Figure 182

To summarise:

(1) *Again, speed of release is the factor of greatest importance* as in all other throwing events, and lift on the javelin is proportional to the square of its speed (as with the discus). Within limits, thinner javelins can be selected and used to reduce the drag factor; but, generally, javelins with the largest planiform area (i.e. their area seen from above or below) generate the greatest lift. Lift increases with an increase in the angle of attack up to 45 deg.; lift equals drag at 42–46 deg., "while the maximal lift-drag ratio is found at an angle of attack between 10–16 deg." (still air).[1]

(2) *The optimum angle of release for the 'aerodynamic' javelins* is seldom above 35 deg. and, generally, the angle should decrease with an increase in release velocity.

[1] J. Terauds, 'Optimum Angle of Release for the Competitive Javelin, as determined by its Aerodynamic and Ballistic Characteristics' (Proceedings of the 4th International Seminar of Biomechanics: *Biomechanics IV*, University Park Press, Baltimore, U.S.A., 1974).

(3) *The attitude angle of the 'aerodynamic' javelin* at release should possibly be a little less than the release angle; the vital thing here is not to present too great an angle of attack to the relative wind. Then, in a good throw, the missile will reduce its angle to the horizontal slightly and maintain that angle until it begins to fall, when it again rotates forward to land almost flat, point first.

(4) *The gliding qualities of the 'aerodynamic' javelin* are especially valuable in the gaining of distance during the second half of flight.

Throwing techniques

Hammer. Technique, in good hammer throwing (Fig. 183), is designed to release the missile at the greatest possible speed at an optimum angle slightly below 45 deg. from a circle 7 ft (2.13 m) in diameter, so that it lands within the prescribed throwing area.

Hammer speed and a rotational pattern are established during (usually two) preliminary swings before the hammer's speed is markedly increased and its plane of motion is steepened progressively during (usually three) turns (Fig. 183 shows only the second and third of these, with a delivery).

The system of man and hammer rotates about an axis passing through the thrower's contact with the ground (Fig. 86). The good thrower works his way across the circle diameter by pivoting alternately on the heel and ball of his left foot (Fig. 183*a*–*h*) (right-handed thrower). Thus, in the course of making these turns, he moves the common axis from the rear to the front of the circle. Finally, he imparts even greater speed to the hammer-head by lifting it powerfully with his legs and trunk (Fig. 183*i*–*l*).

As, in any rotation, a hammer's linear speed will be directly proportional to its distance from the common axis (see pages 73 and 88), in good throwing relaxed arms are used merely as a prolongation of the wire shaft, fully extended in the turns and final delivery—pulled out by centrifugal force (Fig. 183). Its range can also be improved by exerting a centripetal force on it through a *shifting backwards of the hips* (Fig. 184*a*) as distinct from leaning the upper body—which shortens the hammer's radius (Fig. 184*b*).

From Newton's First Law (see page 18) it follows that the hammer would move in a straight path but for the force of gravity and a centripetal (i.e. pulling-in) force exerted by the athlete—a force proportional to the square of the missile's linear speed. If, for example,

a   a1   b   c   c1

d   d1   e   f

g   h   i1

J   j1   k   l   l1 *Figure 183*

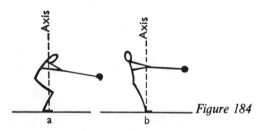

Figure 184

the hammer's speed is doubled, the thrower must then exert four times the centripetal force, automatically increasing an equal but opposite centrifugal (i.e. pulling-out) force. (See pages 47–9).

The athlete accelerates the hammer by exerting horizontal and vertical components of force.

(1) *Horizontally*, he is able to apply force only because of the friction between his feet and the ground—through the reactions of the ground to the forces exerted by his feet. This friction also enables the thrower to accelerate the hammer in this plane through either a linear or flail-like (i.e. circular) movement of the common axis (e.g. the rotational acceleration of a conker on a string in this plane is made possible by moving such an axis, Fig. 185).

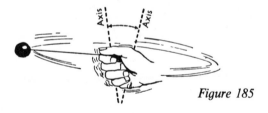

Figure 185

Fig. 186 shows how, in turning, the speed of the hammer-head can be increased horizontally as a result of the thrower's exerting a centripetal force; as, in good throwing, the arms are extended throughout, such a force can be applied only by moving the common axis (Fig. 186). In fact, its movement across the circle is essential to imparting the greatest possible centripetal impulse to the hammer-head, and to this end the weight of the thrower must be maintained over his pivoting leg throughout (for if this axis falls between the feet or over the trailing foot, progression across the circle is impaired).

Tangential acceleration is further improved when the thrower leads the hammer-head (Fig. 187). Here he obtains 'body torque' through

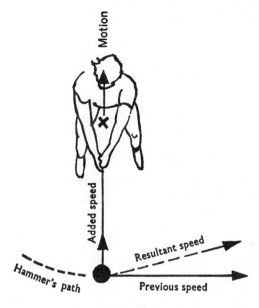

Figure 186

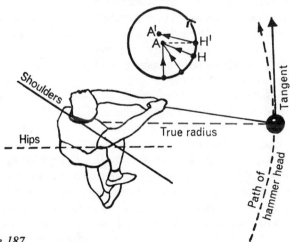

Figure 187

A plan view of a turning hammer thrower. When the *apparent* radius (i.e. a straight line from the thrower's left shoulder to the hammer-head) is at an angle to the true radius, the missile's speed is increased.

When the hammer's axis is moved from A to A', the direction of pull is changed to A'H' and now contains a horizontal component of force in the direction of the missile's motion.

leading markedly with his hips and legs, moving his feet 'fast and early' (Cullum[1]) in the turns. For by this means the thrower continuously moves the hammer's centre of motion *horizontally*, and in a direction parallel to that of the missile itself, urging the hammer forward while it continues to travel in a curved (though not circular) path. The play of the hips 'against' the shoulders fluctuates during a complete turn but whenever the wire shaft is not at right angles to the curve along which the hammer-head is moving (Fig. 187), the hammer will be accelerating and, correctly, the thrower will be 'maintaining contact' through his left arm (Cullum). (Note the reference to 'leading' the hammer-head here, as opposed to 'trailing' it. The latter, to a hammer thrower, indicates a bending of the right arm with a resulting shortening of hammer radius; whereas, to 'lead' the hammer indicates a trunk twist—infinitely preferable).

To re-emphasise: such methods of accelerating the hammer horizontally are possible only because of the friction between the thrower's feet and the ground, and this can attain its greatest value when both feet are in contact with the ground and the hammer-head is below the level of the shoulders. (Maximum friction, here, depends on the pressure between the feet and the ground (see page 59).)

This is particularly true of acceleration through 'body torque' (Fig. 187). In that phase of a turn where the thrower pivots on one foot (Fig. 183*a*), and with only its outside edge touching the ground, horizontal acceleration can therefore be only very small if, indeed, it is at all possible; for in such a position pressure between foot and ground has a minimum value.

(2) *Vertically*, the hammer can be accelerated upwards and downwards during each successive 360 deg. turn, and in good throwing this vertical acceleration increases progressively from turn to turn—and is of vital importance to the delivery (Fig. 183*h–k*).

(i) *Vertically upwards*. The hammer can be accelerated upwards as soon as the hammer-wire is inclined upwards to the vertical, and this acceleration would appear to attain its maximum value shortly after the hammer-head has passed its lowest point, i.e. off the right foot (right-handed athlete) (Figs. 37 and 183*d*1). Here, the force applied to the hammer-head is limited by that which the athlete can exert downwards through his feet (preferably both feet simultaneously) against the ground. Therefore, given the position from which to apply such a force, the limiting factors are the *strength* and *speed* of the athlete.

The direction of the reaction obtained from the ground will be upward with the hammer at its lowest point and will diminish gradually and change more to the horizontal as the hammer-head rises.

(ii) *Vertically downward*, acceleration is achieved by permitting the body weight to drop just before the hammer-head itself drops in its swings or turns. Here, therefore, the limiting factor to acceleration is the thrower's *weight*—which can be lowered with or without contact with the ground.

Fig. 188 illustrates how, with a steepening of the plane of hammer movement and a progressive increase in its linear speed from turn to turn, vertical means of acceleration become increasingly important and horizontal means comparatively less so.

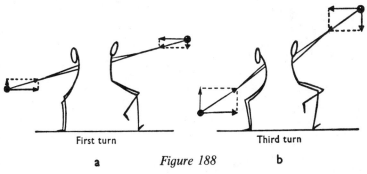

First turn   Third turn

a   *Figure 188*   b

Throwers often jump round on the last turn because the speed of the hammer is too great for their ability to advance their hips and feet in any other way or because they are off balance. However, by this means the hips are never so well advanced—relative to the shoulders and hammer-head—as in a suitably fast pivot on one foot; but for this, of course, the thrower needs tremendous speed and dexterity.

A final acceleration of the hammer can be achieved by simultaneously (a) *lifting* it into orbit while (b) exerting a centripetal force so as to *reduce its radius of motion*; for, assuming no change in the missile's angular momentum (the product of MVR), a reduction in R must be accompanied by an increase in V.[1] (Payne[2] has estimated a 2 per cent increase

---

[1] Because the hammer-athlete system is not isolated from external forces, in fact there can only be a *tendency* towards the conservation of angular momentum.

[2] H. Payne, *Hammer Throwing*, (Amateur Athletic Association, England, 1969), page 61.

in tangential velocity through as little as a 2 inch (5 cm) shortening of the hammer's radius.)

From a position where knees and hips are well flexed, and with the athlete 'leading' the hammer-head (Fig. 183*i*), both legs—and particularly the left leg—drive vertically and the head and trunk are arched back (Fig. 183*j–k*).

This violent change of posture not only lifts the hammer but, by raising the line of action of the athlete's centrifugal force about the feet, also causes a loss of balance away from the missile (Fig. 183*k*); but for this to increase the hammer's speed and to be as *prolonged* as possible, *the thrower must increase his own angular velocity about the common axis*; by accentuating the thrust from his left leg, he must make a conscious effort to accelerate his trunk and head around his left foot (Fig. 189) so as *continually* to shorten the missile's radius about an axis passing through that foot and a point somewhere between his arms (Fig. 183*j–k*).

Figure 189

Discus. If a discus is to be thrown a maximum distance it must be released with the greatest possible speed at an optimum angle—the latter being influenced quite considerably by the aerodynamic factors discussed already (see pages 215–7).

In the sense that both are rotational in character, some similarity exists between this event and hammer throwing. Yet, otherwise, they have little in common. For whereas the hammer is slung from a wire which can only transmit force along the direction in which the wire lies, the discus is thrown from an arm, and whenever the thrower's hand has a firm grasp on the implement there is little limitation to the direction in which that hand can exert force on the discus.

From a position at the rear of the 8 ft 2½ in. (2½ m) circle, and with his back to the direction of throw, the athlete executes several (usually no more than three) preliminary swinging movements, using his entire body—not the arm alone. These movements help to prepare him emotionally for the throw and develop a movement pattern important to the efficiency of the turning and throwing movements which follow.

The thrower then shifts his weight over his left (pivoting) foot, turns and drives quickly across the circle (Fig. 190*a–e*). Here, it is important to use just the correct quantity of spin on this pivoting foot; novices often spin too far, to the detriment of their throwing position, subsequently. In driving across the circle it is also important to maintain a correct relationship between this pivoting foot and the thrower's Centre of Gravity; the faster the movement across, the farther forward of this foot should be the Centre of Gravity. Through failure to maintain this relationship novice throwers often lose balance falling backwards in the throw. (See also pages 63, 64, 67 and 68.)

In this phase (Fig. 190*a–e*) the expert's shoulders turn through approximately 450 deg. and, correctly, he develops maximum controlled angular and linear velocities. In the turn—part pivot, part jump, part running movement—the axis of movement passes through his base— i.e. first his left foot (Fig. 190*b–c*) and then the right (Fig. 190*e*) (see also page 78). A relaxed throwing arm trails fairly wide of the body, encouraging maximum possible speed of movement in the throw which follows; for, for a given angular velocity, the linear speed of the discus will be proportional to its distance from the common axis. (See pages 72 and 86.)

The trailing of the throwing arm also increases the moment of inertia of the upper body relative to the common axis, tending to slow those parts of the body down in their rotation. Today's great throwers build up angular momentum in their hips and legs through a wide leg-sweep during the first half of the turn. When, subsequently, the free leg is pulled in, torque between hips and shoulders is increased—an effect enhanced (in the opinion of some coaches) by a deliberate effort to hold back the upper body by bending the free arm across the chest. But others think that if the free leg is swung out wide so, naturally, should the free arm be extended for balance.

The expert discus thrower also advances his hips and feet relative to his upper body by getting his right foot to the ground again quickly and by positioning his front (left) foot without delay (Fig. 190*d–f*). And this is achieved without raising his Centre of Gravity unduly, and with both

Figure 190   **h**   **i**   **j**

feet off the ground for only an instant—otherwise, when the thrower lands in the front half of the circle, his shoulders will be in alignment with his hips, to the detriment of body torque and the power of his throwing position.

The expert also lands on a flexed right leg and with his weight well over it (Fig. 190*e*). He then adds to the speed of the discus by transferring that weight from rear to front foot, thus shifting the common axis; simultaneously, he stretches and lifts powerfully with legs and trunk and unwinds his upper body and throwing arm through approximately 180 deg. of additional shoulder rotation (Fig. 190*f–i*). All this takes place against a bracing and lifting action of his left leg, the foot of which is placed only slightly to the side of his general line of direction across the circle (Fig. 190 *g–h*); ideally this foot remains in contact with the ground until the discus has left the hand. (See pages 202–6.)

After the left foot meets the ground and the actual throwing movement begins (Fig. 190*f*) the path of the discus describes a spiral curve, first descending and then rising steeply, but inclining more to the horizontal as the point of release (just in front of the line of the shoulders) is approached. Early in its rise the hand has a firm grasp and during this period can exert a vertical or near-vertical force on the implement. In fact, the lifting of the trunk and legs must take place at this time, while the hand can transmit vertical force.

Later, the upper edge of the discus drops away from the wrist and any force applied through the fingers must then pass through the Centre of Gravity of the implement—otherwise it will wobble, to the detriment of its stability in flight. Consequently a series of velocities is given to the discus at this stage, beginning vertically but tending towards the horizontal. A combination of these velocities results in the discus starting its flight with a negative angle of incidence. (See page 222.)

Shot. The technique of the O'Brien style of shot putting (Fig. 192*a*) is simpler than that of each of the other three throwing events, lending itself easily to mechanical analysis through the use of ciné film.

By taking ciné pictures from a fixed camera set on a continuation of the line dividing the circle into front and rear halves, preferably against accurately-positioned background markings, and focused on a point approximately 3 ft (0.91 m) directly above the middle of the circle, these pictures can be projected, subsequently, frame by frame or at other regular intervals of time, and the path of the shot can be plotted.

Then, provided the camera speed[1] is known, it is possible to calculate the (*a*) time taken for the put, (*b*) acceleration of the shot in a sagittal plane, from stage to stage, (*c*) its path across the circle in this plane, (*d*) release speed, (*e*) height of the point of release, (*f*) and angle of projection; and from (*d*) (*e*) and (*f*) compute (*g*), the distance of the put.

Fig. 191 illustrates just such an analysis of a put by Arthur Rowe, Great Britain (former European record-holder), in 1958, where the missile was released (at a point here marked by a cross) 6 ft 6 in (1.98 m) above the ground, at an angle of 41 deg. and at a speed of 41 ft (12.5 m) per second— which (allowing for a point of release 9 in. (0.23 m) beyond the inside of the stop-board) gives a distance of 59 ft 5 in. (18.11 m).

Point of release **x**

Figure 191

The diagram also illustrates the comparatively straight path of the shot from the rear of the circle to the point of release, with fewer undulations and less of a tendency to dip markedly in the middle of the circle than one often sees—proof that all Rowe's various body forces in this plane were acting in the most favourable direction. In this put the athlete applied his forces over a range of over 8 ft (2.44 m) (as against the 7 ft (2.13 m) of the circle's diameter).

[1] An accurate electric clock can be placed in the photographic field to provide a time reference on each frame.

A study of the dots marking the passage of the shot shows that by far the greatest accelerations occurred as the large forces of the legs and trunk were brought into play approximately half-way across the circle, where the distance between the dots increases suddenly and considerably (Fig. 191). A more detailed analysis than is shown here also revealed that the shot's acceleration dropped as the arm thrust, but increased again when the athlete added a final wrist-snap as the shot rolled off his fingers.

The purpose of the glide (Fig. 192*b*–*d*) is principally to 'prime' certain of the muscles needed in the delivery, largely through the creation of torque between hips and shoulders and in the legs (see page 26); *and to complete this at the instant of attaining a putting stance*. It also provides horizontal speed prior to the delivery, although it would seem that only 30 to 40 per cent of this can be utilised *directly* in the put, even in world class performances—due, presumably, to the need to change the direction of effort in delivery.[1] The glide is important, yet not too much importance should be attached to it, as it accounts for no more than 10 per cent of the total distance (a difference between a standing and a complete put which has held fairly constant throughout the event's technical evolution). Certainly, the glide ought never to be executed to the detriment of power of position and control in the delivery, subsequently; i.e. it should never take up too much of the circle, so cramping the putter's delivery; or be too fast, to the point of exceeding his 'critical' speed.

It can be seen that Rowe's glide (Fig. 191) took him rather less than half-way across the circle, permitting a breadth of base suited to his height, horizontal speed and lean over his rear leg.

(Fig. 192*b* illustrates a rotational, 'discus-style' variation based on an assumption of greater early shot speed. Here: (1) the shot should be pressed more strongly against the neck; (2) the timing of a straight thrusting movement after the rotation is difficult as is (3) a quick grounding of the front foot; (4) tall men in particular tend to use up too much of the circle (i.e. the rotation takes up more space than a glide) so encouraging a cramped, upright putting stance with danger of fouling).

The actual putting action must begin immediately the athlete's rear (right) foot comes to rest at the end of the glide, otherwise valuable time will elapse without acceleration being given to the shot. (See pages 202–

---

[1] P. Lay, 'A report on the 6th I.T.F.C.A. Conference in Madrid' *Athletics Coach* (March 1973), British Amateur Athletic Board.

Figure 192a

Figure 192b

204.) As soon as this rear foot lands, its leg can exert an efficient upward thrust and the trunk and shot can be raised.

However, since maximum body force and maximum rotation of the trunk about its long axis are possible only with the other foot used as a point of resistance, the front foot should land only fractionally after the rear foot (0.03 to 0.05 sec. later); here, there should be just sufficient rocking motion from one foot to the other to help keep the common Centre of Gravity moving forward. A slight rock will, in fact, help bring the front foot to the ground; on the other hand, with too much weight over the back leg at this stage, and with the front foot poised long in the air, the athlete will lose much, if not all, the speed built up during the glide.

Contrary to the view that the putting action 'is a movement which begins in the toes and ends in the fingers', in fact *(as in almost all athletic activities) movement begins in the stronger but slower muscles surrounding the athlete's Centre of Gravity and is then taken up, below the hips, at the knees, ankles and feet, in that order; simultaneously, above the hips, it extends upwards through the putting shoulder, elbow, wrist and fingers.* In its summation of forces (see pages 34 and 201), therefore, a technically sound putting action can be likened to the throwing of a stone into a pool of water—causing the ripples to flow outward.

Theoretically, there can be no doubt that, throughout the putting movements in the front of the circle, the front foot should be firmly in contact with the ground, providing the necessary resistance for the hand to exert maximum force both vertically and horizontally. The vertical component of force must exceed the force of gravity to ensure continuous, though varying, upward acceleration. Horizontally, as soon as the hand rises above the centre of percussion the backward thrust of the shot on the hand encourages the front foot to move forward (see pages 204–7).

However, it must be admitted that a majority—if not all—of the world's best shot putters *do* in fact break contact with this front foot fractionally before the missile leaves the hand. This may be to avoid moving beyond the stop-board; for by this means, the athlete reduces some of his forward momentum. Or, the legs may be driving too vertically (possibly because the feet are too close together) or the arm striking too horizontally. Or contact could be broken in an attempt to achieve greater release height. Again, this could happen because of the accelerations developed by the legs and trunk—accelerations which may be too great for the strength of the arm; arm action may have to be delayed until these have been reduced, if not completed (see page 205).

Javelin. The ideal, in this event, is to combine maximum controlled approach-speed with a throwing position which enables maximum force to be applied to the javelin over the greatest possible range (see page 201), releasing it at an optimum angle (see pages 223–5). Throwers are rarely satisfied with their combining of these two largely irreconcilable factors; yet, always, their aim is to obtain an effective throwing position with the javelin already moving fast—and then, with the throwing shoulder travelling at maximum speed relative to the ground, to impart maximum hand speed in relation to the shoulder.

For the greater part of his 14–17 stride (overall) run-up the expert thrower holds the javelin over his shoulder in a position which permits relaxed, balanced running, and accelerates gradually into a horizontal speed governed by his ability to exert full body force, subsequently, in his throwing movements. Approach speed should depend upon body speed and strength (see page 202).

After 10–12 of these running strides he withdraws and aligns the javelin in preparation for the throw, turning and gradually leaning his trunk to the rear to adopt a powerful pulling position (Fig. 193a). The change in the angle of the trunk is particularly marked during the long, so-called 'cross-step' immediately prior to the throwing stride (Fig. 193a–b), where it is essential that the thrower contacts the ground with his right foot (right-handed athlete) before his body weight moves over and beyond this foot.

Here, in a good throw, the athlete's grip will be approximately 4 ft (1.22 m) behind his Centre of Gravity which, in turn, will be to the rear of his right foot (Fig. 193b). The line of the leading leg and trunk at this instant will be about 25 deg. to the vertical, but the angle should depend upon the speed of the run-up, the greater speed requiring a greater angle, and vice versa.

Basically the javelin throwing action can be described as, first, a powerful pull exerted on the missile, followed by a lifting motion, where 'the thrower attempts to run off and away from the rear leg against the resistance of the front leg' (Pugh[1]) (Fig. 193b–h). Beginning as the right foot contacts the ground at the end of the cross-step and with the throwing arm comparatively straight and relaxed, a *pull from the shoulder* is applied as the weight of the body moves forward and the front foot reaches out (Fig. 193c–d). And as this weight moves ahead of the supporting foot, the right leg drives hard to add to this pulling movement and keep the right hip, in particular, moving fast into the throw. In good throwing, this transference of weight against the resistance of the front leg (the foot of which is quickly grounded) occurs without a premature turning of the shoulders to the front; in fact, *the hips twist fractionally ahead of the shoulders.*

So widespread are the feet in good javelin throwing that the rear leg completes its drive before the front foot contacts the ground (Fig. 193d).

---

[1] D. L. Pugh, *Javelin Throwing* (Amateur Athletic Association, England, 1960), page 19.

Figure 193

Trunk rotation occurs mainly by virtue of the front foot's resistance to horizontal motion. A quick turning-in of the rear knee and foot adds to hip speed and coincides with an outward rotation and raising of the throwing elbow (head slightly to the side) which are essential to a final flail-like arm action.

If the trunk is too erect and the throwing base too narrow for the athlete's approach speed, he will lack sufficient range over which to apply his body forces and will tend quickly to rotate in a sagittal plane over and beyond his front foot in delivery, pulling the javelin down (Fig. 194*a*). On the other hand, if he leans back too far and his feet are too widespread, the Centre of Gravity's forward speed will be reduced excessively (see pages 204–8), the hips will not pass over the forward foot and, incorrectly, the trunk will pivot about the hips, shortening the radius of movement in a sagittal plane and, again, pulling the javelin down in delivery (Fig. 194*b*).

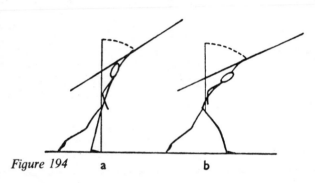

Figure 194   a   b

It is difficult to estimate the actual loss in forward speed of the Centre of Gravity due to the impact of the front foot with the ground, but even in a good throw it seems likely that this will be about one quarter of its original horizontal speed, depending upon the efficiency with which the front foot takes up the shock on impact (see pages 93 and 206). However, it may well be that the throwing shoulder at least maintains, if not increases, its linear speed, because of its distance above the Centre of Gravity.

(M. J. Ellis and H. H. Lockwood agree[1] that the speed of the throwing shoulder increases markedly as the front foot meets the ground, but

[1] M. J. Ellis and H. H. Lockwood 'Javelin throw, John McSorley', *A.A.A. Coaching Newsletter,* Amateur Athletic Association, England, No. 26 (January–April 1964), page 6.

suggest that this is due to the shoulder's rapid rotation about the body's longitudinal axis. In analysing film of one thrower they found that his Centre of Gravity did not describe an arc during the throwing stride, because of his flexed front leg, which kept the Centre of Gravity moving horizontally. They concluded that the hinged effect in this event occurs more in a *transverse* than sagittal plane, commenting, 'Perhaps, whilst the hinged moment effect (in a sagittal plane) is theoretically and mechanically ideal, the stresses that it would place on the thrower are such that the innate protective mechanisms of the body would not allow it to be used, even assuming that the thrower is strong enough to remain rigid.') In all probability *the most valuable effect in the checking of forward motion lies in the 'bowing' of the body—with chest to the front—a movement which rapidly stretches the trunk's flexor muscles, invoking powerful eccentric contractions.*

Because, in good throwing, the athlete's rear foot must break effective contact with the ground before the arm applies its forces, *the arm's* first *pulling movement*, acting at shoulder-level below the point of percussion, must be exerted against the inertia of the thrower's body, so reducing his forward speed. However, once the front foot meets the ground (Fig. 193e) it remains in contact until the javelin is released, and so provides an essential resistance not only to any vertical component of the force of the arm action, but also to those horizontal components exerted, subsequently, above the point of percussion (see pages 202–7).

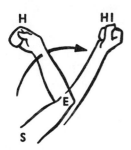

Figure 195

The final flail-like (see pages 35–6 arm action of the good javelin thrower is brought about, first, by outwardly rotating the elbow (Fig. 193) and raising it higher than the hand grasping the javelin— 'leaving that hand behind' (Pugh[1])—before quickly extending the forearm and hand to apply further force vertically and through the javelin's length against a full extension of the front leg.

Fig. 195 illustrates the range of movement at the elbow, and Fig. 196 gives a diagrammatic interpretation of this flailing arm action. SEH approximates the position of the throwing arm during the earlier phases

[1]Op. cit. page 15.

of throwing movement, while SE1H1 is the result of an extremely fast action of the upper-arm, SE1. SE2H2 represents the arm's position at the instant of delivery, where the outward rotation of the elbow permits greater extension than that shown in Fig. 195.

This flailing arm action is superior to a straight-arm, bowling action because:

(i) the muscles acting between the forearm and upper arm, as well as the muscles acting between the shoulder and upper arm, can be used to produce force;

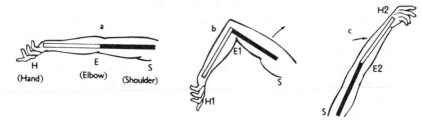

Figure 196

(ii) the small moment of inertia of the comparatively light forearm and hand about the elbow joint does not hinder greater angular speed of the forearm relative to the elbow (although, of course, the moment of inertia of the javelin about this joint must also be considered); and

(iii) in a straight-arm rotation about the shoulder, angular speed would have to be developed against the considerable moment of inertia of the whole arm and javelin.

Thus the essential *pulling* character of a good javelin throw derives from (*a*) the motion of the body in front of the missile, (*b*) the body's rotation in two planes—sagittal and transverse, and (*c*) a final flail-like arm action. This pulling movement can take place over as much as 14 ft (4.27 m) (Pugh[1])—from the moment the right foot lands at the end of the cross-step (Fig. 193*b*) to the instant of release (midway between Fig. 193*g–h*), producing release speeds in excess of 60 m.p.h. (96.54 km.p.h.).

[1] Ibid., page 11.

Appendix

Many aspects of rotational movement important to athletics (much of it involving the conservation of angular momentum) can be demonstrated on a turntable, preferably with a light stool attachment. Some demonstrations also require a weighted cycle wheel.

These experiments have to be confined to movement in a horizontal plane, for a turntable can react only to movement in that plane; but the principles illustrated apply to motion in any plane.

A turntable (1) should be level and stable and as frictionless as possible; of sufficient size to support a variety of positions, yet with the smallest possible moment of inertia. It should include levelling devices—adjustable legs with, ideally, spirit levels. A built-in friction control is recommended, as even a marginally-tilted smooth-running turntable will make demonstrating difficult. A straight line painted across the axis can be a useful guide, in some experiments, as to the extent of rotation.

The cycle wheel (2) should be equipped with two detachable handles which allow the hub to revolve independently. To increase the wheel's moment of inertia (and, therefore, its turning effect on the platform), its rim should be weighted until the whole mass is 8–10 lb (3.5–4.5 kg).

Figure 1

Figure 2

Series A   The effect of a change in 'I' on angular velocity

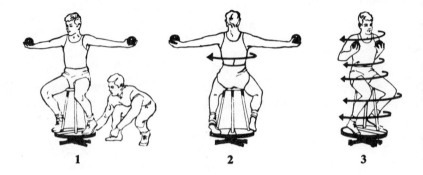

1 Two light shots are held with arms out-stretched and the turntable system is then rotated.
2 Its angular velocity is

3 markedly increased when the arms and weights are drawn in close to the chest; but the total angular momentum of the system remains constant.

Series B   Transference of angular momentum from a part to the whole

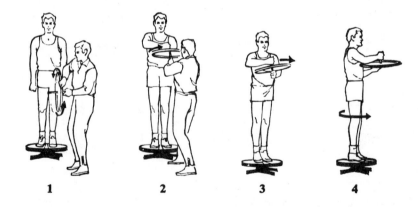

1 The wheel is spun and
2 then, rotating horizontally, is given to the person on the turntable.

3 First kept clear of the body, it
4 is then checked against the chest, trans-ferring its angular momentum to the system as a whole.

Series C **Transference of angular momentum, with emphasis on its directional quality**

1　　　　　　　　　**2**　　　　　　　　　**3**

1 The wheel, spinning in a horizontal plane, is given to the person on the turntable.
2 Thus, the turntable system's total angular momentum is concentrated in the wheel.

3 When the latter is turned to spin vertically, its earlier angular momentum in a horizontal plane, conserved in the system, now turns the table in the same sense. (Since the table cannot react to the wheel's new rotation, the earth absorbs this new reaction.)

Series D **Action and reaction**

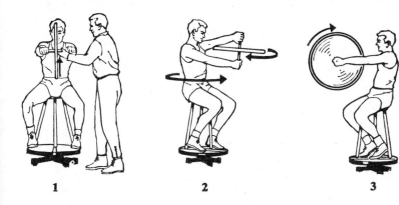

1　　　　　　　　　**2**　　　　　　　　　**3**

1 The wheel, rotating in a vertical plane, is given to the person on the turntable.
2 When the wheel is turned horizontally, the turntable system (of which the wheel is a part) rotates with equal angular momentum but in an opposite direction.

3 When the first position is resumed the turntable stops.

Series E   'Taking up' angular momentum

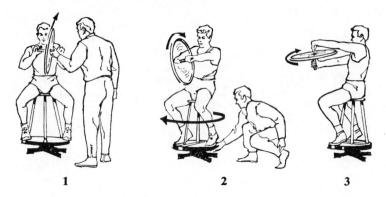

1   **2**   **3**

1 The spinning wheel, rotating in a vertical plane, is given to the person on the turntable and
2 the system is then rotated.

3 When the wheel is turned horizontally to rotate in the same sense as the turntable, it absorbs (i.e. takes up) a quantity of the table's original angular momentum—the amount depending upon the angular momenta imparted to wheel and turntable initially.

a With the wheel's angular momentum less than that of the table, the latter will continue to rotate, but more slowly.

b When the wheel's angular momentum is equal to that of the table, the turntable stops (as shown here).

c When the wheel's angular momentum exceeds that of the table, the latter reverses its rotational direction (thus conserving the system's total angular momentum).

Bibliography

ADAMSON, G. T., 'Some Facts and Fallacies on Fitness Training', *A.A.A. Coaching Newsletter*, Amateur Athletic Association No. 15, July 1960.

ALFORD, J. W. L., 'Sprinting and Relay Racing', Amateur Athletic Association, 1959.

——, 'Middle Distance Running and Steeplechasing', Amateur Athletic Association, 1960.

ARISTOTLE, 'On the Gait of Animals', Vol. II, Book 9, *Great Books of the Western World*, Encyclopaedia Britannica Inc., 1952.

BALL, A. F., 'The Mechanics of Diving', unpublished thesis, Loughborough College of Education.

BARRETT, L., 'The Universe and Dr. Einstein', New American Library Inc., New York 22, 1962.

BRITISH AMATEUR ATHLETIC BOARD, *Senior Coaching Award Coaching Theory Manual*, B.A.A.B.

BUNN, J. W., *Scientific Principles of Coaching*, Prentice-Hall, Englewood Cliffs, N. J., U.S.A., 1955.

COOPER, L., DALZELL, D. and SILVERMAN, E., *Flight of the Discus*, Division of Engineering Science, Purdue University, Indiana, U.S.A., May 1959.

COUNSILMAN, JAMES E., *The Science of Swimming*, Prentice-Hall, 1968.

——, *Principles of Fluid Mechanics Applicable to Swimming*, University of Indiana, 1972.

CULLUM, D. N. J., 'Hammer Throwing', A.A.A. Advanced Course Lectures, Loughborough Summer Schools, 1956–60.

DAISH, C. B., *The Physics of Ball Games*, Hodder and Stoughton, 1974.

DOHERTY, K., *Modern Track and Field*, Prentice-Hall, 1953.

DYATCHKOV, V. M., *High Jumping*, Moscow, 1966.

DYSON, G. H. G., *Body-mechanics without tears*, A.G.M., Mathematical Association, 1956.

——, 'Elevation and Rotation', Royal Academy of Dancing *Gazette* (R.A.D.), September 1955.

——, *High Jumping*, Amateur Athletic Association, 4th edition, 1959.

ECKER, T., 'Track and field dynamics', *Track and Field News*, Box 296, Los Altos, Cal. 94022, USA.

EDINGTON and EDGERTON, V. R., *The Biology of Physical Activity*, Houghton Mifflin Co., Boston, 1976.

ENG YOON TAN, 'Research into the Hop, Step and Jump', National Collegiate Track Coaches Association, 29th Annual Meeting. Published by 'Champions on Film', $303\frac{1}{2}$ SO Main Street, Ann Arbor, Michigan, U.S.A.

FOX, E. L., *Sports Physiology*, 2nd Edition, Saunders College Publishing, 1984.

GANSLEN, R. V., 'Aerodynamic factors which influence discus flights', Research Report, College of Arts and Sciences, University of Arkansas, May 1958.

——, 'Finnish Javelin Throwing', *Scholastic Coach*, 33 West 22nd Street, New York 36, February 1950.

——, *The Mechanics of the Pole Vault*, John S. Swift and Coy., St. Louis, 4th edition 1959–60.

GRAY, JAMES, *How Animals Move*, Cambridge University Press, 1953.

GRIMSEHL, E., *A Textbook of Physics: Vol. I. Mechanics*, Blackie, 1932.

HAWLEY, G., *An Anatomical Analysis of Sports*, A. S. Barnes and Co., New York.

HAY, J. G., 'A kinematic analysis of the high jump', *Track Technique*, No. 53, September 1973, *Track & Field News*.

HILL, A. V., *Muscular Activity*, Williams and Wilkins, Baltimore, 1925.

——, *Living Machinery*, Bell, 1939.

HOPPER, B. J., 'Rotation—a vital factor in Athletic Technique', *Track Technique*, Nos. 9–17. *Track and Field News*.

——, *Notes on the dynamical basis of physical movement*, St. Mary's College, Twickenham, London, 1959.

——, *The Mechanics of Human Movement*, Granada Publishing, 1973.

HOUSDEN, E. F., 'Mechanics applied to Discus Throwing', *Discobolus*, The Discus Circle Magazine, No. 8, December 1959.

——, 'An analysis of the effects of the acceleration of the free leg in various athletic events', *Coaching Review*, Royal Canadian Legion, March 1966.

KOMI, P. V., 'Neuromuscular performance. Factors influencing force and speed', *Scandinavian Journal of Sports Sciences*, Vol. 1, No. 1, August 1979.

KRAUSE, J. V. and BARHAM, J. N., *The Mechanical Foundations of Human Motion*, C. V. Mosby Co., Saint Louis, 1975.

KUZNETSOV, V. L., 'Mastery of Javelin Throwing Technique', *Track Technique* No. 2, December 1960, *Track and Field News*.

LINDHARD, J., *Theory of Gymnastics*, 2nd edition, Methuen, 1939.

MCINTOSH, P., and HAYLEY, H. W. B., 'An investigation into the running long jump', *Journal of Physical Education*, November 1952.

MUIR, J., *Of Men and Numbers*, Dell Publishing Company, New York 17, 1962.

PAYNE, HOWARD, *Hammer Throwing*, Amateur Athletic Association, England, 1969.

PEARSON, G. F. D., *Athletics*, Thomas Nelson, 1963.

PHARAOH, M., 'Observations on Discus Throwing', *A.A.A. Coaching Newsletter*, Amateur Athletic Association, No. 4, April 1957.

PUGH, D. L., *Javelin Throwing*, Amateur Athletic Association, 1960.

ROGERS, E. M., *Physics for the Inquiring Mind*, Princeton University Press, 1962.

SCHUPPE, HANS, *Physik der Leibesübungen*, Ferdinand Enke Verlag, Stuttgart.

SIMONS, J. C., 'An introduction to surface-free behaviour', *Ergonomics*, 7 January 1964.

STEINHAUS, A. H., 'The Physiology of Exercise', Series of lectures, Chicago 1948.

STUKELEY, W., *Memoirs of Newton's Life,* Taylor and Francis, 1936. (From a manuscript now preserved by the Royal Society, London.)

TARRANT, G. T. P., 'Mechanics of human and animal activity', *School Science Review,* No. 78, December 1938.

TERAUDS, J., *A Comparative Analysis of the Aerodynamic and Ballistic Characteristics of Competitive Javelins.* Ph.D. dissertation, 1972. University of Maryland, College Park, Md., U.S.A.

WEBB, P., *Bioastronautics Data Book,* Webb Associates, Yellow Springs, Ohio, 1964.

WELLS, K. F., *Kinesiology,* Saunders, 1950.

WHITNEY, R. J., 'The strength of the lifting action in man', *Ergonomics,* Vol. 1, No. 2, February 1958.

WILKIE, D. R., 'Man as a source of mechanical power', *Ergonomics,* 3 (1960), p. 1.

WILLIAMS, M. and LISSNER, H. R., *Biomechanics of Human Motion,* W. B. Saunders Coy., 1962.

WILT, F., 'Run, Run, Run', *Track and Field News Inc.,* 1965.

Index

The following abbreviations are used in addition to the ones in common use in designating specific athletics events:
   Diving: (div) Running: (run) Throwing: (thr)